THE PHILOSOPHY OF
ARISTOTLE

BARBARA JANCAR
ASSISTANT PROFESSOR OF GOVERNMENT
SKIDMORE COLLEGE

MONARCH PRESS

Published by
MONARCH PRESS
a Simon & Schuster division of
Gulf & Western Corporation
Simon & Schuster Building
1230 Avenue of the Americas
New York, N.Y. 10020

Standard Book Number: 0-671-00506-5

Library of Congress Catalog Card Number: 66-28637

Printed in the United States of America

CONTENTS

ARISTOTLE'S LIFE AND HERITAGE

Aristotle was a product of Greek culture. Before the Greeks came into the Mediterranean world, man was primarily oriented toward death and built his monuments in honor of death. The zigurats of Babylon and the pyramids of Egypt testify to the hold of death upon these early civilizations. To the Greeks, however, life was the most significant fact in the world, and human life was the greatest wonder on earth. The Greeks were the first people to play. Their famous Olympic Games are witness to their boundless enthusiasm for living. Their art speaks of the pleasure they derived from the form of the human body. The Greeks were also the first philosophers. Man was a miracle above the other creatures because he possessed what they called *logos*. *Logos* in Greek means a word by which a thought is expressed. It can also mean the thought itself, or reason. The Greeks were the first people to say that the world was knowable, because they believed in man's power of reason. They had no idea of changing their own life or the world around them through the knowledge acquired by reason. The world was something to be understood and admired as it was. Through understanding the nature of the universe and the nature of man, a Greek believed he had the key to understanding man's own place in the scheme of things.

THE IONIAN SCHOOL

In classical times this school was famous as one which sought scientific answers to questions about nature. Because the school was mainly concerned with observing nature, its followers were called *phusikoi* or natural philosophers. *Phusis* is the Greek word for nature, from which is derived our word physics.

THALES AND ANAXIMANDER: Some six centuries before Christ, on the island of Miletus in the Aegean Sea, a man called Thales asked the question: "What is the world made of?" He had looked around himself and seen a world where things were chang-

5

ing all the time. The tide came in and went out. A tree grew where a seed had been. He thought there must be something unchanging and permanent beneath all the change. Beneath the world of life and death there must be some basic substance which explained and made possible everything else. Instead of turning to religion, Thales tried to give a scientific explanation and decided that the first substance was water. His pupil, Anaximander, said that the first substance was a lump of matter which had no form, shape, or definite character of any kind. He called this first matter The Unlimited. Its chief characteristic was that it was always in motion. How did our world evolve from this shapeless lump? Anaximander's theory was that the world is a battlefield where opposites are constantly fighting each other, encroaching on one another. At some time in the past while basic matter was whirling through space, four basic opposites—hot and cold, and wet and dry—separated themselves out. The cold and wet went into the center of the whirling mass of matter to become the earth. The hot and dry moved toward the edge and formed rings of fire around the mass. Mist rising from the earth prevented the rings of fire from being seen on the earth. Man could only see the flames peeping through the fog in the forms of the sun, the moon, and the stars. But even before man appeared, the heat dried up the wet to form land. Life was the result of the action of heat on moisture. Life first appeared in the ocean; eventually man evolved from fish that took to dry land. This theory may well be considered a precursor to Darwin's account of evolution.

ANAXIMENES: Another pupil of Thales named Anaximenes held that the world was not made of either water, or indefinite matter. It was made of air. Observing how air condensed to form rain, he said that the earth and ocean were formed that way. The wet fell toward the center, while the purer air remained in the heavens. Like the other early philosophers, Anaximenes believed that the universe was alive in the same way that man is alive. He accounted for man's particular form of life, the life of reason, by saying that the soul of man was formed from the very pure air which had remained at the farthest edge of the universe.

One problem which these early philosophers faced was why the first substance of the universe, be it water, matter or air, formed the world at all. What first set things in motion? Since they thought all matter was alive, they said that the first substance was *self-moving*. Not only did it cause motion in other things, it was the cause of its own motion. It *produced* life and was life at the same time. Because it moved itself, they said it was divine.

HERACLITUS

Later philosophers continued the Ionian tradition. Following in the steps of Anaximander, a thinker from the city of Ephesus in Asia Minor by the name of Heraclitus held in the fifth century B.C. that the world was the scene of the conflict of opposites. He too was impressed by the instability and changing character of the physical world. But he disagreed with Anaximander's view that the strife which characterizes the world is something disorderly or unjust.

CONCEPT OF UNITY: "Strife," he said, "is the justice of the world." The existence of this conflict of opposing forces, in his view, is essential to the existence of the One, or God. In accordance with this attitude, he held that "ever-lasting fire," not air, or water, or the unlimited, is the essence of all things, because it exhibits the most continuous state of tension. "All things are in flux," he said. Being the most fluctuating of all things, fire is therefore the essential reality of the universe. Heraclitus explained change by saying that it is the upward and the downward path of fire by virtue of which the universe came into being. The relative stability of the world, he said, is due to different "measures" of the ever-lasting fire, some being kindled (burning upward) and some burning out (going downward) in more or less equal proportions. The balance between the upward and downward paths of the different "measures" of fire forms what Heraclitus called the "hidden attunement" of the universe. This is an attunement of opposite tensions, he said, "like that of a bow and a lyre." Thus Heraclitus saw the harmony of the world as the resolution of many diverse tensions in the unity of the one reality, which is fire. This concept of unity in diversity, of the One as Many, is Heraclitus' most significant contribution to philosophy. He himself felt that his special "Word," or message, to mankind was the knowledge that "all things are one."

IMPORTANCE OF REASON: A second aspect of Heraclitus' philosophy is his idea of the One, or God as an all-ordering Reason, a universal law present in all things. This view led him to emphasize the value of man's reason, which he considered the fiery element in man and thus a moment of Universal Reason. In his "Word" he urged men to live by reason. He was one of the first philosophers to suggest that we cannot rely wholly on our powers of observation. Our senses often trick us. Only by trying to see the world from the viewpoint of Universal Reason, he said, can man understand the hidden laws of the universe that "all things are one," and that "War . . . is the father . . . of all things."

PYTHAGORAS AND THE PYTHAGOREANS

A second school which greatly influenced the course of Greek philosophy, and particularly Aristotle's famous teacher, Plato, was the school of Pythagoras of Samos, another island in the Aegean Sea. Little is known about the life of the school's founder. It seems Pythagoras left his native Samos about 530 B.C. and settled in Croton, a Greek colony in southern Italy. There he founded a religious brotherhood. Legend says that Pythagoras performed miracles. He was also very interested in mathematics, and seems to have been the first man to treat mathematics as a science. One of his contributions to mathematics is known to us today as the Pythagorean Formula: the square of the hypotenuse of a right triangle is equal to the sum of the squares of the two sides. The importance he gave to numbers was upheld by his followers, many of whom thought numbers were divine.

PYTHAGOREAN PHILOSOPHY: First, Pythagoras believed in the transmigration of souls. Each soul comes from God, in Whose image it is made, and to Whom it will at last return when it has been cleansed of sin. Until that time, each soul enters into the body of a plant or animal, stays there until it dies, and then enters another body, and then another. Second, if God and the human soul have similar natures, then the structure of man and the structure of the universe must be based on the same principle. The human soul is the cause of order in man, as God is the cause of order in the universe. His soul, which makes man one complete being, is finite; it has a definite form. The One which unifies the world must likewise be definite, i.e., finite and limited, else its form could not be reproduced in miniature in the soul of man. This view of the relation between God and man made the Pythagoreans identify order, goodness and beauty with the idea of Limit or Form, and disorder and evil with the Unlimited or Formless. Their word for universe was *kosmos,* which itself meant order or arrangement. Finally, the similarity between the whole and its parts can be expressed in terms of some proportion supposed to exist between the whole and its part, and the part and its parts. One result of Pythagoras' interest in proportion was the numerical ratios of the octave (2:1), the fifth (3:2), and the fourth (4:3) in the musical scale. As the musical scale is defined and limited by these numerical ratios, so every whole is made by the action of Limit (order) upon the Unlimited. The correct proportion between the whole and its parts was the cause of beauty in the object, and was called *harmony,* meaning perfect arrangement. Aristotle in his *Metaphysics* attacks the latter Pythagorean idea that numerical ratios can be the cause of anything.

NUMBER IS THE FIRST SUBSTANCE OF THE UNIVERSE: The realization that all things are numerable, and can be related to each other in a numerical proportion is one factor which led the Pythagoreans to their emphasis on the value of number in explaining the world order. If musical harmony is dependent on number, world harmony must also be dependent on number, they thought. Most probably they assumed that the conflict of opposites in the world (which the natural philosophers had observed) could be resolved in terms of number. If, as they thought, Limit is what gives form to the Unlimited and can be expressed in a numerical proportion, number must obviously play a significant role in the world. Such thinking contributed to the Pythagorean position that all things are numbers. But to understand this theory better, we must also look at their view of numbers. Most scholars agree that the Pythagoreans thought of numbers spatially. For example, in their view one is the point; two is the line; three is the surface; and four is the solid. To say that all things are numbers is thus another way of saying that everything that exists consists of points, or units in space, which taken together make a number. In making number the first substance of the world, the Pythagoreans most likely transferred these mathematical conceptions to material reality. Consequently, they said that points, lines, and surfaces are the real units from which all bodies in the world are made. Every material body, in fact, is a solid (i.e., it is an expression of the number four). It is difficult to say which aspect of Pythagorean science most influenced the theory that basic reality is number: their research into the nature of musical sound or their geometrical view of numbers. That their theory was taken seriously is evident from the fact that Aristotle devotes a good part of his work on the nature of being to the refutation of the idea that mathematical concepts have a concrete, substantial existence.

THE IDENTITY OF HARMONY WITH GOOD ORDER: This was the main contribution to Greek philosophy by the Pythagoreans. They approached all things with the purpose of finding the right relation between the whole or the One, and its parts (the Many). Medicine, for instance, was the science which brought about harmony, or the good ordering, of the parts or vital fluids of the body. Pythagoras' view that health was the right harmony of the body became the ideal of Greek medicine. One of the problems of this distinction between the whole and its parts, and the One and the Many (a problem which Heraclitus did not have) is that Pythagoras could find no way of explaining how the Many could have come from the One. The question of unity and diversity plays a large part in Aristotle's own philosophy.

MATTER AND FORM: The difference between the Ionian School and the so-called Italian School of Pythagoras lay in their different approaches. The Ionians asked, "What is the world made of?" The Pythagoreans asked, "What is its structure?" Thus, the Ionians said the basic world substance was some kind of self-moving matter. The Pythagoreans saw number or form as the first principle. Both schools were led to make a definite distinction between matter and form. Aristotle inherited this problem of the relation between matter and form. His solution provides the key to his philosophy.

In thinking of matter and form, we must not make the mistake of thinking that form simply means the shape of an object, and that matter means the stuff from which the object is made. To think in this way would be to misunderstand the problems the Greek philosophers were trying to solve. The Greek word for form comes from a verb which can mean both *to see* and *to know*. The form of anything was that which was knowable about it. When you wanted to say what was knowable about an object you gave it *logos* or definition. But no object is the same as its definition. The Greek philosophers were trying to find some way of making their system of language fit the structure of thought to reflect accurately the nature of reality. The early Ionian philosophers thought the problem was relatively simple. Just divide up the natural world into its elements, and you will have found the nature of reality. By the time of Heraclitus, men were thinking that the question was more difficult. Perhaps our senses cannot be trusted to tell us about reality. Only the way we think can give us any information about the nature of things. The Pythagoreans thought things were best understood through their intelligible structure. They said that what could be known about an object was what you could say about it in numbers.

PARMENIDES: The real break between language and thought on the one hand, and the sensible world on the other, came with a pupil of the Pythagoreans named Parmenides (c. 540–470 B.C.). Parmenides was particularly impressed with the vital contrast which existed between Being and Non-Being. The basic tenet of his philosophy reveals his fundamental approach to the problem of being. "It [i.e., Being]," he said, "is." "Non-Being is not and cannot be thought." In other words, man cannot think something which is nothing. He cannot think Non-Being. This means that whatever I say, or whatever I think *is;* it exists. Reality is not primarily what can be experienced by the senses. It is what you *think* it is, as stated in language. For reasons which follow, the sensible world, the world which is familiar to all of us, is not, in Parmenides' view, the real world at all. The result of this theory was to divide philosophy henceforth into two camps. Some said that all sensible things were thought. Others held that all thought was sensible things. No one could say that the sensible world and the world of thought were one world any longer. Reason and sense had split the world in two.

BEING IS ETERNAL AND INDIVISIBLE: It would be a mistake to believe that Parmenides' important distinctions between reason and sense, and truth and appearance made him an idealist. His notion of Being was not an abstract concept. He thought of Being as a space-filling mass. Being is the full, he said; Non-Being is therefore empty space. From this basic idea he derived his other theories of being: 1) Being always is. It cannot have a beginning nor cease to be, because it cannot come from Non-Being. 2) Being is continuous and undivided. Being is one and indivisible because it is everywhere the same. Since Being is, there is nothing that exists which can divide it. 3) Being is unchanging and unmoving. The fact that the verb "to be" in Greek means both "to be" and "to exist" (the distinction between the two meanings had not yet been made clear) supported Parmenides' argument that there can be no change and no motion. "To change" means that something becomes what it is not. Since "to be" meant "to exist" for Parmenides, he said that it was impossible for something which is, (i.e., exists) to become what it is not (i.e., not to exist). Similarly, Being is unmoving; "to move" means that something moves into a space where something is not (i.e., does not exist). But Being is the full. Therefore, empty space, or a space where nothing is (a space of Non-Being) logically cannot exist.

TRUTH AND APPEARANCE: Parmenides was the first to make the distinction noted above between truth and appearance. It is clear that the type of Being which he describes is one that is completely foreign to that which experience shows us. Parmenides held that only that perception is true which shows us an unchanging Being. Since our senses tell us of a world of change and decay, (i.e., of Non-Being in his view), Parmenides said that they are the cause of intellectual error. They only show us what *appears* to exist. They tell us nothing about the one, indivisible, unchanging Reality. The only way, he said, we can know the nature of reality is through the structure of thought.

EMPEDOCLES: Parmenides' theory of the unreality of change could not long go unchallenged. The philosophers who came after him were left with the problem of reconciling the unchanging world of Being with the changing world in which we live. For no matter what anyone might say, common sense indicated that there was a world of change, and this world had to be in some way real. One attempt to resolve the problem was made in the fifth century B.C., by a man named Empedocles, who came from the town of Akragas in Sicily. Parmenides had reasoned that the world we can see and touch is unreal. But he had not said that matter was unreal. Rather he had held that Being was an indefinite, space-filling, unchanging and eternal mass. Empedocles tried to reconcile the world of change with unchanging Being by saying that the world as we know it is composed of four basic material particles which are themselves unchanging and indestructible. He called them "the roots of everything"; they later came to be called elements.

CONCEPT OF ELEMENTS: According to Empedocles, the four elements were earth, air, fire, and water. The objects of the physical world, he said, are made up of a haphazard combination of these four elements. Although the elements never change their nature, the different ways they can be combined result in the coming-into-being of different physical objects. Objects cease to be when the elements of which they are composed separate. What causes the elements to combine and to separate? Since Parmenides had upset the notion that there could be a self-moving substance, Empedocles explained the phenomenon of change by returning to the concept of the conflict of opposites familiar to the Ionian philosophers and putting it in a new light. Since motion cannot be caused by matter, Empedocles said that it was caused by two opposing forces acting upon matter from the outside. These two forces are the forces of Love and Hate, that is, of attraction and repulsion. The balance between the two keeps the world stable.

ANAXAGORAS: Empedocles posited two forces outside the world of the elements as the cause of motion. Despite their names of Love and Hate, he thought of these forces in physical and material terms. It was the contribution of Anaxagoras of Clazomenae in Asia Minor (born about 500 B.C.) to introduce the concept of Mind as the cause of change and becoming. He admitted that there was a difference between the sensible world and the world of thought. But one was not more "real" than the other. The problem was simple: what was not matter was Mind. The formation of the world was the imposition of Mind, or order, upon the chaos of matter. Although it is not clear whether Anaxagoras thought of Mind as something essentially intellectual or essentially material, most scholars agree that he was feeling his way toward a theory of causation based on a purely intellectual principle. Thus, his theory is of great importance for the later philosophies of Plato and Aristotle, both of whom conceived of Mind in nonmaterial terms.

THE ATOMISTS

A third philosophy to try to resolve the paradox of unchanging being and a changing world was that of a school which came to be called the Atomists. This school was the most radical of all. It agreed with Parmenides that the sensible world was not the real world. But if you divide the world into its smallest indivisible parts you will reach reality, they thought. The best known philosophers of this school were Leucippus of Miletus, who lived around 435 B.C., and Democritus of Abdera (a village in Thrace in what is today northern Greece), 460–370 B.C. Both these men took the Parmenidean idea of the One, which was the unity and reality of the universe, and gave all its characteristics to many little "ones," which they said composed the material world. "Atom" means in Greek "that which cannot be broken up." Like the element of Empedocles, it was limited, eternal, and unchangeable. It differed from Empedocles' elements in that there were many more atoms, and the Atomists considered them more fundamental than the elements. Many atoms, for instance, composed the element of water. Democritus was faced with the problem of how these tiny particles could move in space. It will be remembered that Parmenides had held that Being was the full, the space-filling, and Non-Being, the empty. Democritus revised this theory. Empty space, he said, actually exists. Accordingly, he conceived of the atoms as tiny particles moving in infinite empty space, as dust particles move in a ray of sunshine. The chance combination of these particles occurred when one atom moved from its course and bumped into another one. Aristotle blamed the Atomists for not giving any reason why the atoms should move, and he is partly right. The Atomists returned to the Ionian idea of a self-moving substance, saying that due to their varying sizes and weights, the atoms are in a state of rotary motion for all eternity.

SECONDARY AND PRIMARY QUALITIES OF ATOMS: The Atomists made the distinction between those qualities belonging to the combinations of the atoms themselves and those which *appear* to belong to them because of the way in which they are perceived. The Atomists thus maintained Parmenides' distinction between truth and appearance. Primary qualities, they said, belong to physical objects; these are such qualities as size and shape. Secondary qualities are merely qualities which convention and custom say belong to objects. These are qualities such as color, taste (bitter, sweet), temperature (hot, cold), and so on. The primary qualities are in the object; secondary qualities are relative and depend upon the perceiver. What might taste sweet to me, for example, might taste bitter to someone else. Everyone does not see the same hue of blue when he looks at an autumn sky. The Atomists thought that such things as sweetness and color merely express the way a particular object affects the perceiver. A rose does not really have a sweet smell. It just *seems* to smell sweet.

THE STUDY OF MAN—THE SOPHISTS

While philosophers were arguing about the nature of reality, a number of teachers were traveling all over Greece claiming that they could teach anyone all there was to know about man. These teachers were called *Sophists*. The word comes from the Greek word, *sophia,* meaning wisdom. The wisdom of the Sophists was not connected with such questions as "What is reality?" The Sophists were more practical. They were interested in human nature and man's actions in the world. They appeared in the Greek world in the fourth century B.C. at a time when Athens was engaged in a life-and-death struggle with Sparta. Unrest was in the air. Long-established values were being questioned and the whole city-state system was being subjected to intense study. For the first time, morals and ethics came to the forefront as subjects of scientific investigation. The Sophists claimed they could teach a man to be a good speaker, a good ruler, a good anything. But they were openly skeptical that anything like real goodness actually existed. "What is justice? What is truth? What is man? Why should we obey?" they asked. The world is changing all around us. Our own faculties of sense and smell have been shown to be useless in telling us what the world really is. What is bitter to one man is sweet to the next. Obviously, then, what is just to one man must be unjust to the next. There are no objective standards or values. It all depends on the way you look at it, on your position in society. "Man is the measure of all things," they said.

THE FIRST SOCIOLOGISTS: Athens had become the center of a wealthy empire to which people from all over the known world came. It was also the port from which many Greeks set sail to colonize new lands around the Mediterranean Sea. There was growing contact between different civilizations. The great Greek historian, Herodotus, had traveled far and wide and had returned to write of the various customs he had seen in his travels. The Sophists shared his appreciation of foreign cultures. They concluded that every system had its own type of justice. What the Athenians called law was a product of their tradition; other people had their traditions. Values and moral codes varied from culture to culture.

NATURE AND CONVENTION: In their questioning of cultural and political values, the Sophists brought a new problem into the world. If all law is based on man-made tradition, what is the relation between law and the nature of man? The Sophists put the two ideas of *phusis*, (nature) and *nomos* (convention or tradition) in opposition to each other. Some of them were the first of a long line of thinkers to hold that civilization had corrupted the nature of man. Since all men are naturally equal, society creates injustice by making some men slaves and other men despots. Other Sophists took the opposite view. Nature means the survival of the fittest; by making laws civilization only tries to soften the struggle to which man by nature is fitted. Real justice is the rule of the stronger. The conventional justice of a given society is simply the means whereby those who are unfitted to survive *can* survive. Whatever their approach, the Sophists were essentially relativists in political science. There is no best state; one society is as good as another. Difference in constitutions depends upon variables, such as geographic location, or the idea of justice which a particular society has.

THE BAD NAME OF THE SOPHISTS: The Sophists' teachings were becoming popular in Athens at a time when the city-state was engaged in a life-and-death struggle with its great rival, Sparta (431–404 B.C.). The Athenian government did not welcome the Sophists' activities in the war-torn city. They were accused of corrupting the values of Athenian youth, of mocking the traditional religion of Athens, and of undermining the morals of the city. Governments and people are inclined to be much less tolerant of new ideas in a moment of crisis, and the Sophists earned a very bad name. Some of them were banished from the city (banishment being a traditional Athenian punishment for political offenders) for their "dangerous" teachings. The student should not conclude, however, that the Sophists as a whole were a destructive element in Greek society. The great philosophers among them, such as Protagoras and Gorgias, were truly an educative force and helped to broaden the outlook of the average Greek citizen.

SOCRATES

Although many men in Athens thought the Sophists had gone too far in their new ideas, there was only one man who took up their challenge. Socrates is one of the mysteries of the classical world. No other teacher created such a deep impression upon his followers; yet he did not write a single word. He is the only man who was ever condemned to death by the citizens of Athens because of what he believed. But it seems that it was not so much what he said, but the character of the man which at once inspired deep loyalty among his followers, and aroused the suspicions of the city authorities. Although the great Greek historian, Xenophon, and others wrote about him, our most interesting source of information about Socrates comes from his famous pupil, Plato. The Socrates of Plato's dialogues seems to have been a unique person. He did not claim to be wise. In fact, he always said he was in search of wisdom. Like the Sophists, he went around asking embarrassing questions. What is wisdom? What is virtue? What is justice? Unlike the Sophists, who were thought to have wanted answers for rationalizing a course of action or persuading an audience, Socrates really wanted to know. Time and time again he proved to the Sophists that they did not know what they were pretending to teach. And he firmly believed that the values they denied really existed. Socrates was one of the first to appreciate the importance of definition for human knowledge. He did not think of a definition as a purely abstract or symbolic statement, however. For him, a definition conveyed the living spirit or essential character of what it was supposed to define. He taught that everything in the world has a definite meaning, which is not just the logical expression of its being, but denotes its intrinsic value as well. The meaning of anything, therefore, is not what we think it is. It exists objectively. Justice, for instance, would still be justice, even if there were no human beings to be just. Knowledge is "seeing" this vital meaning behind the appearance of things. It is penetrating the mystery of life. Thus, it is only through this process of learning "to see" that we come to know ourselves.

PHILOSOPHY IS A WAY OF LIFE: Modern man is inclined to think of mind, or the "thought process," as an abstraction. Socrates thought mind was a very real thing. He also thought the *meaning* of things was more real than the actual object in which the meaning was contained because it alone was not subject to change and decay. For example, he thought the idea of man more real than any living man. For this reason, the world of things was a better or worse world in proportion to how close it came to fulfilling its own meaning. In his view, for instance, man becomes good (i.e., the best sort of human being) by trying to fulfill in himself what it means to be a man. Socrates did not think of philosophy, therefore, as a system of logical and abstract statements. Philosophy was not concerned with mere propositions. Philosophy meant a life by which a man actually became his own meaning (i.e., reached self-fulfillment) insofar as it was humanly possible.

SOCRATES' MISSION: It is clear from Plato's dialogues that Socrates thought of himself as a man with a special mission. Philosophy, he said, is not only the best existence but the only real existence for man. It presupposes an objectively existing absolute "good for man" which can only be known by the mind, and from which all human action receives its value. This "moral ought" has to be experienced, if it is to be the meaningful "best" for any one man. Thus, the philosopher has to lead a certain kind of life. As mind alone can go behind the façade of the senses to grasp the essential meaning of existence, the "moral ought" or the ultimate value in man lies in a life of knowing. The good life is a life of knowledge. Insofar as a man realizes in himself the "ought" which is human perfection, so far has he climbed up the long road from superficial knowledge of the sensible appearance of things to perfect insight into the meaningful essence of things as they exist in all their purity in the incorruptible world of ideas. At the end of the road there comes the vision of the Absolute Good in which virtue and knowledge are united as the One which is the source of all being, and whose light lights everything which comes into the world. When the philosopher has had such a vision, he has already experienced eternal life. Death no longer terrorizes him, for he knows he will live through it. Socrates saw himself as the embodiment of this true philosopher. In the course of his life he went through the necessary discipline until at the end he knew he had seen a glimpse of the meaning of life. Absolute Good was something so real to him that he did not flee death, although he twice had the chance to do so. Socrates believed that his escape would make his life meaningless. To him death was but the last step on the way to immortality.

SOCRATES' DEATH: A man to whom an eternal truth is so real that he is not afraid to die is an uncomfortable man to have in a defeated state which is trying to reconstruct a war-torn economy. Moreover, Socrates had shown his moral courage in opposition to the state several times during his service as a member of the Committee of the Senate by refusing to prosecute persons contrary to the Athenian laws, or without just reason. In 399 B.C. he was brought to trial on the charge of "impiety," and put to death, after refusing to go into voluntary exile, or to escape from prison. The heroic way in which he met his death was vividly described for all time by Plato in his famous dialogue, *The Phaedo.* Socrates' life was an intensely personal and almost religious experience. We know that he was conscious of his particular mission in life from the record of the speeches he made in his own defense at his trial which has been given us by Plato. But, as we said earlier, Socrates left no writings, and it is doubtful he ever developed any philosophical system. He only knew he was looking for an ultimate reality beyond time and space. And he knew this reality was really there. He believed that it could be found through a method of questioning and answering which has since been called the Socratic method. If the philosopher really wanted to know the truth, he should join up with other men like himself who were also eager to find the truth. They would choose a subject for discussion. Through questions and answers about the subject and topics related to it, the essential meaning of the subject would shine forth. It is also questionable whether Socrates thought of the theory of Ideas. Beauty, goodness, and truth were not ideas. They were living principles which were present in all things. Plato took the life and method of Socrates and made a philosophy from them.

PLATO

As with so many of the earlier philosophers, little is known about the life of one of the greatest philosophers of all times. We do know that he was the student of Socrates for many, many years, and that he did not start to write until after Socrates' death. It is impossible to give an account of Plato's philosophy here. The subject is too big. There are perhaps four aspects of his philosophy the influence of which his pupil Aristotle never completely escaped. All four of these elements belong to the more religious side of Plato's thought.

PERFECTION: The first aspect was Plato's desire for wholeness and perfection. There was just one world, the world of ideas. The sensible world was merely an image of the real world, full of imperfections and decay. But the real world was a whole, and perfect entity. Plato did not distinguish between knowledge, virtue, and being. With the artist's eye for seeing everything in its completeness, he said that the meaning of a thing was the same as the goodness of that thing, which was the being of that thing. In human affairs, for example, "virtue *was* knowledge." The truly good man was the man who had knowledge of the truth. Thus, the truly good man was the only man who could properly be said *to be,* insofar as he approached the absolute truth of man, his ideal human nature. Plato has been considered the first philosopher to make ethics a part of philosophy. But nowhere does he distinguish the object of ethics from the object of knowledge. The good and the true are but two aspects of the whole, in his opinion. Things are good insofar as they participate in their proper thought or Idea. When we think, however, we can only think in terms of definitions, which are themselves universal concepts which express characteristics common to many individual objects. For Plato, *logos,* the universal concept, contained the nature of being.

THEORY OF IDEAS: From this desire for wholeness comes the famous Platonic theory of Ideas. The world about us is imperfect. It is constantly coming into being and going out of being. It seems impossible that anything which really *is* should be part of such a world. When we look at a beautiful statue or a beautiful girl, we cannot say that either of them is perfectly beautiful. Yet, there is something beautiful about them. What is it that makes them beautiful? Plato says it has to be something which is itself perfectly beautiful, so beautiful that it never can change. The wholly beautiful is the essence or Idea of what it is to be beautiful. It is Absolute Beauty. In the same way, things are true because the Idea of Truth is present in them. A chair is a chair because it participates in the essence of chairness, which actually exists beyond the reach of the sensible world. Were there no Ideas, there could be no world as we know it.

THE REALITY OF THE IDEAS: If we consider Plato's Ideas abstractions, we shall never grasp his meaning. But if we think of how a great artist sometimes manages to catch the vital meaning of an event on his canvas, we are coming closer to Plato's theory. Take another example. How many of us have known someone for years when, suddenly, one day something happens, and we see him for the first time as a "real person." His personality has become alive and full of meaning in a way which has nothing to do with his appearance or his attitude. Our two minds seem to be looking directly at one another. We feel we have a real contact with that person. Plato's Ideas are similar to this something alive, yet not a part of the sensible world, which we seem to see in our friend.

THEORY OF KNOWLEDGE: Plato's theory of knowledge follows from his concept of the Ideas. Since the Ideas are eternal, learning is but a process of recollection. Plato thought there was something different from our body which would outlive our human lives. He had had experience of that something in knowing Socrates. As Socrates was sure, so Plato was sure that our minds were eternal. The sight of a sensible object recalls to our minds that moment in eternity when we "knew" the Idea of that object. The sight of a horse recalls the Idea of a horse, for instance. As knowledge is recollection, so it is also a purification. Plato thought we failed to grasp an Idea because our minds were imprisoned in the shadow world of the senses. In one of his most beautiful myths Plato compares the process of knowing with the experience of a man who has lived all his life watching shadows on the wall of his cave. One day something urges him to turn toward the entrance of the cave. The sunlight shining through the entrance almost blinds him. Gradually he becomes accustomed to the light and makes his way out of the cave. Finally, he stands in the pure sunlight. No longer is he living in the world of shadows. He sees things in their wholeness as they really are. Knowing is disciplining yourself to become accustomed to the pure light of truth.

PLATO'S ACADEMY: The process of knowledge brings us to the last aspect of Plato's thought. Socrates had lived the life of the philosopher. His life had become the Ideal on which all other philosophical ways of life would be patterned. Socrates had shown the dangers of this life. Men could only become perfect if they knew the truth. And they could only know the truth by giving up all the pleasures which bound them to the sensible world. The reward for such virtue was eternal life. Plato's Academy was the result of Plato's belief in the philosopher's way of life. It was a group of like-minded men bound together in the common purpose to find eternal life. In his Academy Plato tried to institutionalize the philosophical journey which had been the life of Socrates.

SUMMARY OF ARISTOTLE'S
INTELLECTUAL HERITAGE

The foregoing outline of philosophical thought before Aristotle gives some idea of the complex problems Aristotle had to solve. He was still living under the impact of Socrates' life and death. No matter how far his thought developed, Aristotle was never able to dismiss the religious insight into the nature of the universe which had been Socrates'. From the natural philosophers through Plato he inherited the two unsolved "natural" questions: What is the nature of reality? How do you account for change? From the Sophists and particularly from Plato he inherited the problems of human existence: What is the nature of man? What is his function in life?

ARISTOTLE'S LIFE

Aristotle was born in 384 B.C. in the Macedonian town of Stagira on the northeast coast of the peninsula of Chalcidice, or what is now called Thessalonika. He was born at a time when the Greek city-state system was already in decline. Athens, the city where the Greek genius had flowered, had been conquered by the city of Sparta in 404 B.C. During the years that followed, Greece was torn by the struggle for leadership between Sparta and the city of Thebes. Sparta was eventually defeated in 362 B.C. After her own defeat, Athens went through a period of dictatorship under a council known as the "Thirty." With the victory of Thebes she became once more the champion of liberty in Greece. While the Greek city states were gradually growing weaker, a new power was rising in the north, the kingdom of Macedonia. Aristotle's father, Nicomachus, was the court doctor and friend of the King of Macedonia, Amyntas II. Amyntas' son, Philip II, reorganized and increased the power of the kingdom. His son, Alexander, made the name of Macedonia famous in history by his lightning conquest of a huge empire stretching from Greece to the Indian Ocean. Aristotle himself probably spent his childhood at the Macedonian capital, Pella.

FAMILY: The young boy's interest in natural science came both through his race and his family. Stagira was an Ionian colony and Aristotle was an Ionian Greek. It is no wonder he followed the great scientific tradition of his forefathers. His family was of noble origin with a tradition of medicine. His father was a member of the Asklepiad family, which claimed to be descended from Asklepios, the Greek god-physician, who was said to be the son of Apollo and a mortal princess. We are told that the family trained its sons in medicine. Probably Aristotle had some medical training and helped his father perform surgical operations. His mother's family came from Chalcis in Euboea, where Aristotle was to spend his last days. Unfortunately, both parents died when Aristotle was quite young, and he was put under the guardianship of a Macedonian official, Proxenus.

> **COMMENT:**   It is important to note that all his life Aristotle enjoyed the protection of the Macedonian court, first under Philip II and later under Alexander. Perhaps this is one of the main reasons why Aristotle was able to exert such an influence over the intellectual world of his time.

PLATO'S ACADEMY: When he was eighteen, Aristotle entered Plato's Academy at Athens. He remained at the Academy until Plato's death in 347 B.C. It is difficult to imagine the influence Plato had over his pupil, but something of that influence has been discussed above. It is also hard for us to put ourselves in the atmosphere of the great school which Plato founded. We know that the Academy was literally *the* center of learning for the Mediterranean world into which Aristotle was born. The fame of the Academy and that of its founder brought men from all over the world to discuss the urgent questions of the day. We know these men visited the Academy because Plato mentions them in his dialogues, and even named some of them after the visitors. One who was so honored was Theaetetus, the man who is said to have discovered solid geometry. The astronomer, Eudoxus, came all the way from his home in Cyzicus in Asia Minor in 367 B.C. to discuss astronomy with Plato. In his dialogue named after the great Sophist, Protagoras, Plato shows us his interest in the Sophist's view of life. Then, too, Plato was a man who traveled far and wide. In the course of his travels he had come in contact with the Pythagoreans in Sicily, and with the Sicilian medical school of Philistion. It was from the Pythagoreans that Plato got his interest in numbers, which was to lead him in his later life to suggest that numbers were the basic principles of all things. In short, the Academy at Athens was truly cosmopolitan, reflecting the many influences of travelers from abroad.

The second fact about Plato's Academy was his method of teaching through discussion. The Academy aimed to put Socrates' way of life and his method into practice. Abstract problems were discussed with an enthusiasm which might amaze a visitor from the modern world. One effect of the dialectic method on Aristotle was to make him distinguish between that kind of knowledge which could be gained through discussion and that which could be acquired through observation and deduction. Probably because there was so much discussion, Aristotle had a chance to learn and examine thoroughly all the theories of the earlier philosophers. He also gained a respect for their wisdom, as his frequent references to the "opinions of the wise" show. Another effect of the discussion method was to make both Aristotle and his fellow students realize the value of definition and orderly thinking. An argument has no value unless you define your terms and argue in a systematic way. At the time of Aristotle's entrance into the Academy, there is reason to believe that Plato was working on a standard formula of argument. In such an atmosphere, it is not surprising that Aristotle should have developed his own tools for argument.

The third fact to be remembered about the Academy was that its students were working on every type of problem. The impact of the many ideas that were in the very air of the Academy must have left a deep impression on Aristotle. We know that Plato was particularly interested in the Pythagorean theory of numbers about the time Aristotle came to the Academy. Plato had also turned from his original concept of the Ideas as that which had meaning and value in an object to a more workable theory of the Ideas as universal principles. When we wonder why Aristotle devotes two books of his *Metaphysics* to showing that neither the Ideas nor numbers can be called substances, we must remember the background of the Academy.

Aristotle remained at the Academy for about twenty years. Probably he did not remain a student all this time, but began lecturing and teaching. We know he did some writing during this period, but unfortunately most of his early work has not survived the passage of time. From the fragments which have survived, we can see how deeply Aristotle was under the influence of his teacher during these early years.

ARISTOTLE LEAVES ATHENS: When Plato died in 347 B.C., his pupil, Speusippus, was elected to succeed him as head of the Academy. Apparently, there was a great deal of friction between Speusippus and Aristotle, who did not like Speusippus' interest in Plato's theory of numbers. At the same time Aristotle's presence had become not welcome in Athens. The Greek Confederacy had fallen to pieces. It was not the moment for a man who was known to have connections in Macedonian court circles to be in democratic Athens. Thus, for both personal and political reasons Aristotle decided to accept the invitation of a fellow student, Hermeias, to live at his court at Assos, a town on the slopes of Mount Ida in Asia Minor. Hermeias had risen from a slave to become the owner of a large mining property on Mount Ida. With the money earned from the mines he had purchased the title of prince from the Persians and now was a ruler in his own right.

Aristotle never returned to the Academy. Apparently, Hermeias gave him a great deal of liberty in organizing the small group of Platonists he had gathered at his court. Aristotle quickly became the leader of the group, directing discussions and giving lectures. This small group was later to form the core of the school that Aristotle himself founded at Athens. While at Assos, Aristotle married Hermeias' niece, Pythias. She gave him one daughter, whom he named after her mother.

After three years at Hermeias' court Aristotle moved to Mitylene on the island of Lesbos in the Aegean Sea. He was probably persuaded to go there by another fellow-student at the Academy, Theophrastus, the future author of a celebrated book called *Characters,* which had a great influence on English writers of the seventeenth century. Little is known of Aristotle's activities at Mitylene. Many scholars think he did most of his research on biology during this time. It is probable that his friend, Theophrastus, helped him collect his material.

TUTOR TO ALEXANDER: Aristotle remained on Lesbos until 342 B.C. He then accepted an invitation from Philip II of Macedonia to become tutor to his son, Alexander. Aristotle had not been at his new post very long when he heard of the capture and crucifixion of his friend, Hermeias, by the Persians. Aristotle was so shaken by the death of his friend that he composed a poem in his honor. This action did not meet with the approval of the Greek world, as Hermeias had been suspected of plotting with the Greeks' Macedonian master, Philip. We tend to think of Aristotle as a hardened intellectual with no emotional reactions. Aristotle's defense of his friend in the face of Athenian disapproval is proof of the value he attached to friendship. On the practical side it was probably Hermeias' contact with Philip which caused the Macedonian king to send for Aristotle to teach his son.

We know little about Aristotle's education of Alexander. Judging from the *Politics,* we can be sure that Aristotle thought the education of kings very important. We know that he wrote one short work for his pupil on the subject of monarchy, and another on colonies. It was the fashion of the time to hire philosophers to teach king's sons. Plato had tried to teach the young tyrant of Sicily. Aristotle tried to teach Alexander, apparently with little success. Alexander was more inclined toward a life of action than a life of study. When Philip died in 336 B.C., relations between Aristotle and his pupil had already become quite strained. When Alexander set off to conquer the world, Aristotle returned to his native town of Stagira.

THE LYCEUM: Aristotle's life at Pella was not all unpleasantness. It was probably at Pella that Aristotle turned his thoughts to politics and decided to make an anthology of Greek constitutions. He also made the acquaintance of a man who was influential at the Macedonian court by the name of Antipater. The acquaintance ripened into friendship. When Alexander left for the East, he left Antipater regent of Greece until his return. Antipater encouraged Aristotle to return to Athens and promised him his support.

So it happened that Aristotle returned to Athens in 335 B.C. His return marks the high point of his career. On the outskirts of Athens, a little to the northeast there stood a grove which was sacred to Apollo Lykeios and the Muses. Here Socrates used to come and spend a few quiet hours. Here Aristotle founded his own school to be known the world over as the Lyceum.

There has been some question as to why Aristotle did not return to the Academy. Speusippus had died, but the Academy had already elected one of Aristotle's old friends, Xenocrates, as head. It was obvious that the world-renowned teacher of Alexander could not accept a position lower than head of the Academy. It was fitting that he open his own school. Since he was by this time the recognized leading philosopher and teacher of Greece, Aristotle immediately announced that he was the successor to Plato and his school, the successor to the Academy. In a short time, the Lyceum had taken the place of the Academy, whose students were applying for admission. The solitary reign of the Academy was over.

Aristotle's work at the Lyceum was the fruit of his years of research and analysis. During his years at Athens he seems to have written or revised most of his major writings. He completed the classification of the sciences, developed his own system of logic, and carried most of the sciences to a point which they had never reached before and were not to reach again for a long, long time. At the same time the influence of his ethical and political theories was being felt in Athens and throughout the Greek world.

Following in the Platonic tradition of learning by discussion, Aristotle seems to have written most of his works which have come down to us as lecture notes from which he talked to the students. Apparently, Aristotle was an organizer. Study hours were not free but were planned at the Lyceum. Tradition tells us that Aristotle gave his most serious lectures in the morning. In the afternoon he spoke on more popular subjects, like rhetoric, in order to attract

the crowds that came out from the city to hear him. Like the
Academy, the Lyceum had a spirit of its own. Aristotle laid down
the rules by which both students and teachers lived. These rules
were to survive long after his death. Under Aristotle, Plato's idea
of a common life shared by friends in search of wisdom became
the basis of the first university in Europe.

ARISTOTLE'S INFLUENCE: As was the case with Plato, it is
impossible for us to realize the influence which Aristotle's teaching
and personality had over his students. Aristotle seemed to live
his teaching. His followers, called Peripatetics because they used
to walk around the arcades of the Lyceum discussing philosophy,
showed little influence of Aristotle's teaching. Once the man was
gone, it seemed to be difficult to recapture the original meaning of
his words. It was not until the Middle Ages that Aristotle became
alive again and spoke to the Schoolmen with the same energy he
had put into his teaching at the Lyceum. Thus, Aristotle's teaching at the Lyceum did not give rise to a new philosophy. Rather
it marked the ultimate achievement of Greek philosophy.

HIS LAST YEARS: The death of Alexander in 323 B.C. shocked
the entire Greek world. Once again Aristotle was *persona non
grata* at Athens. A charge of "impiety" was brought against him.
Rather than have Athens "sin twice against philosophy" (Socrates
had been accused of the same crime), Aristotle turned his school
over to his old friend, Theophrastus, and fled to his mother's home
in Chalcis. He died in Chalcis from a stomach disease at the age
of 64 in 320 B.C. Aristotle must have been a lonely old man in the
last years of his life. Exiled from the school to which he had
given so much, he withdrew more and more into himself. In one
of his last letters he writes that he had become more and more
attracted by "the wonderland of myth."

Aristotle was buried beside the body of his wife, as he requested in
his will. His daughter, Pythias, his adopted son, Neandor, his son
by his mistress, Nicomachus, and his mistress all survived him. For
each he made special provision in his will. It is wonderful that
Aristotle's will has come down to us, for it proves once more how
very human he was. He not only provided for his family, but
he freed his slaves. Antipater was appointed executor of the estate
to see that everything was properly carried out. Always an organizer, Aristotle did not forget anything which might contribute
to the welfare of those he loved after his death.

ARISTOTLE'S WORKS AND METHOD

Aristotle's known writings form such an impressive body of knowledge that it is hard to believe he wrote many more books than have come down to us. The entire complex of his works falls roughly into three parts.

THE FIRST GROUP OF WRITINGS

These belong to Aristotle's early period. The works in this group are of a popular nature and were published by the philosopher himself. Unfortunately, only fragments of them survive today. Most of our knowledge about them has come from comments made by later Greek and Roman scholars. The great Roman orator and thinker, Cicero, is one of our best sources of information about these earliest writings of Aristotle. According to a list of his writings which dates from the third century A.D. there were nineteen of these more popular works. We may assume that they were written during Aristotle's early years at the Academy when he was still under the influence of his teacher, Plato, for they all were written in dialogue form. A dialogue is a work written in the form of a conversation between a teacher and his students, or friends. The titles of some of these dialogues show the direct influence of Plato. For instance, Plato's great dialogue on love was called the *Symposium*. Aristotle named one of his dialogues the *Symposium*.

Among the earliest dialogues were one called the *Grylus*, which discussed rhetoric or the art of public speaking, and another called the *Eudemus*, which discussed the nature of the world in much the same terms as Plato's work, the *Phaedo*. The *Eudemus* accepts Plato's theory of the transmigration of souls and the view that learning is recollection. Another work called the *Protrepticus* is an invitation to a prince of the island of Cyprus to study philosophy. In those days, philosophy was considered as useful and necessary

27

a science as physics and chemistry are today. The *Protrepticus* served Cicero as a model for one of his works, and it was well known throughout the classical period and the Middle Ages.

The most significant of Aristotle's earlier writings is *On Philosophy*. It is thought that Aristotle wrote the work while he was living at Hermeias' court at Assos. The book is important because it contains Aristotle's first attack on Plato's theory of Ideas, particularly on his later theory of ideal numbers. The dialogues *On Monarchy* and *On Colonies* were written while Aristotle was tutor to Alexander at the Macedonian court of Pella.

In addition to these dialogues about which we have some information, there are many about which we know next to nothing. Early lists of his writings mention such works as *On Justice, On the Poets, On Wealth, On Prayer, On Education*, and *On Pleasure*. Probably all these works formed the basis for Aristotle's later more finished treatments of the same topics. During this early period, Aristotle also composed poems, such as the one he wrote in honor of Hermeias.

THE SECOND GROUP OF WRITINGS

This group contains notes and collections of research material which were incorporated into the third group of works, the scientific writings. Again, all of this second group has been lost in the passage of history. Only one of the books written during this period of Aristotle's research has come down to us. This is the famous *Constitution of Athens*. We know that Aristotle collected and wrote down all the Greek constitutions of his day. It is possible to gain some idea of the wealth of material Aristotle must have collected on every kind of subject because the lists of works said to have been written by him, which were drawn up in classical times, contain some 200 titles!

THE THIRD GROUP OF WRITINGS

Almost all the writings of Aristotle which are familiar to us today fall under the third group of his works known as the scientific writings. It is generally agreed that most of them were written as lecture material and notes for the use of his students, while he was teaching at the Lyceum in Athens. As we noted earlier it was while he was at the Lyceum that Aristotle completed his classification of the sciences as we have them today. He divides the entire field of science into three parts: the theoretical sciences, the practical sciences, and the productive sciences. We shall see later what he meant by these names. Today, we divide Aristotle's scientific works into eight parts, each with its own subject matter and its own method of procedure. This division follows Aristotle's own system of breaking down the different sciences according to *what* each studied and *how* it studied that topic. The eight sciences are logic, physics, metaphysics or the science which comes "after physics," biology, psychology, ethics, politics, and finally aesthetics or the science of art. Although we do not call all these subjects "sciences" today, we have not developed any new method by which to classify the two fields of philosophy and science. We have only added new sciences to the ones Aristotle set up. Aristotle's contribution to science becomes clear when we remember that he was the first person to make a systematic classification of the various disciplines of human knowledge. He was the first to realize that it was impossible to study anything without first knowing what it was you wanted to study and finding out the best method to study that particular subject.

LOGIC: The science of the *logos* is the science of definition and argument. Aristotle's logic is perhaps his greatest contribution to both science and philosophy. He himself did not consider logic a separate branch of study but thought of it as an *organon* or tool to right thinking. You cannot find out the truth unless you can reason from sound principles in a systematic fashion. Aristotle's logical system is his answer to the problem of the relation of the structure of language to the process of thought and the nature of reality. *The Categories* and *On Interpretation* deal with the nature of individual terms and simple statements. These are the raw materials of language. *The Prior Analytics* introduces the student to what Aristotle considered the essence of argument: proving that the individual fact is what it is because of why it is. It is relating the definition of anything to its cause. This method of proof Aristotle called the *syllogism*. Now, all syllogisms, like all arguments, are not the same. They differ according to the nature of the principles on which your argument is based. In the *Posterior Analytics* Aristotle tells us how to argue scientifically. He discusses how we can use the syllogism so as to be sure that the outcome of our argument will be the truth. If we want our result to be the truth, the grounds or principles of our argument must be both true and necessary. This means that they must be principles derived from our experience of the nature of things. In the last group of the logical works, Aristotle turns to those kinds of arguments which do not satisfy the requirements of scientific reasoning. In the *Topics* he discusses that form of argument which is based on the dialectic or conversation. The grounds of such an argument are principles derived from the nature of the thought process that are not rooted in objective experience. They are thus essentially opinions, the opinions either of "the many" or "the wise." In the *Sophistic Elenchi* Aristotle discusses arguments which are not really arguments at all. The Sophists made two kinds of mistakes, he says. The first is a mistake in language. They think they have a premise for an argument, where there are no grounds for it at all. Second, they make mistakes in thinking. From a true premise they think they are arguing in a scientific fashion, but this is not really the case. It was Aristotle who gave the word sophism its meaning of a fallacious argument. A sophism is a trick used instead of a sound argument to prove the point you want to prove. We shall look a little further into Aristotle's logic when we come to discussing his own philosophic method.

PHYSICS: Aristotle wrote many treatises on physics. It is important to remember that physics did not mean the same thing to the Greeks as it means to us today. Physics comes from the Greek word for nature. Thus, the best translation of Aristotle's well-known work which has been called the *Physics* would be the *Study of Nature*. For Aristotle's writings on physics contained his philosophy of nature and his observations of the natural world. Of Aristotle's writings on nature the best known to us are the *Physics, On the Heavens, Of Generation and Corruption,* and his work on the influences of the four elements, fire, air, earth and water, upon the heavenly bodies, or the *Meteorologica*. Aristotle was the first to separate the study of weather from astronomy. Much that he includes under meteorology is still part of that science today.

METAPHYSICS: The third discipline is what Aristotle called first philosophy, or the science of being, but which is commonly called today, *metaphysics*. Aristotle's work by that name contains his concept of the nature of being, and what it is *to be* essentially.

BIOLOGY: The fourth discipline in Aristotle's list of sciences is biology, or the science of life. In many respects Aristotle did his best work in this science, as it was the phenomenon of life which interested him most. The titles of his biological works show the range of the philosopher's interests in the world of living things. *The Parts of Animals* is an introduction to biology. Then follows another book which many scholars believe Aristotle did not write, but which recent research has put back on the list of Aristotle's writings. It is called *On the Motion of Animals*. Other books on natural history include *On the Origin of Animals* and *On the Gen-*

eration of Animals. Ancient lists of the philosopher's works contain many other titles, which are not considered to have been written by his pupils or friends. These titles illustrate the kinds of problems which Aristotle had his students work on at the Lyceum. Examples are *On Color, On Plants, On Hearing.*

COMMENT: There has been much discussion of the many mistakes Aristotle made in his observation of living things. One can excuse some of these mistakes by saying that the limited scientific experiment never seems to have occurred to the Greek mind. Nevertheless, it is curious that Aristotle should have thought that women had fewer teeth than men, when the simplest observation would have shown him otherwise. Again, with all his theories of dynamic change it is hard to see how he could have failed to develop some theory of evolution. Yet he specifically rejects Empodocles' view on the subject. On the other hand, we should not underestimate the enormous amount of accurate research Aristotle carried out in the field of biology. He was the first to classify animals into genus and species. He also discussed the question of pangenesis with much perception. As a question that has played a large role in the development of modern biology, it is concerned with whether animals are completely formed in the embryo from the moment of their conception, or whether the different parts develop as the embryo grows. Aristotle held the modern view that the parts of the animal are formed in stages as the embryo grows in size.

PSYCHOLOGY: Despite the fact that Plato played a large role in the development of the concept of the soul, Aristotle still remains the founder of the fifth branch of science, psychology. He was the first to consider the problems of the human psyche as a separate discipline. His best known work in this field, *On the Soul,* defines what a soul is, and then takes up the functions of the soul specifically related to man, such as sensing and knowing. His other works on the same subject have been collected into a book with the title, *Parva Naturalia.* This book discusses such topics as *Sense and the Sensible, Memory and Recollection, Sleeping and Waking Dreams, Prophecy in Sleep, On the Length and Shortness of Life, On Youth and Old Age, On Life and Death,* and *On Breath.*

ETHICS: . The sixth discipline in Aristotle's classification of the sciences is ethics. Ethics belongs to the practical sciences, to that branch of knowledge which is concerned with human action. Three books on ethics which have been at various times attributed to Aristotle have come down to us: the *Eudemian Ethics,* the *Nico-*

machean Ethics, and the Magna Moralia or Great Ethics. Only the first two were written by Aristotle. The oldest lists of Aristotle's writings give only one book on ethics, entitled simply Ethics. Until recently scholars did not think that Aristotle wrote the Eudemian Ethics but attributed this work to one of his pupils, Eudemus. At the present time it is generally believed that Eudemian and Nicomachean refer to two of Aristotle's pupils who edited these "textbooks" on ethics. Some scholars, however, believe that Aristotle named the Nicomachean Ethics after his son, Nicomachus. The Magna Moralia was probably written by followers of the Peripatetic School in the early third century B.C. Of the two works by Aristotle, the Eudemian Ethics is considered to have been the earlier work. Some think it might have been written at Assos during 348 and 345 B.C. The Nicomachean Ethics contains Aristotle's mature thinking on the subject.

Although the study of ethics was already becoming a separate science when Aristotle first came to the Academy, it was Aristotle who separated the study of virtue from the study of knowledge definitively. Ethics comes from the Greek word, ethos. It means primarily, custom or habit, and secondly, character. Ethics is the study of those habits which go to make a good character; it is the study of morals as they relate to the individual.

POLITICS: The seventh science, politics, is the study of morals as a system of behavior in a society. The question in ethics is: "Is there a set of values by which the individual may act wisely and well?" The question in politics is: "Is there an integrated system of values as expressed in the power structure of a community which will enable society to live well?" Politics is the ethics of the political system, and is discussed in Aristotle's work by that name, the Politics.

AESTHETICS: The last branch of Aristotle's scientific system is that of the productive sciences. Artistic creativity, or rather the nature of the art object, forms the subject matter of Aristotle's eighth discipline, aesthetics. Under this heading come two works, On Rhetoric, and the Poetics.

The word, rhetoric, comes from the Greek word, rhetor, a public speaker. As its title suggests, the book teaches the would-be politician or lawyer the art of persuasion through words. As a creative science, its aim is to produce the emotion desired by the speaker in his audience, and to sway the listeners to his opinion. Its aim is not to teach a man to speak the truth. This is the aim, properly speaking, of logic. Nevertheless, Aristotle considers a sound argument an essential part of the art of public speaking. The *Rhetoric* was widely read in classical times, but it has little relevance to present-day problems of speaking to a mass audience. Public speaking was very important in the Athenian law courts. Naturally, there was a definite method of speaking with which citizens wanted to be familiar. As every Athenian had the chance to become either the judge or the lawyer for a case, it was in his interest to know the rules of the game.

If the *Rhetoric* has had little influence in modern times, the *Poetics* has inspired more criticism than any other of Aristotle's works. It is the first work that we have on the philosophy of art.

PHILOSOPHIC DEVELOPMENT

As it is not within the scope of this book to discuss all the works of Aristotle, we have selected the five most important ones. They are the most important for two reasons. First, they contain the basic elements of Aristotle's philosophy. Second, they have had the most influence on the subsequent development of philosophy from the classical period right down to modern times. The works which will be discussed are the *Physics*, the *Metaphysics*, the *Ethics*, the *Politics*, and the *Poetics*.

PLATONIC REBELLION:　　A word should be said about Aristotle's personal development as a philosopher. The five books listed above were written during his years spent at the Lyceum. When we read the concise, dry, scientific statements found in these works, which lack poetic and dramatic flavor, we must remember that they are the fruit of Aristotle's mature years. Recent research has shown that the young Aristotle shared Plato's almost religious view of the Ideas. There is considerable evidence that Aristotle's interests as a philosopher shifted as he grew older. From being concerned with the transcendent, non-sensible, and unseen world of the Ideas, Aristotle developed a consuming passion for the facts and things of this world. In this sense, he was the first philosopher to be confronted with the problem of the relation of religion to science. Up to the end of his life, he seems to have believed that science, at least his science, did not explain satisfactorily the vital question: "Whence and what is life?" As he wrote in one of his last letters, he withdrew more and more into the "wonderland of myth," the Bible of Greek religion. He was never able to renounce the Platonic vision of a world which was essentially spirit.

THE IMPORTANCE OF CONTEXT: A second aspect of Aristotle's development is his own consciousness of his place in philosophy. Aristotle may be said to have invented intellectual history. No matter what subject is under analysis, he always takes care to trace the history of the development of that concept from its origins down to his own time. The opinions of "the many and the wise" who went before are crucial to him. After he has looked at the historical background of his subject, he proceeds to show what *his* contribution to the solution of the problem is. Socrates' self-awareness was based on the sense of divine mission. Aristotle's grew naturally out of his view of change. In a matter-of-fact way he simply fitted himself into the general scheme of things.

ARISTOTLE'S METHOD

To speak of Aristotle's method is to do the philosopher an injustice. Aristotle would have been the last person to say that he had a particular method, believing as he did that every science has its own subject matter and its own method of procedure. Nevertheless, his philosophy does seem to be inspired with a way of looking at things that is distinctly Aristotelian. Much has been written on this subject. The views on Aristotle's way of approaching philosophy which are expressed below are but a few among the many which could be suggested.

LANGUAGE: Aristotle, like many of his fellow Greeks, firmly believed in man's capacity to know. For him it may be said that the crucial fact was that man was able to know and understand the universe in which he found himself. As the function of a knife was to cut, the function of man was to know. The world would have existed if man had not been born into it, but it would not have been *known to exist.* Thus, man and man's knowledge were the focus of Aristotle's philosophy.

Aristotle held that there is nothing unnatural or even supernatural in man's ability to know. Man is a rational animal as a bird is a winged animal. It is no more surprising that a man should know than that a bird should fly. As birds fly in formations which are suited to their function of flying, so man lives in cities which are suited to his function of knowing. Knowing requires communication and communication requires language. Society provides the necessary condition for man's knowing, namely, the possibility of communication through language.

In Aristotle's view to be able to say exactly what something is, is *to know*. It does not mean "to reason." We reason about something before we know what it is. Once we can say what a thing is, there is no longer any need to discuss it. It is no coincidence that the Greek words for "to know" and "to see" are closely related. "I have seen" in Greek is the same thing as "I know." Knowing is seeing things as they are. When our newspapers talk about "clarifying" a situation, meaning by this that they want to enable us to understand it better, Aristotle would have understood just what they mean.

"To know" means to be able to see something so that you can say exactly what it is. Unfortunately, however, it is not easy to say precisely what something is. If we want to say what the maple standing just outside the front door of our house is, we can say what all maples are, and make a few statements about how this tree is different from other maples we have seen. Yet we have not said exactly what this particular maple is. We have only been talking in generalities. Life deals with individual concrete things, but reason deals with universal concepts. How can you bridge the gap between the two?

Plato tried to bridge the gap by his dialectic method of discussion. He believed that if you talk round a subject long enough, and look at it from every angle, suddenly the intrinsic characteristic, i.e., general meaning, of that subject will shine through. You will "know" what justice is, for example. Aristotle thought this method a good one in matters which did not concern things which "were always or for the most part" in a particular way. Plato's method was good for ethics, for instance, but Aristotle did not feel it satisfied the requirements of science, or rather theoretical science, such as physics or mathematics.

THE ANALYTIC: Aristotle called the method he invented analytics; we call it logic. Analysis means "breaking up." The analytic is the breaking up of an argument into its individual terms and the examination of what those terms mean. Analysis is thus not a science in its own right or a particular method of approach. It is a process common to all the sciences. It is the basis of scientific investigation, because it answers most closely the requirements of the process of thought. We reason by the addition and subtraction of terms in a thought sequence.

The process of analysis falls into two parts. There is first the process of discovery and then the process of demonstration. During the process of discovery we conduct an empirical investigation of the subject matter. We collect data and material necessary for the final proof. Reason enters into this first process insofar as we choose that material which is relevant to our subject. But it is when we come to the proof that the correctness of our thought sequence becomes vitally important. How to determine whether the thought sequence is a good one or a poor one? Aristotle's answer was the syllogism.

SYLLOGISM: Aristotle's definition of a syllogism is as follows. "A syllogism is a formulation of words in which, when certain assumptions are made, something other than what has been assumed necessarily follows from the fact that the assumptions are such." An example of the simplest kind of syllogism is this: when A equals B, and B equals C, then A equals C. There are others which are much more complex. The advantage of the syllogism is that it expresses the relation of the terms with which we reason to one another without referring to any subject matter. A, B, and C can be anything. No matter what they represent, the thought sequence will be a good one, so long as you keep A, B, and C in their proper place.

The value of Aristotle's invention cannot be over-emphasized. By using the variables, A, B, and C, he broke up the process of thought into its several parts. The danger lies in the fact that it is possible to reason from false premises to a logically correct conclusion. Right thinking can become independent of what is thought.

WORDS AND THEIR COMBINATIONS: In the use of the syllogism, however, it is impossible to let the variables stand. There comes a time when they have to represent something, if the thought process is to be meaningful. In the *Categories*, Aristotle analyzes the nature of individual terms, which can be put in place of the variables, A, B, and C, and their relation to one another. First, he discusses things that can be said "without combination." He examines single words or words in pairs that do not form a sentence. The fundamental term is substance, the individual object which alone can be the subject of definition, for example, man. All the other terms depend on substance and are attributed to substance. There are nine of them: quantity (how many men); quality (what kind of men); relation (like, unlike); place (where); date (time); position (standing, sitting, etc.); state (armed, dressed, etc.); action (heating); and passivity (being heated). Second, he takes up terms and their contraries. In Aristotle's opinion, contraries are necessary in any account of change. There are four classes: correlatives (as in the concept of half or double, the other part of half an apple is "opposed to the first part"); opposites (good and bad, black and white); contraries (this means a positive state and its absence or privation, for example, sight and blindness, hearing and deafness); and finally affirmative and negative (true and false, "is" and "is not"). Toward the end of the *Categories* he defines those terms which identify change: generation (birth); destruction (death); increase (growth); diminution (growing smaller); alteration (as when something cold becomes hot); and change of place (walking, etc.). In *On Interpretation* Aristotle analyzes pairs of terms which can be put together to form sentences, which are made up of subject (man) and predicate (runs). There are four kinds of basic sentences: 1) a man runs; 2) a man does not run; 3) a not-man runs; and 4) a not-man does not run. Aristotle develops from these four basic kinds of sentences all the other more complex forms. Finally, in the *Prior Analytics* Aristotle takes up the combination of terms in groups of threes: two propositions or premises, and a conclusion. This is the syllogism.

PRINCIPLES OF ARGUMENT: To show the relation of terms in a syllogism it is not enough to know what your terms are. They have to have something in common one with the other which will serve as the basis of your picking those particular terms in the first place. You cannot reason without some common ground of argument. Earlier, we showed that Aristotle held there were three kinds of syllogism: the scientific syllogism, the syllogism based on opinion and conversation, and the syllogism which is not a syllogism. In general, the kind of syllogism or argument you have depends on the principles you choose as the basis of your argument.

THE SCIENTIFIC SYLLOGISM: ITS TERMS AND SUBJECT MATTER: In the *Posterior Analytics* Aristotle shows there are five subjects with which science is concerned: 1) what a name refers to, for example, to what does the word "table" refer; 2) whether this particular thing, like a table, exists; 3) what it is, i.e., its definition; 4) what are its basic properties. A table has legs and a top, for example. 5) Why it is. Now we know what a thing is when we can say why it is. It is the purpose of science to show the connection between an object and its cause. To show the connection between the "that" and the "why" is what Aristotle calls demonstration. Every scientific inquiry begins at stage two, for we usually know what a word refers to, otherwise we would not use that word. And we usually know that the object is, otherwise we would not choose to find out "what it is." This means that we start with a number of observed facts, as the subject matter of our inquiry. The most significant fact of all the observed facts (i.e., the fact which all the other facts have in common) determines what kind of inquiry we have. For example, in physics we start with the most significant fact that the world is in motion. In psychology we start with the fact that man has something which makes him alive. In metaphysics we start with the fact that things are. Thus, every science has its principle distinctive fact which sets it apart from all the other sciences. Every science has its own subject matter. Part of a scientific inquiry consists in classifying particular facts under the chief fact with which they are most closely associated.

THE PRINCIPLES OF SCIENCE: In any thought process the the only way we can reason with the facts we have on hand is, as we have said, to find their common ground. This common ground Aristotle calls *archai* or first principles. *Arche* is the Greek word not only for "principle" but also, and more commonly, for "rule" or "command." An *arche* of any science is the principle which controls and regulates the facts of that science. But we must not confuse the meaning of *arche* with our modern concept of a scientific law. Scientific laws offer explanations, which can be expressed in quantitative, measurable terms, of the way our universe behaves. Their validity rests on the fact that they can be proven on the basis of experimental observation and measurement. Aristotle's first principles are not explanations. They are universal, self-evident truths assumed to be rooted either in the nature of things or the nature of thought. For example, Newton's laws of motion explain the various phenomena associated with mechanical motion. Aristotle would look for the first principles of such motion in an examination of the general factors necessary to produce motion in the first place. His *archai* are thus akin to axioms whose truth is so evident at first sight that no further proof is required.

What distinguishes scientific principles from principles based on opinion and conversation is that they are based on *experience*. Aristotle tells us that the fact that scientific principles are based on experience makes them true and certain. These principles are not something that are the result of reasoning. They are determined by a process of induction and intuitive perception. This means that first we look at a sufficient number of individual facts. We see what these facts have in common and wherein they differ. After looking long enough we become aware of the principle that governs all those facts. It is necessary to realize that Aristotle was very insistent on the importance of observation. His *Politics* begins: "Observation shows us." Science is true because it is based on objective experience. It is rooted in the nature of reality. If a first principle does not answer to the nature of reality, it is not a first principle. We must observe once more, perceive more accurately, and test our observation. This is the basis of all scientific experiment.

DEMONSTRATION: Once you have grasped the principle which governs your facts, it is a simple step to the definition of the particular subject matter you have chosen. Aristotle's favorite example of demonstration is the reason for the eclipse of the moon. First, we see there is no light on the moon. By seeing an eclipse often enough, we hit upon the universal truth that whatever has something between it and its source of light loses its light. We then think, the moon has the earth between it and the sun. Therefore, the moon has no light. We have reasoned from the particular fact to the universal truth or principle and *back again* to the fact. The scientific syllogism or demonstration consists in reasoning from the principle back to the fact. Once we know the why, the what is nothing but a restatement of the why. The eclipse of the moon is its loss of light due to the earth's coming between it and its source of light, the sun.

DIALECTIC SYLLOGISM: As stated earlier, some syllogisms are not based on principles derived from experience but upon the structure of thought. For this reason, Aristotle tells us, they cannot be true and certain. For our thoughts sometimes can be true and sometimes not. Metaphysical and ethical syllogisms are based on such principles. Ethics especially is rooted in what is thought. Its foundation is opinion. When Aristotle defines happiness, for example, he says we have to begin with the views that have generally been held about happiness. Since Aristotle is aware that reasoning based on what people *think* is liable to error, it is not strange that he considers tradition so important. What most people have thought over a long period of time is less likely to be wrong than what some person thinks up on the spur of the moment. There is wisdom in the accumulated thought and mythology of the ages. In accepting opinions as the basis of argument, Aristotle is careful to say which opinions he thinks are most foolproof. First, he accepts the opinions of the "many" either as expressed in tradition or as expressed collectively, for example, in an assembly of citizens. Second, he accepts the opinions of the "wise," of those men who have spent their lives dealing with difficult problems and solving some of them. Third, when he rejects the opinions of the "wise" in general, he will turn to the opinions of those few who are respected as the "wisest among the wise."

SYLLOGISMS WHICH ARE NOT SYLLOGISMS: Finally, there are types of reasoning which neither follow the rules of right thinking nor are rooted in principles which can be shown to be based on either experience or opinion. Such are the syllogisms of the Sophists whom Aristotle makes the target of his book refuting their methods, the *Sophistic Elenchi.*

THE SIGNIFICANCE OF ARISTOTLE'S LOGIC: So familiar are Aristotle's concepts of induction, first principles, category, demonstration, syllogisms, and definition that it is hard for us to look back to a time when the implications of the interrelation of language and thought were not well understood. Aristotle's analysis of language as an instrument whereby man could arrive at an accurate understanding of observable facts opened the door to the development of science. His classification of the sciences according to subject matter and first principles made scientific inquiry possible.

KNOWLEDGE AND REALITY

We have seen that Aristotle believed that the possibility of knowing scientific truth was based on our experience of individual facts. Language is the tool which helps us state what we know about nature in an accurate and meaningful way, but it is dependent on our observation of nature. The question arises, "How can we be sure we know anything?" In terms of what are we to understand the world in which we live?

NATURE AS PROCESS: Like the Greek philosophers before him, Aristotle did not consider the world static and inactive. He thought that the fundamental fact of the universe was change. We can only understand nature if we look at natural things from the standpoint of the dynamics of change. What Aristotle called motion, or change, we shall call process.

PROCESS AND FUNCTION: It is clear that nothing is isolated and complete in itself in this world. Everything is involved in some kind of process. An acorn, for instance, is part of the process which ends in the oak tree. Coal is the outcome of the process which started with green plants. It is also plain that an object is related to its process by virtue of how it acts in the process. Aristotle has no mechanical theory of change, which explains motion in terms of forces of attraction and repulsion *outside* the object. To him, each thing in the world has an *internal* tendency to act in a certain way, that is, to perform a definite *function.* The performance of its function is the reason for a thing's existence. Function determines the kind of process to which it will belong, (i.e., the conditions of its functioning,) as well as the end product of that process.

KNOWLEDGE BASED ON FUNCTION: Aristotle considers function the key to understanding the natural world. We understand change when we understand how things subject to change function. Second, we understand the function of individual things when we know how they actually behave in a given process. Third, we know what an individual thing is insofar as we understand its functioning in that process. This means that Aristotle views the structure of reality as a system of interrelated functionings on the part of those elements which belong to the system. Scientific knowledge is thus basically a knowledge of function.

THE STRUCTURE OF THE NATURAL WORLD: If nature is to be understood in terms of the different kinds of functions of its various parts, the universe can be classified on the basis of function. Life, for example, is a function, since it is the characteristic behavior of certain kinds of natural beings. Non-life is also a function. The first major division of nature, therefore, is between animate objects (those that have life) and inanimate objects (those that do not have life). Observation shows us, however, that not all living things have the same kind of life. Aristotle thus proceeds to classify animate beings according to the kind of life each has. He makes his classification on the theory that some kinds of life are more complex and include other kinds. The result is a classification of animate organisms on an ascending scale. On the bottom rung are all plants and lower animals. These possess only a nutritive form of life. They simply vegetate and reproduce. On the next rung are those animals which not only perform the basic function of self-preservation, but they also have the ability to react to their environment through the use of their senses. This form of life Aristotle calls sensitive life. Most animals belong in this class. On the top rung in the order of living things is man, who has both the faculties of sense and the faculty of mind. In possessing the power to know, man is unique among natural beings.

KNOWING AS A FUNCTION: Man's function of knowing is but one among the many functions which are to be found in the natural world, although it is the most important one. This means that the way man knows will have something in common with other kinds of functions, and particularly with the functions of other living things. For example, knowing is similar to the vegetative function of a plant in that it is dependent on the world for its operation. It is similar to the sensitive function of other animals insofar as it is a response to the world based on an ability to discriminate between objects. A dog does not react in the same way to everything he meets. His eyes and nose tell him what to avoid and what to approach. In an analogous way, man also distinguishes between different objects of knowledge. Moreover, just as the senses (for example, the eyes) cannot be mistaken about their proper objects (in this case, color and shape), unless they are injured, so the mind cannot be mistaken about those things which are the direct object of its knowing. We can be mistaken in our reasoning, but we cannot make a mistake in knowing a tree as a tree, or a man as a man.

KNOWING AS A PROCESS: Knowing is not only a function, in Aristotle's view, it is also a kind of process, since it is the functioning of mind. To understand what Aristotle means, we must turn to his general explanation of the process of motion in animals. In his work, *On the Soul,* he distinguishes essentially four factors in this process (Aristotle actually describes only three factors, as he puts the animal which is moved and his instrument of motion in the same category. For purposes of clarity, I have divided this category in two): 1) There is the animal which is moved—for example, a dog. 2) There is the instrument by which the bodily organs of the animal are moved—his legs. 3) There is the stimulus presented by the environment—a bone. And 4) there is the desire awakened in the animal by the presence of the bone to go and get it. Aristotle views the action of living things as a *response* to some kind of a stimulus *outside* the organism. But the *actual movement* of the organism proceeds from an *internal* impulse or drive. As mentioned earlier, Aristotle sees a drive, or *horme* in Greek, implanted in every natural thing to behave in a certain definite way. In animals, this drive appears as a desire for or rejection of something in the environment. Human beings also act from desire; and their basic desire, the philosopher tells us, is "the desire to know." But men possess the capacity of mind. Hence they are not limited to reacting to an immediate and present stimulus—as the dog reacts to the bone, for example—but can act from a desire which has been modified by reflection and deliberation. Men can bring their intelligence to the service of desire.

The process of knowing has characteristics similar to the process of motion observed in animals, according to Aristotle. But since knowing is the highest type of natural process, the philosopher finds knowing difficult to describe in terms of the simpler motion of inanimate, vegetative, or animal life. For this reason, he chooses to describe knowing in terms of what he believes to be the next highest natural process, the process of seeing. In *On the Soul,* Aristotle devotes a good deal of space to an analysis of seeing, which he derives from his view of the way living things seem to move. We have already described the four factors involved in the process of animal motion. In *On the Soul*, Aristotle attempts to explain how these four factors are present during the actual moment of seeing.

SEEING: The four factors involved in the process of sight are 1) the one who sees—man; and 2) the instrument by which he sees —his eyes; 3) that which is seen, the object of sight—a tree; and 4) the desire within man which prompts him to see. Aristotle explains the actual moment of sight by saying that our eyes become one with the object at which we are looking. This means that in some way our eyes receive the *form* and *color* of the object (for instance, a tree) *abstracted* from the actual material of which the tree is made. We can understand what Aristotle means when we think of taking a colored photograph. When the shutter clicks, light passes through the lens and registers the image of the scene we are photographing in full color on the blank film. The film has abstracted what can be seen or the "seeable" from the scene, namely, its form and color. The scene itself is there on the film exactly as it is in reality, except that it is without its material features. The trees are no longer made of wood; the lake is without water. Yet, in a certain sense, the snapshot *is* the scene we photographed. Seeing is similar to taking a picture. It is the process of perceiving the seeable in the natural world. As the image of the scene photographed remains on the film inside the camera, so the image of the tree we see remains in our eye. The process of seeing is complete with the actual seeing. There is no end product other than the seeing. For this reason, Aristotle does not call seeing a process in the proper sense of the word. Process always involves an end product. But seeing is an end in itself.

SEEING AS A POTENTIAL: Seeing involves the seeable and that which can see, namely the eyes. A tree would exist if we were never there to see it, but it would be only *potentially* seeable. In the same way, our eyes are always able to see, but we do not see, unless we are *actually* seeing. When we are asleep, for instance, we see nothing. Seeing occurs when the seeable and that which can see meet. There is the old question: "When a tree falls in the woods, and there is no one around, does it make a noise?" Aristotle would answer that the noise was potentially there in the form of wave lengths, etc. But unless there were someone there to *hear* the noise, and to register what could be heard, there would be no real noise. A noise becomes heard and a tree seen, when the proper sense organ *actually* hears or sees.

KNOWING: The four factors involved in knowing are similar to those involved in seeing. They are: 1) the knower—man; 2) his instrument of knowing—mind; 3) the knowable; and 4) that which moves us to know.

THE OBJECT OF KNOWLEDGE: The objects of seeing are particular things which are in the natural world. The objects of knowledge, however, are completely separated from the material world by the process of abstraction. First, the imagination stores away various images we have received from experience in the memory. Although these images are immaterial, they have not yet become mental. They become mental when we grasp the common image which gives meaning to different seemingly unconnected sense-impressions we have in our memory. For example, we see three-cornered objects and store their images in the memory. The day comes when we perceive that these three-cornered objects are triangles. The difference between the images of the three-cornered objects and the concept of a triangle is the difference between the individual image perceived by the imagination and the mental image which is the object of knowledge. There are two things to notice in Aristotle's theory. 1) We *cannot* know without the aid of concrete images derived from sense experience. Knowing is rooted in our contact with the world around us. As everything in the world is part of a system of relationships, so we too are dependent on the natural world for our source of knowledge. We could not know if we did not live in the kind of world that can be known. And the world could not be known if we were not here to know it. 2) The object of knowledge, the mental image, as an abstraction from reality, is necessarily a generalized concept of reality. This concept, however, is not a subjective invention of our own minds; it is actually present in particular things as their form. For example, the concept of triangle is a general definition which fits any three-cornered object. And we can safely say that *any* three-cornered object *is* a triangle. The concept which expresses the essence of anything is always general. Knowledge, Aristotle insists, can only be of universals. It can never be of particulars. As the seeable is form and color separated from matter, so the knowable is the essential nature of types of objects abstracted from matter.

THE KNOWER AND THE PROCESS OF KNOWING: The instrument by which we see is an organ of the body, and the object of seeing is form and color seen in matter. Consequently, seeing takes place through the intervention of matter. Aristotle believes that the instrument by which we know, namely, *nous* or mind, has to be immaterial, since the objects of knowing are themselves immaterial forms present in the mind. Thus, he explains the activity of knowing by saying that the mind *becomes* the image or concept it is actively knowing. Seeing requires the material organ of the eyes. What is seen therefore is only a photographic likeness of the object of sight. But mind becomes *its own content*. For this reason, says Aristotle, mind has the ability to become all things. It follows from this that mind must be without form or structure. Mind could not become the same as what is thought if it had a particular form, for then the perception of mental images would be distorted by the form our minds happened to have. In seeing, Aristotle remarks, our eyes are blinded by too much light. If our minds were material and had form, they too would be hindered in their operation of knowing all things.

MIND AS CAPACITY AND AS CONTENT: If something is formless and immaterial, can it be said to exist? Aristotle says that mind exists as a faculty or power. As the eyes have the ability to see, but do not really see until they are moved to see by contact with a seeable object, so mind, in one sense, is the capacity to know. Mind does not actually know and in another sense, does not exist, however, until it becomes one with the knowable. Mind, when it is functioning, is thus the same as the contents of its knowledge. Functioning mind is therefore what it knows.

WHAT MAKES US KNOW?   In his account of knowing, Aristotle does not give a clear answer to this question. How do we know things that have not come within our experience? How do we learn? In one passage of *On the Soul* Aristotle suggests that, in some way, we have two minds. One has the power to become all things. This is the passive mind. The other has the power to make all things. This is the active mind which may be compared to the function of light in the activity of seeing. As light makes it possible to see the visible world, so, Aristotle suggests, the agent intellect, (as later scholars called it) has the power to illuminate the knowable world and make us understand. What this mind is and from where it comes Aristotle never makes clear. Scholars have worked on this problem over the centuries and are still no nearer to discovering Aristotle's view on the subject. At one point the philosopher tells us that the mind that creates all things is divine, separate from the material world, and immortal. Because it is not passive (i.e., since it does not *become* anything but it is always *creating*), it is eternally active and is the highest form of activity we know. Whether this active mind is one supreme Intelligence or is particular to each one of us Aristotle never tells us.

THE RELATION OF THOUGHT TO REALITY: Aristotle's view of nature in terms of function and of thought as the highest kind of function is one solution to the problem of how thought is related to reality. Since thought is a natural function, the structure of our thought must correspond with the nature of reality, for it *is* one kind of reality. Moreover, thought depends on the world for its source of facts; it is rooted in the world. On the other hand, though thought cannot do without concrete images, the thought process or knowing takes place apart from the natural world in the activity of our minds. In this sense, knowing is independent of the world, and is seen to be an activity different from all other natural activities. The possibility of error lies in this separation of mind from reality. For Aristotle, the link between thought and the natural world is the definition. An accurate definition expresses the actual nature of the object it defines. It is an object of knowledge and thus part of the process of knowing at the same time. In this way, the nature of things and the structure of thought become one in the act of knowing.

THE *PHYSICS*

DEFINITION OF NATURE: Aristotle nowhere tells us exactly what he means by nature, but the way he uses the word in the *Physics* suggests two basic meanings. 1) The Greek word, *phusis*, comes from the verb, *phuo*, meaning to grow, to produce, to generate. Our word, nature, comes from the Latin verb, *nator*, to be born. Nature, in English, suggests something fixed and given, a starting point. Human nature, for instance, is the sum total of qualities with which a man starts when he is born. It is what distinguishes him from the other creatures. Aristotle would agree with this view, but would improve upon it. Human nature sets man apart from the world about him not only in the sense of identifying the characteristics common to man, but also in the sense of differentiating the principle of human behavior. The *phusis* of anything is its capacity to realize all that it can possibly be. It at once determines *what* anything will become and how it will realize that end. Nature, as something inside and present in a natural body, is, in Aristotle's view, that body's *principle of motion.* 2) The second way in which Aristotle uses the word *nature* refers to the *sum total of objects* which possess their own principle of motion. Man-made objects are thus excluded from the world of nature. The wood in the chair, for instance, is a part of nature, for it has the tendency to age and decay. The chair itself is not a part of nature. You can destroy the chair by taking off its legs, but the chair does not have any inherent tendency to undergo change. Aristotle excludes artificial objects from nature, but he definitely puts lifeless bodies in his natural world. Stones belong to nature, because they have a tendency to move downwards, for example. He argues that stones would not fall to the earth if they did not possess the ability to do so. It is the nature of stones, in other words, to be subject to the law of gravity. The ability of chairs, on the other hand, to fall toward the earth is not part of the nature of chairs, but a function of the matter from which chairs are made, namely, wood, marble, or stone.

Aristotle never satisfactorily solves the relation of mind to nature. On the one hand, he sees mind as a part of nature; knowing is the function of a natural body (i.e., man). On the other hand, mind is not part of nature in the sense that mind is not subject to change. Mind, as we suggested in Chapter II, is the act of understanding. It is therefore an activity, not a process. One either knows or he does not know. There is no beginning, middle, and end of knowing. It is a single act which is outside time, space, and motion. For this reason, mind, in Aristotle's view, could be considered something divine. Aristotle's psychology and ethics illustrate the difficulty he had deciding just what mind was.

ORGANIZATION OF THE *PHYSICS*:   The *Physics* was originally meant to be the first in a series of works dealing with the natural world. Books I and II define the subject matter of natural science, and discuss the *archai* or first principles of that science. They contain an analysis and general definition of motion. In Books III to VIII Aristotle takes up the movement of natural things which are without life. He develops a general theory of motion. He continues his discussion of nature in *On the Heavens, On Generation and Corruption,* and the *Meteorologica.* The first work examines the movement of the stars, and the nature of what Aristotle considered the basic elements, fire and earth. In *On Generation and Corruption* Aristotle analyzes absolute change, the processes of coming into being and going out of being. In the *Meteorologica* Aristotle deals with many subjects included in the modern science of meteorology. The discussion of that part of the natural world which exhibits the motion we call "life," Aristotle leaves to his biological works. As the main points of Aristotle's natural philosophy are found in the first four books of the *Physics,* we shall concentrate on these books.

BOOK I
SUBJECT MATTER AND
FIRST PRINCIPLES OF NATURE

INTRODUCTION: Aristotle begins the *Physics* by saying he plans to study nature. In accordance with his method, he says it is important at the outset to discover the first principles, causes, and elements of nature. To do this, we must first determine what the subject matter is. There have been many different views on the subject matter, however. There is a real question of whether objects subject to motion and change actually exist. Aristotle is quick to point out that Parmenides did not believe the natural world was real. Aristotle says he disagrees with Parmenides' view that there is only one first principle, and therefore one kind of reality, the unchanging, permanent and eternal reality of thought. Aristotle tells us to reject this view and to trust our own eyes. Observation shows us that the things around us really do exist.

Parmenides had had such an influence on Greek thought, however, that it is not enough for Aristotle to brush off Parmenides' philosophy with the statement, "Things that change do exist. We see them." He must prove Parmenides wrong by logic and reasoning. To make his proof, Aristotle turns to an analysis of the meaning contained in the words, "One" and "Being." His argument is long and complex, and needs only be summed up here.

REFUTATION OF PARMENIDES: The first part of his argument is based on the many ways of saying something exists. Parmenides says that everything that exists is One. Does he mean that everything is of one substance, of one quality, like redness, or of one quantity, like the number one? If he says that everything that exists has all three of these components, then he admits that everything that exists is not one but many. For example, if you hold that everything that exists is basically fire, red, and one, you are saying three things about its existence. Everything will have a plural being. If, like Parmenides, you say that everything that exists has only one substance, for example, fire, and then describe this substance as being limited or unlimited, you have already given two types of existence, namely, substance and quality.

The word, "One," is equally misleading. It has at least three meanings. A line, for example, is one, but you can divide it an infinite number of times. Second, one thing can have two names. For example, we call a human being both "man" and "rational animal." Third, a thing ceases to be one in the sense of a unit broken up into its parts. For example, a man ceases to be one man when you break him up into bones, muscles, and veins. He reverts to his various constituent parts. Aristotle concludes that there is no way Parmenides can say everything is one.

A QUESTION OF GRAMMAR: Aristotle points out that Parmenides and his followers did not understand grammar correctly. It is true you can say that "to be" and "to be one" are the same thing. But a thing can be one, and still have many things "attributed" to it. For example, one man may be educated, tall, fair-haired and rich, all at the same time. He still remains "one" man.

In the same way that he did not understand the use of "one" in a proposition, so Parmenides did not understand the use of "to be." Depending on the way it is used in a sentence, "to be" can mean "to exist" and "to be such and such." For example, you can say, "a man is," meaning, "he exists." You can also say, "a man is white." Whiteness, however, is a quality which does not have an independent existence apart from individual substances. There are white horses, white men and white chairs. But you cannot see whiteness as you see a white horse. There is a difference between whiteness and the thing in which whiteness is. When you say, therefore, that the horse is not white, you are saying "the horse is not-white." The horse continues to exist even though he is not white. He exists in his quality of not-whiteness. Similarly, when you say, "the man is not sitting," you do not mean, "the man does not exist." He simply does not happen to be sitting at this moment. Whiteness and sitting are not necessary to the existence of anything. They are what he calls accidental qualities. That which exists as a substance, as a concrete, individual, thing, however, cannot be an accidental quality of anything else. There is no such thing as a human horse, for example. We must distinguish between those things which exist independently and those things which can only exist in something else, like whiteness. It is thus impossible for everything in the world "to be one," for the universe is made up of separate individually existing things which cannot be made qualities of anything else.

> **NOTE:**   We may think that Aristotle has gone into questions of grammar and definition a little more than is necessary. But he evidently believes that the point he makes is one which was not well understood by philosophers before him. Moreover, he is eager to refute Parmenides in order to put his own arguments in a favorable light. Needless to say, Aristotle's interpretation of Parmenides is biased and much too simple. Most scholars on the Greek philosophers before Socrates agree that Aristotle misrepresents Parmenides' thought in this section.

FIRST PRINCIPLES: After showing that both logic and experience require that the world of individual moving things actually exists, Aristotle turns to the problem of the first principles of motion. He tries to determine what causes change.

To set the context for his own theory, Aristotle reviews the opinions of the natural philosophers who went before him. He notes that their ideas on what the first principles of nature are fall into two categories. Some held that motion was first produced by the action of external contrary forces, for example, love and hate, upon a single mass of substance. Others thought that the separate individual things which emerged from the first primeval mass of matter were originally present as qualities of that matter. Aristotle points out that both these views assume that the first substance started to change because of the presence of contraries, either as external forces or as internal qualities. By contrary qualities, Aristotle means hot as opposed to cold, wet as opposed to dry, etc.

ARISTOTLE'S TWO FIRST PRINCIPLES: Aristotle concludes that a change to any state assumes that there is an opposite of that state. Water cannot become hot, if there is no not-hot, or cold. If we are to bridge the gap between something which is now cold and not yet hot, we must suppose that that which is now cold contains the possibility of becoming the contrary of cold (i.e., hot). Change is only possible if contrary qualities exist. A man cannot become pale, if he is already pale. But a man who is sunburned can lose his sunburn and become not-burned or pale. Thus, in everything that exists there are present contrary or contrasting qualities, one of which actually *is* at a given moment, and the other which now is not, but *can be*. Aristotle's two first principles are a pair of opposites.

Obviously, there is more than one first principle, but there cannot be an unlimited number of first principles. 1) If there were, nature would be unknowable, for it is impossible to know the infinite. Knowing requires definition, the setting of limits. 2) We could say that there are only two first principles, substance and its opposite non-substance or nothing. Furthermore, 3) if we can limit ourselves to only two or three first principles, it is better; the simple explanation is always preferable to the complicated one. Again, 4) it is evident that not all contraries are fundamental, in the sense of being universally present. Black and white, for example, are not present in all phenomena. This means that we must concern ourselves only with those contraries which are evident in every case. Aristotle believes, however, that there are more than two first principles, for he finds it difficult to see how two contraries can act directly upon each other. How does whiteness act on blackness, he asks, and make it white? The answer is, it can not. Whiteness has to be *in something*. It cannot act on what is not, or blackness, for that does not yet exist. The third principle must therefore be some kind of material substance in which the opposites inhere. But before Aristotle commits himself to three first principles, he examines the problem more thoroughly.

THE PROCESS OF CHANGE: Change means either coming into existence or becoming this or that. For example, a man becomes cultured. This means that the uncultured became cultured. The uncultured man is the thing out of which comes the cultured man. In this process of change, what remains throughout is the man. But non-culture does not remain, nor does culture remain as an independent entity. For we have a new compound being as the outcome of the process, namely, a cultured man. The product of change has thus two elements: the basic *material,* man, and *his form,* culture. But a third element has to be assumed in the change process, the *absence of form,* which in this case is non-culture. For the cultured man was first not-cultured. He did not possess the form of culture.

THE THREE FIRST PRINCIPLES: MATTER, FORM, AND PRIVATION OF FORM: There must be something out of which change takes place. This "out of which" Aristotle calls matter. In the case of a bronze statue, the "out of which" is the artist's material, bronze. Upon the bronze is imposed that "which is to be," or form, in this case, the statue. The result is the compound object made of matter and form, the bronze statue. Thus, in one sense, there are only two first principles, the matter which is your starting point, and the form the matter is to assume. Form and matter, however, are not sufficient to explain change. The statue was made from bronze which first *was not* a statue. The contrast between opposites is not between the statue and the bronze. The contrast is between the non-statue, the lump of bronze, and the statue. In order for something to change, it must change from not having a particular form into having that particular form. Aristotle concludes that there are therefore three first principles: 1) the underlying substance out of which the change takes place; 2) the form which is imposed upon it; and 3) the absence of that form which the underlying substance possessed at the beginning of the process.

FIRST MATTER: The problem arises as to what matter really is. How are we to think of matter? Everything which is the subject of change at a given time is also the end of a change cycle. A chair comes from wood, which comes from an oak, which comes from an acorn. How are we to identify that which persists in all these change processes? We can trace matter back to the four first elements: fire, water, air, and earth, but even these are not first matter. They too can be resolved into opposite qualities: hot-moist, or cold-dry. It seems that the first "out of which" always escapes us. Aristotle tells us that we should not try to separate first matter in this way, but we should consider it the same way we consider the relation of the bronze to the statue. First matter cannot be thought of as a particular something, like an element. Rather it has to be understood as that which can potentially assume a form. It is the ground of all being which possesses the capacity to become a concrete individual thing. The nature of matter is to be a subject for form.

FORM AND MATTER IN THE WORLD: Aristotle stresses the point that although matter and form can be separated in our minds, they do not exist separately in the natural world. Everything that exists is composed of matter and form. Matter without form cannot really be said to be except in the sense of being a subject capable of receiving form. Everything around us has its definite structure. Aristotle puts off the question of whether forms can exist apart from matter, saying it is the proper subject of another science which he variously calls theology, first philosophy, and sometimes the science of being.

ANSWER TO PLATO AND PARMENIDES: Aristotle ends Book I by showing that neither Plato nor Parmenides understood the three first principles. Contrary to what Parmenides thought, things do change because they are composed of matter which happens to be without a certain form and thus can assume that form. Parmenides did not grasp the principle of absence of form. Plato came nearer, but he did not separate the principle of matter from the principle of absence of form. He thought absence of form was a fundamental characteristic of matter. The truth is that the concept of matter and the concept of absence of form are two different things. In being simply the subject for form, matter is eternal and imperishable. As the starting point of coming-to-be and the end point of perishing, it is always the something which persists through every change process.

BOOK II
NATURE AND THE
MOVEMENT OF NATURAL THINGS

INTRODUCTION: In Book I Aristotle proved that the subject matter of natural science, namely change, really exists, and set forth the three principles which form the basis of any change process. In Book II Aristotle examines the nature of change itself. First, he determines what things can properly be said to fall within the scope of natural science, and what the nature of those things is. Second, he distinguishes natural science from sister subjects such as mathematics. Finally, beginning with Chapter III, he turns to an analysis of the conditions necessary to produce change. Most of Book II is given over to a discussion of the process of change.

NATURE AS THE IMPULSE TO MOVEMENT: Some things exist by nature and some are man-made and artificial. Aristotle calls those things natural which have a principle or tendency to movement or rest within themselves. "Nature," he tells us, "is the principle and cause of motion in those things . . . in which she exists essentially." It is an internal impulse to movement. This impulse exists only accidentally in artificial objects, like a bed, insofar as they are made of natural materials. Everything natural, however, possesses an inborn tendency to move or be moved in a certain definite way. Thus, even the elements can be said to have an impulse to move, in that they rise and fall in space, and undergo change. Living things move by change of place, growth, change in size, generation and decay. The internal impulse to movement which natural things possess does not have to be demonstrated according to Aristotle. Its existence is obvious to anyone who uses his eyes.

NATURE AS FORM AND FUNCTION: Aristotle states that there are two main views about nature. Some say that the nature of a thing is the same as its matter. The nature of the bed, for instance, is the wood from which it is made. Moving from the object at hand to the ultimate "nature of things," they hold that "nature" is the eternal matter which is the ground of all being. Others hold that the nature of anything is found in its form—in the "what a thing actually is." Aristotle agrees with this view. Matter is the subject of form, but form is what makes anything *be* a particular kind of thing. Form, in this sense, is the end product of the change process, the final state of a natural body. Nature, however, also implies generation, coming-to-be, and reproduction. Beds cannot reproduce, but man can beget man. Thus, Aristotle says nature is the form of anything in two ways: 1) it is the final state of a natural body, the "what" that that body ultimately becomes; and 2) it is the principle of behavior by which a natural body realizes its ultimate form. The two concepts are related. Nature, as function, is what Aristotle calls the "path" to nature as the end of the natural process. For example, man becomes man by virtue of his human nature. But when we say of a famous person in history, "He really was a man," we mean that that person realized within himself those qualities of human nature which are the goal of human life. Nature is the power to move toward a definite end, and the end itself.

PHYSICS AND MATHEMATICS: Having defined what nature is and in what kind of things nature is to be found, Aristotle describes the scope of natural science by determining its relation to the other sciences. Other sciences study matter and form. In what way is physics different from these? He concludes that mathematics studies forms, such as triangles, lines, and points, in abstraction. This means that mathematics studies physical forms separated from matter which have no independent existence. Physics, on the other hand, must study matter and form together, since it is the science of concrete existing things. As medicine or any art must know both the nature of that art (its form) and the matter which is the subject of that art, so natural science must study the principle of motion of a natural body and the matter in which this principle is found. In natural science, matter is related to form as means to an end. The basic concern of the scientist, is the *nature*, or impulse to movement, of natural objects. For example, a scientist first asks why or what makes a tree grow. His second question will be "Of what is the tree made?" Natural science is distinguished from metaphysics in that physics studies forms *in* matter. Metaphysics studies pure forms existing *independently* of matter and the natural world. The difference between metaphysics and mathematics is that the former studies forms existing independently of matter, and the latter studies forms *abstracted* from matter which have no separate existence of their own.

THE FOUR CAUSES: In Chapter III Aristotle discusses the factors which he considers essential to explain the existence of any natural body. It is impossible to say what a thing is, without knowing "why" it is. To ask why is to ask "what brought this thing into being?" Aristotle's four causes are so famous in the history of intellectual thought that we will use the word, "cause," in referring to the conditions necessary to a thing's existence. The Greek word which has been translated as "cause," however, actually means "responsible." In asking why a thing exists, Aristotle means, "What factors are responsible, i.e., account for the existence of any natural body? What questions must the natural philosopher ask to understand the 'why' of a particular phenomenon?" Aristotle thinks there are four questions that should be asked.

1. Out of what has a thing come? The "out of what" is known as the *material* cause.
2. What is it? *What is it meant to be* is known as the *formal* cause.
3. By means of what is it? By what agent? The agent is known as the *efficient* cause. For example, the father is the efficient cause of his son.

4. For the sake of what is it? For what end? The purpose or end state of a thing is known as the *final* cause. For example, a man walks for the sake of health. Health is the final cause of his walking.

THE RELATION OF THE CAUSES TO EACH OTHER: Aristotle says that all the causes are related to each other. In the natural world of organic and inorganic matter, it is impossible to separate them. Indeed, some of them seem to overlap. For example, in defining nature, we saw that the form or structure of anything can also be its end state, or "for the sake of what." The definition of anything includes its function and the goal toward which that thing is moving. A child grows into a man. We understand what a child is in terms of what he will become, namely, a man. Again, the formal-final cause may also be the efficient cause. Such is the case of reproduction, where man, the formal-final cause, fathers— is the efficient cause of—the child. The important thing to note in this example is that the efficient cause or agent may be the *same in kind* but never the *same in number* as the formal-final cause. Man does not beget himself. He begets another human being *like* himself. No universal concept such as human nature exists apart from the matter in which it is found. Thus, the form, man, as found in one type of matter, begets another form, man, found in another type of matter. The second man has a similar nature but is obviously not identical with the first.

RELATIONS BETWEEN CAUSES IN LIFELESS BODIES: In instances less dramatic than reproduction, the same relations between causes exist. Each natural body, says Aristotle, has a tendency to move toward a certain place unless it is prevented from doing so. He gives two examples. Earth moves downward, fire upwards. The being in a certain place of an inanimate body (its final cause or end state) is included in its definition or form, as the end of the movement. Second, the inclination or ability to move toward that place can be considered in part the efficient cause of the thing's movement. The efficient cause is not only found inside the body, but is also present as an external force. Aristotle argues that earth would not move downward when acted upon by an eternal force if it did not possess the tendency to do so. There is an interaction between the external conditions in which an inanimate body finds itself and its internal nature.

TYPES OF EFFICIENT CAUSES: Aristotle ends his discussion of causation by listing the various ways an agent may be said to cause anything to be. 1) The agent may be a *specific* cause, for example, the doctor, or he may be a *generic* cause, for example, a professional man; 2) There is a difference between the *proper* cause and the *incidental* cause. A statue, for example, is said to be made by a sculptor, and incidentally, by a particular sculptor, Michelangelo. 3) A cause may be sometimes *actual* and sometimes *potential*. For example, while the builder is building a house, he is the *actual* efficient cause of the house. When he is not building, he is a *potential* efficient cause, in the sense that when he chooses to do so, he can build a house at some indefinite time in the future.

CHANCE: After describing the causes which he considers fundamental to the understanding of any happening, Aristotle asks whether there is not a fifth cause, namely, chance. Early philosophers gave chance a place in their systems, but they did not explain it. Others said it was something divine. Aristotle thinks the question so important that he devotes the rest of Book II to an inquiry of what chance is, and its relation to natural necessity.

THE NATURE OF CHANCE: At the beginning of his discussion Aristotle distinguishes those events which occur "always or for the most part" and those extra-ordinary events which may happen once in a mililon years. Nature has a tendency to move toward a definite end. Man has a purpose to do a certain thing. Man's purpose and nature's movement toward a certain end are both expressions of the usual and customary in the natural world. It can happen, however, that the end I want to achieve is brought about accidentally without any particular action on my part. For example, I go to the market to buy food. Buying food is the purpose or final cause of the trip to the market. By chance, I meet a friend who repays me $100 which he borrowed some time in the past. Of course, I am glad to have the money repaid, but my getting $100 is not the purpose of my morning outing. It is only a "lucky break." By chance, my friend happens to go to the market at the same time on the same day. He, too, has a different purpose for his visit than repaying me the loan. But our paths cross, and I have my loan repaid.

DEFINITION OF CHANCE: In this story of Aristotle's which I have put in a modern setting, one cannot say that there was no reason behind the chance meeting. In fact, what actually happened was that two different and separate events, each with its own set of four causes, happened to come together at the same time. Factors which were responsible for one happening crossed over and affected another event, without being an essential part of that event. Aristotle thus distinguishes between *direct* causation, which can be completely explained by the four relevant causes, and *indirect* causation, where causes linked to one event influence a second. He consequently defines chance—or, as he calls it, luck—in human affairs, as "the incidental production of some result by a cause that took its place in the chain of causes . . . without the result being contemplated [i.e., planned]." My receiving $100 was incidental, that is, not part of my purpose in going to the market. People have called luck vague because it is impossible to predict a result outside of a planned (purposeful) action.

LUCK AND CHANCE: Aristotle next distinguishes between luck and chance. Luck, or *tuche* in Greek, is part of human affairs and human intentions. Nature, however, cannot be said to have intentions. She only has tendencies and processes. Aristotle says chance (*to automaton* in Greek) is the interruption of a process which produces an unusual result. For example, monstrosities in nature are a result of chance. Something interrupts the natural chain of causation when a two-headed baby, for example, is born. In this example, chance is understood as an occurrence which has no purpose in itself. Chance is an event which deflects things from their proper end, and contributes nothing to some other end.

NATURAL NECESSITY AND PURPOSE: Chance as that which prevents something from reaching its natural end raises the final question of Book II. What is the role of necessity and purpose in nature? Can nature be said to have a purpose?

PURPOSE IN NATURE: In approaching the problem, Aristotle first asks whether the final cause may not be left out of a theory of causation, since it is already included in the "because" which is the form or nature of anything. His answer is no. The essential nature of a natural body can only be fully understood in terms of its purpose, that is, in terms of the function it is supposed to perform. Form as the aim of a natural process is a distinct factor in causation. Purpose is the ultimate "because" of natural change.

Is there any reason for saying nature has a goal? Why cannot the rain rain, and the sun shine, not because the sky is cloudy or clear but just by chance? Empedocles argued for a theory of natural selection on the basis of chance. The survival of the fittest means that those who happen to be more fit survive; the less fit perish. Aristotle rejects any theory of evolution. Things either occur by chance or they occur "always or for the most part," which is the opposite of chance. You must admit that things which occur "always or for the most part" occur either by chance, or not by chance. If they occur not by chance, then they occur for a purpose. Monsters occur by chance because they are not among those things which are always or for the most part. Man, on the other hand, survives because he is meant to survive. To argue that he is a result of chance is to argue that he does not exist always or for the most part, but only sometimes. This, of course, is absurd. Because most things in nature seem to occur most of the time and exhibit a pattern of change which can be broken up into the four causes, Aristotle argues that nature must have a purpose. Order and conformity to type imply purpose. All causation is directed toward an end and the end of each natural body predetermines the form and the material of that body. Aristotle's view that nature has a purpose is called *natural teleology*. *Telos* is the Greek word for end. Teleology is the science of ends or purposes.

NATURAL PURPOSE AND ART: Aristotle makes his explanation of purpose in nature more clear by relating natural purpose to artistic creation. In any process of human creation, there is a definite end to be achieved. In order to achieve that end, the artist has to go through certain steps to bring this end about. For example, if you want to build a house, there are certain steps you have to go through in order to bring the house into being. Natural processes are similar to the process of human creation. Art can thus be said to imitate nature in the way art works come into being. If art is for an end, nature must even more be for an end. One has only to look at the work of swallows, ants or bees, who have no conscious purpose, to realize that they nevertheless act according to a purpose. Mutations and man-faced oxen are simply nature's failures, the miscarriage of purpose. If all had gone well, the monster would have been a man. When nature fulfills her purpose, man begets man and nothing else. The natural end of anything is to conform to its type, to become what it is designed to be.

NATURAL PURPOSE AND DIVINE PLAN: In this section of the *Physics* Aristotle does not raise the question of what the ultimate purpose of nature is. To say that everything acts for a purpose is to suggest that there is some overall plan according to which things function. The most logical plan that Aristotle could suggest would, of course, be a divine plan. The nature of Aristotle's God, however, does not permit Him to take much interest in the world. Aristotle would seem to believe that natural purpose is explainable simply in terms of conformity to and survival of types. This explanation leaves out the reason why conformity to type should persist. Why should man beget man, or a dog, a dog? If nature has a purpose, as it does in Aristotle's system, there must be some explanation which goes beyond the purely natural world to account for that purpose. In this respect, Plato is more satisfactory. He held that a type persists because there is an eternal Idea of that type in the supersensible world. Man begets man according to the form of the Ideal Man existing in the world of pure being. The Medieval philosophers followed in Plato's footsteps, and said that type persists because its Ideal Form is an everlasting thought in the Mind of God. Aristotle's natural teleology does not include either of these views. Type is present in each individual natural body as its final cause, and as an element of its form, or nature. But to say that man begets man because it is his nature to beget man is to give no real explanation as to why the human race continues to exist. Yet Aristotle offers no other solution.

NATURAL NECESSITY: In the final chapter of Book II Aristotle turns to the question of necessity in nature. In what way are things said to have to be? Do bricks have to become a house. Do materials determine the outcome of a natural process? Aristotle says that function, the purpose for which something exists, imposes necessary requirements upon a given object. Natural necessity is a question of form, not matter. If we ask why a saw is like it is, the answer is, "in order that it may have the essential character of a saw, and serve for sawing." This purpose could not be served unless it were made of a strong material. Therefore, a saw must "necessarily" be made of a strong material. Similarly, in building a house, the "purpose-serving," materials, i.e., stone and cement, must be present if the house is to be built, and fulfill its purpose of a house. "It is the goal, which determines the purpose, and the principle of causation is derived from the definition and rationale of the end." This is true in nature, as well as in the world of Art. If "this is what a man is," says Aristotle, then there must necessarily, "antecedently be such and such things" in order for him to be such a being. Purpose, the final cause, regulates what things have to have been and have to become in order to fulfill their functions. Consequently, natural necessity derives from the purpose for which anything exists. The end of any process determines the other factors in that process.

MATHEMATICS AND NATURAL NECESSITY: Aristotle compares natural necessity to mathematics. In mathematics, if the axioms are true, then the conclusion follows logically of necessity. In the natural world, the physical object may be compared to the axiom. *If* a certain thing exists, *then* certain conditions necessarily have to be present. They are an inevitable consequence of the nature of that particular thing.

BOOK III
MOTION AND CHANGE

INTRODUCTION: In Book III Aristotle examines the nature of motion, as a prelude to an investigation of other concepts connected with motion, such as place, time, and empty space. It has been explained that nature is the principle of movement. But we cannot know what nature is until we know what motion is.

> **COMMENT:** The Greek word for motion is *kinesis,* from which is derived the English word, kinetic. When we speak of kinetic energy, we mean energy resulting from motion. Aristotle uses *kinesis* to refer both to motion and to change.

OBSERVATIONS ABOUT MOTION: Aristotle starts out with his usual matter-of-factness by observing that there *is* such a thing as motion. We know this from experience. Second, motion is something we think of as continuous. Continuous means something unbroken which can be divided an infinite number of times; for example, a line is continuous; a point is not. Third, motion cannot take place except in relation to place, time, and empty space. And fourth, motion is not to be considered a series of "moments"; it is progress from this to that.

WHAT MOTION IS: Motion, Aristotle says, is not a substance; it cannot exist apart from what moves, or changes. That which changes always changes from one state into another state, or from something into something else. Motion thus has two poles. You will recall that Aristotle's first two principles of motion were a pair of opposites, which may be compared to the north and south poles, or to positive and negative charges. Motion is passage from one of these poles to the other.

POTENTIALITY AND ACTUALITY: Aristotle refers back to his statement, made in Book I, that anything which changes has the ability or potentiality of changing into what it becomes. A table *can* become white but it is not in the nature of tables to become chairs. In the natural world, tadpoles can become frogs. They cannot, in the sense that it would be contrary to their nature if they did, become fish. This ability to move or change in a certain way, which observation has shown to be a normal way for a particular natural body to behave, Aristotle calls the *potentiality* of that body. For example, a stone falls into a pool. The potentiality of the stone is its capacity to fall. When it has fallen into the pool, Aristotle says that its potentiality has been made actual. Actuality is the realization of the potential. The actuality of the stone is the completed action of falling into the pool. Motion is the transition between the potential and the actual. Aristotle gives the example of building a house. The potentiality of the motion is the bricks and stones which can be made into a house. The actuality of the house is the finished house. The motion of building makes real the potentiality of the bricks and stones. Thus, the actual building process is what Aristotle calls motion.

THE RELATION BETWEEN THE POTENTIAL AND THE ACTUAL: Aristotle develops his theory. The same physical body may be potential to something and actual to another thing at the same time. It can be the end of one natural process and the beginning of another. Water, for example, can be potentially hot, but actually cold. Things do not act in isolation; they act and react on one another. Thus, everything which can be moved, can cause motion, and vice versa. Change is a vast chain of individual processes linked together by mover and moved, the potential and the actual. Everything which is moved is moved by something else which is moved by something else, and so on back to the first unmoved mover who starts the chain reaction.

INERTIA: Unfortunately, Aristotle did not understand the concept of inertia, which is so important in the history of science. It states that a body in motion will go on of itself at the same speed and in the same direction, unless some new force acts upon it. For this reason, he had difficulty explaining the motion of anything thrown, such as the path of a ball. He thought that anything moved was kept in motion by constant physical contact with its source of motion.

THE UNMOVED MOVER: From Aristotle's theory of motion it does not follow that that which moves something else is itself moving at the time it causes that something to move. His view is simply that that which causes motion is itself capable of being moved at some time, since, by definition, everything in the natural world must be able to be moved. For example, the object which moves our eyes to see may not be moving at the time. His theory does imply, however, that the ability to be moved by an unmoved object only belongs to a living organism. In the mechanical world, he says, nothing can move something else, without itself being moved by a third body at the same time. For example, the stone falls into the pool and "moves" the water because it has been thrown, or because a landslide has caused it to become loosened

from the bank. The landslide might have been caused by unprece-
dented rains, which were caused by other phyical factors, and so
on back to the First Unmoved Mover whom Aristotle considers the
initial cause of all movement, and whom we will discuss later. On
the other hand, if the stone was thrown, it might have been thrown
by a child's arm, which was "moved" by its mind to throw the stone.
The mind was moved by an "unmoved mover," namely, the picture
of a stone being thrown which was present in the child's mind, and
which "moved" his mind to desire his arm to throw the stone.

MOTION A FUNCTION: Aristotle makes it clear that motion
is never the end of motion. It is the function of a body which is
able to move, as long as it is moving. *Before* anything starts to
function in a particular way, it cannot be said to be in motion.
When it has reached the end of its functioning, it is no longer in
motion. Motion is an incompleted action in the process of being
completed.

ACTIVE AND PASSIVE AGENTS IN MOTION: In the next
chapter Aristotle looks more closely at the relation between the
mover and the moved. Any process of motion involves two factors.
There is that which causes motion, which Aristotle calls the active
factor. There is that which undergoes motion, the passive factor.
This raises the question as to whether in any change process there
are actually two movements instead of one. Aristotle says there is
only one act of motion, for movement only takes place in the passive agent, that which is moved. The mover's action is the cause of
motion in the moved. For example, when a teacher teaches, he is,
hopefully, causing learning in his class, but he is not himself being
taught at the same time. The motion of learning takes place in
the pupil. The teacher's teaching is actualized in the pupil who is
taught. The change takes place in the pupil. Aristotle realizes that
this distinction between active and passive agents is entirely relative. The thruway from New York to Buffalo is the same road as
the thruway from Buffalo to New York. It depends from which end
you start. The thruway remains the same road throughout. Similarly,
one can distinguish the different aspects involved in motion, but
there is only one movement or change taking place at a particular
time. Whatever change does occur, occurs in that which is potentially movable (i.e., in the passive agent).

> **COMMENT:**   It is important to realize that Aristotle's con-
> cept of motion applies not just to movement from one place
> to another, such as walking. It is something more general. In
> *On the Soul* Aristotle lists four kinds of movement: 1) Change

of position (for example, walking and the orbits of the stars); 2) change in state (becoming hot or cold); 3) decay; and 4) growth. Coming-into-being and going-out-of-being are not movements, because the opposite of substance, or something, is nothing. To have motion you have to have some *thing* which can be moved, and this thing has to be *somewhere*. In another place, Aristotle lists only three kinds of movement: 1) change of place; 2) change of quality (black becoming white); and 3) change of quantity (growing from four feet to six feet). Coming-into-being and perishing are considered absolute changes. In the first case, something is which was not; in the second, something is not which was.

INFINITY: In Chapter IV Aristotle turns to the subject of infinity (that which has no limits, the unlimited), as it relates to the concepts involved in the study of nature: motion, space, and time. As is his custom, he reviews the opinions of the philosophers before him, as the first step to making his own definition.

Pythagoras and Plato held that the infinite had an independent existence, and was not an attribute of anything else. It was something which could be known by the senses and was located in no particular place. The Pythagoreans, Aristotle says, identified "the unlimited" with "the even," while Plato associated the infinite with both the objects of sense, and the Ideas. The natural philosophers thought there was some kind of infinite or formless first substance, or else an infinite mass of first particles. Anaxagoras suggested some infinite mixture of these infinite first particles as the nucleus out of which the different elements were separated. Democritus, according to Aristotle, found the unlimited "in his hodgepodge of multishaped atoms." All these philosophers agreed that the infinite is some kind of beginning or first principle. The natural philosophers even believed it was divine and self-moving.

ARISTOTLE'S THEORY: Aristotle agrees that the infinite must be a principle, because it is something which cannot be measured by any other principle, being itself without form or limit. Since it is a principle, it can have no beginning and no end, because it cannot come into being from anything else. He gives five reasons for the existence of a general belief in the infinite. 1) Time is generally considered as being endless, that is, without limit. 2) Size, width, length, and height can be divided an infinite number of times. 3) The process of birth and reproduction suggests that new organisms come from some storehouse of infinite material. 4) There can be no absolute limit, for everything limited has to be limited by something else. 5) The fifth reason Aristotle considers the most important of all—people have always been able to conceive of a beyond.

THE USE OF THE WORD INFINITE: In his characteristic method, Aristotle first looks at the ways in which "infinite" can be used in a sentence. He says there are basically two ways. *No limit* may mean that you have thought of something of such *size* that it would be foolish to try to go from one end to the other. You would never be able to do it. *Absence of limit* means that you can add or divide something an infinite number of times. "No limit" refers to space. "Absence of limit" refers to numbers.

> **COMMENT:**   Aristotle's definitions of the infinite should be carefully noted, if the reader is to understand the arguments which follow. Perhaps a better translation of the Greek word, *apeiron,* might be "unlimited," in the sense of without set limits, without concrete shape. *Apeiron* does not mean "without limits," in the sense of "beyond the concept of physical limits." When God is described as infinite, for example, it means that the concept of limit does not apply to Him.

DEMONSTRATION OF THE EXISTENCE OF THE INFINITE: Having examined the linguistic usage of the infinite, Aristotle proceeds to the next step, demonstration. First, the infinite does not exist as a substance because by definition it is not bound by size or number. It must therefore be an attribute, not a substance. Furthermore, numbers do not themselves exist. Finally, if the infinite exists substantially, it must be entirely indivisible, or divisible into infinities, both of which possibilities are absurd.

AN INFINITE MATERIAL BODY DOES NOT EXIST: Observation shows us that an unlimited body cannot be a compound of a definite number of elements. Second, the unlimited cannot be made of one simple element; an infinity of air, for example, would mean that fire, water, and all other elements of which there was a limited amount would be swallowed by the infinity of air. Experience shows us that this cannot happen. Finally, our experience of place (up and down, sidewise and backward) shows us that there cannot be an infinite body, for it could not move in place.

THE INFINITE MUST EXIST IN SOME WAY: If there is no such thing as an infinite body, there still must be something called the infinite for three reasons. 1) If there were no infinite, there would be no infinite series of numbers. 2) If there were no infinite, it would be untrue that you can divide a finite space an infinite number of times. 3) If there were no infinite, there would be a beginning and end of time, which Aristotle thinks is inconceivable.

THE INFINITE IN SPACE BY WAY OF DIVISION: Aristotle concludes that the infinite must exist as a potentiality, something that can be and is in the process of being realized, but never actual. If you take the second reason for the existence of the infinite, you will see it is possible to divide a line into an infinite number of parts. You can take a line twelve feet long, take half of it, and then halve the halves, etc. But you will never be able to divide the line into indivisible parts. In actual practice, once you get down to divisions as small as millimeters and smaller, you can no longer see the parts of the line, and your experiment would probably stop. But there still remain tiny parts of that line which can be divided further. In this sense, Aristotle tells us, the infinite exists as a day exists. It is continuously coming into being and never wholly realized. A day passes from one moment to the next, with each past division of time giving way to the next minute. Days pass into days on into infinity.

THE UNLIMITED IN SPACE BY WAY OF PROPORTIONAL ADDITION: This is the same as the infinite by way of division. If you add or subtract equal parts from a finite whole in a constant ratio, you will never be able to subtract the entire whole from the whole or add up the parts to make a whole. If I have an apple, and eat half of it, then eat half of that, then half of that, etc., I will never be able to eat up the entire apple. Always some piece will remain. Similarly, if I take half an apple, and add to it a fourth of an apple, then an eighth, then a sixteenth, a thirty-secondth, a sixty-fourth, and so on into infinity, I shall never be able to add up the parts to make a whole apple. In each case an infinite series is contained in a finite whole.

DEFINITION OF THE INFINITE: Aristotle concludes that the nature of the infinite is incompleteness. No form of the infinite exists as a whole at the same time as does the whole to which it is related. The infinite is always that which is beyond. Thus, "the unlimited is the open possibility of taking more." The whole, or "all," is that from which nothing is missing. There is no "more" in a whole. In order for there to be a whole in which no "mores" exist, it must of necessity have a limit.

THE INFINITE IN NUMBER: The characteristic of space is that its maximum is limited by the concept of a whole. Its minimum is unlimited. There is always one more division. Number is the other way around. Its minimum is limited by the number one, i.e., unity or wholeness. But as you can divide a whole an infinite number of times, so you can add wholes together an infinite number of times. There is always the possibility of adding one more number. The point is, you never actually add on that one more number. Mathematicians, for example, says Aristotle, do not work with actual infinite magnitudes. They always ask for, or imagine, a line of length "x," meaning a line of any length they please.

THE INFINITE IN TIME: Time is like space in that each unit of time is infinitely divisible. You can divide an hour an infinite number of times. It is like a number in that you can keep adding hour to hour, on into infinity.

THE INFINITE AS POTENTIALITY: Aristotle ends his discussion of the infinite by saying that it is related to a finite whole, as the material cause of anything exists with respect to its formal cause, for example, as bronze exists with respect to the statue, before it becomes the statue. The infinite is pure potentiality, always realizable, but never realized.

BOOK IV
PLACE, EMPTY SPACE, AND TIME

INTRODUCTION: Book IV discusses the difficult concepts of place, empty space, and time. It will be remembered that earlier Aristotle listed the characteristics of natural things as motion, space, empty space, and time. Now he returns to a discussion of these characteristics. In the first half of Book IV, Aristotle determines the meaning of place and empty space. The definitions enable him in the following books to explore the relation of these phenomena to motion. In the concluding chapters of Book IV (10–14) Aristotle develops his theory of time.

PLACE: Place and motion are terms which express the relations of objects to one another. Moving things are "in motion." Unmoving things are "in place," or "in position." The terms are a pair of opposites, place or position being the opposite of movement. All natural things must be in place or in motion. They cannot be in both at the same time; they cannot be both in place and in motion; and third, nothing can be in motion or in place except with respect to the third factor—time.

COMMENT: The Greek word which Aristotle uses for place is *topos*, from which we get our word topical; for example, the topical map of the world means both the physical concept, "space," and the more common word, "place." It also has some of the meaning of locality. The forest nymphs, for example, were thought to have a special *topos* where each one lived. In Book IV, Aristotle is not concerned with the abstract physical concept of "space" but with "place," or point of rest, as opposed to the act of motion.

THE FACTS OF PLACE: As always, Aristotle starts out with observable facts. For two reasons we know that place exists. First, we know from experience that whatever exists exists somewhere, that is, it exists in a definite place. Second, we know that everything that exists either is moving or is capable of moving from one place to another. Moving from place to place, or locomotion, is the most elementary and universal kind of motion there is. The fixed stars and planets have only this form of motion in common with other things in motion. Although these two observations indicate that place exists, can we say that place exists independently of the object which is said to be "in place"?

ARGUMENTS FOR THE INDEPENDENT EXISTENCE OF PLACE: There are three arguments for the independent existence of place. First, it is obvious that one thing can take the place of another. A car can take the place of the car in front of it at the stoplight, for example. Second, all the elements exhibit a tendency to move toward their particular place. For example, fire moves upward and earth downward. Upward, downward, sidewise, right and left thus seem to exist in the objective world and are not dependent upon human perception for their being. The place which is the end of a directed motion must therefore exist independently of the object which is moving toward that place. Third, the idea of place is contained in the idea of empty space. When philosophers talk about empty space, they assume the existence of place. Empty space is really a place where nothing is.

   COMMENT: The passage described above gives an indication why Aristotle never discovered the law of gravity. He thought of a natural tendency as an inner-directed impulse to movement on the part of a physical body. In his view, things are propelled by their own inner nature. The concept of gravity is a "pull" idea. Objects fall to the earth, because they are pulled by the force of gravity, not because their "nature" propels them. It is clear from Aristotle's statements that fire moves upward and earth downward, that concepts of "pull" and mechanical attraction are foreign to his way of thinking.

Indeed, his understanding of the physical world seems to be based upon his biological observations rather than upon his investigation of inorganic matter. Apparently, he was fascinated by that vital "something" which is present in all living organisms and makes them grow. Most probably, he derived his concept of the nature of inorganic bodies as an inner tendency to movement from his principle of life, which he considered the inner impulse to growth in living organisms.

WHAT IS THIS THING CALLED PLACE? Place is not a body but it can contain a body. What is it? After listing the many problems connected with the concept of place, Aristotle turns to his own analysis.

He begins by giving an example similar to the one which follows: Suppose someone wants to know where you are at this moment. You might answer, "in the universe, on the earth, in the USA, in New York, in my apartment, in the study, at the desk." Your answer shows that you are not in one place, but in a whole "nest of places," each one contained in another, like letters in envelopes. There is a place you have in common with the rest of the natural world—the universe. There are all the intermediate places, and finally, there is your particular place—the place you are occupying at your desk, where there is nothing else but you at the present time.

A DIGRESSION: At this point, Aristotle takes up the various meanings of "place" and what it means to be the limit of something. Place, for instance, can mean the room in which something is. But what does it mean, "to be in something else"? After the digression, Aristotle continues his inquiry of the meaning of the place which things have in common, and of particular place.

PARTICULAR PLACE: Particular place assumes some kind of container that an object can move "into," or "out of," or simply "be in." It separates the particular object, such as a book, from its general environment. Particular place is that place which immediately contains the object in question.

DEFINITION OF PLACE: Place, Aristotle observes, can be one of four things: It can be 1) the form of a body; 2) the matter of the body—for example, water; 3) the space between the outer edges of the containing body—for example, the inside of a pail of water; or 4) the containing surface itself—in this case, the actual sides of the pail. Place cannot be form. Although the sides of the pail happen to be the boundary of the water, they are not the limit of the water but rather the limit of the surrounding container. Place is not matter, for matter cannot be separated from its form. If you pour the water out, the place where the water was will be filled with air, a new material. Place is not the space between the sides of the pail, because that space would not exist if the pail had no sides. If you move a bookshelf from its place, the bookshelf does not carry its place with it. It finds a new place, and air takes its former place. The only solution is that place is the limit of the body which immediately surrounds the object. We must think of place, says Aristotle, as an immovable pail and consider the pail a movable place.

To make his explanation of place more clear, Aristotle gives an example of a boat on a river. The boat is in the running water, as if it were in a pail, or movable place. The river as it runs between two shores may be said to be the real place of the boat, as the two shores provide the first unmoved boundary. Aristotle finally defines place as "the first unmoved limit of a surrounding container." It is the boundary of the first unmoved body which surrounds the object. Place has to be unmoved or else you could not describe a particular place. As we saw in the case of the water in the pail, you can always empty the water out and fill the same unmoved space with air.

THE UNIVERSE AND PLACE: From this definition of place, it follows that for anything to have a "where," it must not only exist but must also have something in which it is contained. The universe, however, is the sum total of existing things. It is the whole in which everything else is contained. Consequently, the universe cannot properly be said to be contained in anything else. This means that the universe is not "in place."

THE UNIVERSE IS NO PLACE: That the universe is no place raises one problem in Aristotle's cosmography or theory of the universe. Aristotle thought of the universe as a nest of concentric and hollow rotating spheres which are in contact with one another. Immovably fixed in the substance of each of these spheres, between its inner and outer limit, is the heavenly body, or heavenly bodies as the case may be, which belong to that sphere. In Aristotle's system, the earth is a relatively small sphere at the very center of the universe. At the outer edges of the universe is what he calls the first heaven; it contains what are today known as the fixed stars. Each of the spheres in between this first heaven and the earth contains one of those heavenly bodies which the Greeks thought had a characteristic motion all its own, such as the sun, moon, or the planets. (Planet, in Greek, means "wanderer.") After some rather complex calculations, which we need not go into here, Aristotle concludes that the heavens are made up of fifty-five revolving spheres. When he adds the spheres of the four elements (earth, fire, air, and water), he arrives at the grand total of fifty-nine spheres, which together constitute the entire universe. Aristotle thought the matter from which the heavenly bodies are made is different from that of terrestial bodies, and is free from every kind of change except that change which he considers the most elementary, namely, circular motion. Because the heavenly bodies move in a circular motion, Aristotle said that their motion is eternal (his reasons will be given later), although not identical, one with the other. He thus treated the individual motion of each of the "wandering stars" as a separate problem. In his view, the fixed stars have no independent motion. They are carried around by the rotation of the first heaven once in every twenty-four hours. Each of the moving stars, however, revolves in its sphere in a direction different from, and consequently with a motion distinct from, that of the first heaven. They all derive their motion from the uniform rotation of that heaven. Aristotle explained the motion of the first heaven by saying that it was caused by a First Unmoved Mover, whose characteristics will be explained later. The problem which arises from his view of the universe is the following. If the universe is not "in place," how do you account for the fact that all of it rotates? How can something which is no place, revolve (i.e., change its place)? Aristotle somewhat begs the question. If place is the boundary of the first unmoved body which surrounds an object, he says, the place-universal cannot be the rotating mass of the heavens. Everything, including the outermost sphere of the universe, must be in place. For this reason, he suggests that the place in which the universe is contained is "the extreme limit of the heavens, which is at rest, and which is in contact with the heavenly mass which moves." What this "extreme limit" of the universe is, Aristotle does not tell us.

IMPORTANCE OF ARISTOTLE'S CONCEPT OF PLACE: Aristotle's concept of "place" is limited by his theory of the universe. Nevertheless, he was the first to realize that place is a relative concept. Place and motion exist only as relations between physical bodies. There can be no place or motion without things that can be placed and moved. Moreover, Aristotle's concept of place is a frame of reference, starting from the immediate place of the particular object to the universal place, the outer heaven of the universe.

VOID OR EMPTY SPACE: Place is where *something* is. Is there such a place where *nothing* is? Does empty space exist? To put it another way, is there such a thing as a place in which at a given moment there is nothing filling it? Aristotle sets forth the arguments for and against the existence of empty space. Anaxagoras denied that empty space existed. He tried to prove this thesis by showing that air was a body, although it was not seen by the senses. Aristotle thinks Anaxagoras missed the point. What he should have tried to prove was that no place exists where there is neither air nor any other kind of matter. On the other hand, those who say there is such a thing as empty space give three arguments for its existence. 1) There could be no movement if there were no empty space for bodies to move "into." 2) Contraction can only be explained by the existence of empty spaces between particles. And 3) nothing could grow or expand without empty space into which to grow. In addition to these arguments, the Pythagoreans advanced the theory that empty space was breathed into the heavens to create the spaces between the stars and planets.

THE MEANING OF EMPTY SPACE: The problem of empty space requires a definition of terms. Some philosophers use the term, "empty space," to mean a place where there is no body which you can touch and see. In their view, even empty space filled with color is still a void, if there is nothing "heavy or light" in that place. These people would seem to argue against the theory that empty space is a place which is absolutely empty of all matter. Plato's idea of empty space was similar to the view described above. He thought empty space was a place where there was no body which was composed of matter and form. To Plato, void meant "absence of form." The same concept of empty space led philosophers to believe that the formless void was the first matter of all physical bodies. Aristotle feels that this definition of empty space does not take into account physical bodies which cannot be separated from their matter.

ARISTOTLE'S VIEW OF EMPTY SPACE: Aristotle holds that these proofs in favor of the existence of a void do not really prove anything. As *place* does not have an independent existence of its own, so *empty space* does not. Empty space is only a place where there might be a body, but where there now is not. Motion does not have to be explained by the theory that empty space exists, as Parmenides tried to do. Observation shows us that bodies can change their place and take the place of other bodies. We do not have to explain the motion of whirlpools and wheels by a theory of void. Whirlpools form vortices because air and water change place in rapid succession. Similarly, expansion and contraction do not require the independent existence of a void because place has no independent existence. The body does not grow into a rigid place where air is. As it grows taller, it simply takes the place of air in that space into which it grows.

REFUTATION OF FIRST ARGUMENT: Aristotle proves empty space does not exist by refuting the above-listed arguments. He emphatically rejects the *first argument* in favor of empty space, that motion is impossible unless there is empty space for bodies to move "into." (It will be remembered that Parmenides said that motion did not exist, precisely because it required the existence of empty space, and empty space, in his view, was Non-Being.) Aristotle offers many ingenious arguments in refutation of this viewpoint, the three most significant of which are given here. His arguments are based on his theories of motion and place. 1) We know, he says, that every natural motion has a determinate character. For example, elemental, inorganic bodies, such as fire and water, tend to move in a definite direction to a definite place toward which their nature impels them to move. Why should natural bodies move one way rather than another, unless there existed a determinate goal, a "place to which," which oriented their movement? Empty space, in Aristotle's opinion, is limitless; "it has no top, bottom, or middle." Moreover, it is undifferentiated; it has no direction, such as up or down. By definition, therefore, limitless, undifferentiated vacancy cannot be the cause of motion, because it is not able in any way to orient the behavior of physical bodies. To use a modern example, there could be no gravitation if a field of gravity did not exist and there were only "undifferentiated, limitless vacancy." Furthermore, in Aristotle's view, if there were no determinate "place" that conditioned the behavior of inorganic bodies, we would be unable to describe the specific nature of these bodies. Natural tendencies to movement are differentiated by their goal of movement, and in their turn, differentiate the physical bodies which exhibit them. Aristotle concludes that "either nothing has a natural tendency in any direction or that what does condition movement is not empty space."

An even more interesting argument than the one described above is the one based on time, rate, and distance. The speed of a body is inversely proportional to the density of the medium through which it moves, and directly proportional to its weight. If water, for example, offers twice the resistance of air, a body should take half the time it took to travel the distance in water to travel the same distance in the air. But in a vacuum there is no resistance. Therefore, a body should take no time at all to travel through empty space. Moreover, a heavy body should take the same time to travel through a vacuum as a light one. This is impossible. Nothing moves in no time, and if there is no time span which can be divided or measured, there is no question of a heavy body moving slower than a light one.

REFUTATION OF SECOND ARGUMENT: Aristotle next refutes the argument that no physical space exists apart from its material contents on the basis of his concept of place. A piece of wood, for example, displaces its own bulk in water and in air. Similarly, if we see a space which seems to be empty—i.e. where there seems to be no heaviness or lightness—there can still be bulk, as distinct from the other qualities, as in the case of air.

REFUTATION OF THIRD ARGUMENT: The third argument can also be shown to be false. There are no empty spaces inside bodies. Aristotle first shows that the hypothesis of a void does not help explain the facts. Void can only be conceived as being in a body in two ways, as small separate voids between particles, or as something diffused throughout the substance. The first case is nothing but the problem of whether a void exists between bodies in miniature. And we have shown that it does not. In the second place it is no longer *empty space* in which movement takes place, but empty space would itself be the cause of movement and act like an elevator. But a void cannot move or be in place, so the second theory is as false as the first one.

Aristotle says we can explain contraction and expansion as we explain changes in quality. The body which is contracting must be able to be contracted in the same way in which water is potentially hot. What changes in water are the qualities of hot and cold. The matter remains the same. The matter likewise remains the same when things contract or expand.

CONCLUSION: In view of all these arguments, Aristotle finally concludes that empty space does not exist.

TIME: The fourth and final characteristic common to all physical bodies in Aristotle's view is time. He has shown that empty space both in our modern sense of a vacuum, and in the sense of no place at all does not actually exist in the natural world. He now proceeds to show the dependency of place, motion, and time upon each other. Aristotle notes that it is obvious that bodies move from one place to another in time. This fact leads him to develop a theory of time.

THE PROBLEMS RELATED TO TIME: The concept of time presents many difficulties. In the first place, time seems to be composed of "no-longers" and "not-yets," of past and future. How, therefore, can we say that time actually exists? Second, time seems to be something divisible. When anything divisible exists, it follows that if the whole exists, its parts must exist at the same time. But some parts of time are in the past and some in the future. Moreover, "now" is not a part of time, for you cannot say that time is made up of many "nows." Third, the terms used to express time present difficulties. How do you define "before" and "after"? When does a "now" cease to be a "now"? Fourth and last, Aristotle observes that philosophers before him have not been successful in defining what time is. Some thought it was the movement of the universe as a whole, while others thought it was the heavenly sphere. These theories present many problems. For instance, if time is the movement of the universe as a whole, then the individual movements of lesser bodies must constitute different times. Observation shows us, however, that there are not many times but one time for the whole universe.

TIME IS NOT MOTION: Time seems to be a kind of motion or change, but it cannot be the same as movement. For it has been shown that motion occurs only in the moving thing. But time is the same everywhere and related to all things in the same way. Second, time itself cannot be faster or slower, but is itself the standard by which things are said to be fast or slow. It is obvious, therefore, that time is not some kind of motion.

TIME IS RELATED TO MOTION: On the other hand, time cannot be separated from motion because we are only aware of time passing, when we are aware of some change taking place. While we are asleep, for instance, we are not aware of change, for when we wake up it does not seem to us as if any time had actually passed. On the other hand, if we are in a dark room and thinking dark thoughts, we are aware that time is passing, because things are going on in our minds.

TIME, THE MEASURE OF MOTION: Motion is a passage "from here to there." We are conscious of motion through an awareness of a change of place. We are conscious of time from the experience of a "before" and an "after." Aristotle shows how time and motion are related by an example like the one given here. Two of us start out at the same time from New York to go to Washington. I reach Baltimore as you pull into Washington. There is no doubt about it; you have traveled *more* than I have; not only have you traveled a greater distance, but you have moved more than I have. You have traveled *faster*. I know you have moved more, because, in the interval between the "now" *before* we started and the "now" *after* we stopped, you traveled more miles. It is clear that time was what measured your progress of motion. Aristotle is now ready for his definition of time: "Time is the number of motion in relation to before and after." Aristotle says time is a *number* in the sense of a counting or measuring of motion. Time is not measured by motion nor is it separate from motion. It is not movement, but that by which movement can be measured. "Time is the countable thing the we are counting" in movement. It is the measurable aspect of motion.

SIGNIFICANCE OF ARISTOTLE'S THEORY OF TIME: Aristotle's concept of time is noteworthy because, as was the case with his understanding of "place," he thinks of it as something relative. It will be remembered that the view that time is a relative phenomenon was not generally accepted in scientific circles until Einstein revolutionized classical physics with his theory of relativity.

THE "NOW" IN TIME: After defining what time is, Aristotle passes to an analysis of the meaning of "now" in time. He tells us that we know something is moving when we see it at different points along the path of its movement. In the case of my trip from New York to Washington, for example, I know I have moved a certain distance when I arrive in Baltimore because I no longer am in New York. The "now" when I was in New York is thus different from the "now" that I am experiencing in Baltimore. We know that time has passed because we are able to call many different moments "now." Yesterday at 5:30 I was living in "now." Today, I call 6:30 "now," and tomorrow morning will be "now" when it comes. We can think of "now" in the same way as we think of a point on a line, or a moving object. We perceive change of place by recognizing different points along the path of the change. We know motion by observing the moving object. We perceive the passage of time by experiencing different "nows."

THE MEANING OF "NOW":   "Now" is related to time in two ways. In the first place, it divides time; it divides the past from the future, and in so doing, it provides limits to different periods of times. For example, the "now" that marks the beginning of an hour sets off the "now" at the end of the hour, as the points at the ends of a line define the length of that line. Second, "now" gives time continuity; it provides the link between "before" and "after." We must not think, however, that in performing this function, "now" forms a part of time anymore than a point forms part of a line. In following a moving object along its path, "now" marks the ever-changing position of that object. Nevertheless, each succeeding "now" divides the past from the future. Consequently, if we included "now" in the continuum of time, there would have to be a break in time to account for the interval between before and after. But experience shows us that time is uninterrupted. "Now," therefore, cannot be a part of time, for the same reason that a point is not part of a line. There is no least indivisible time as there is no least indivisible line.

OTHER ASPECTS OF TIME: Aristotle now turns briefly to a discussion of other aspects of time. For example, time is not faster or slower, but the same everywhere. Second, time and motion are interdependent, as both are measured by the other. Time is known through motion and motion is experienced in time.

"IN TIME": Next, Aristotle takes up the question of what it means to be "in time." "In time" can mean one of two things. "To be in time" can mean existing when time also exists. Second, "to be in time" can mean to be a part of time, as there are parts of numbers or as something which can be counted. When time, for example, is considered as a number or measure, "now" and "before" exist in time in the same way as the unit, and the odd and even exist in number. They are elements of time. Events, however, are "in time" as something which can be measured by time. They are contained in time, as a body is contained in its place. Each event is in a nest of "times," and each body is in a nest of places. As regards the first way something can be "in time," to be in existence while time is passing does not necessarily mean being subjected to time. Some things are outside the control of time, like thought, for example. Once you know something, you know it now and forever. Likewise, something can be in existence where motion and place are, but does not have to be actually in motion, or constantly in place.

Since events exist in time as being measured by it, it follows that there must be a period of time which is longer than any event which has happened, is happening, or will happen in the future. Time, in this sense, is seen as something infinite. Second, observation shows us that things which exist in time are affected by it. Aristotle thus considers time a destructive force. What is counted in time is motion, and motion changes a thing from its present state to another condition. Man is born and he dies in time. It is time which wears him down, and time which eventually brings about his death. If time is a force of decay, it follows that things which are eternal are not "in time." They do not undergo change, and thus cannot be affected by the passage of time.

TIME AS THE MEASURE OF REST: Since time measures motion, it also measures rest or the end of motion. Obviously, everything which is in time is not always in motion. Time, however, does not measure all types of rest, but that kind of rest which is the end or beginning of a motion of a body which is capable of movement. What cannot move, cannot stop moving; it has no beginning or end of not moving. Thus, growth, decay, and other forms of motion can be measured by time. Aristotle thinks the dead are also in time, because they once lived in time. Only those things which never move (a geometric proof, for instance), or were never contained in time (the gods, for instance) are not measurable by time. Eternal being and non-being are not in time.

THE OBJECTIVITY OF TIME: The last chapter raises the interesting question of the relation of time to consciousness. Does time exist apart from consciousness or is it purely subjective? If our minds could not count time, would there be anything outside us which was objectively countable? For instance, if mind did not exist, would numbers also not exist? It seems that without the existence of minds to count, there would be no such thing as counting. Time would therefore seem to exist as something entirely dependent upon our minds. Aristotle holds that time exists independently of our experience of it. The process of change does not depend upon our recognizing that things change. Growth, decay, and motion would take place without us. Since time is the measurable aspect of *any* change that occurs, it follows that time must exist in the objective world.

TIME IS THE MEASURE OF CONTINUOUS MOVEMENT: If time is the "counting of continuous movement," of what kind of movement can time be said to be the standard measure? Are there different times, because there are different kinds of movement? Aristotle says no. It is the lapse of time which is counted by two "nows." And these "nows" are everywhere at once, regardless of the movements taking place. But if you want to pick a standard movement which time should measure, Aristotle suggests taking movement in a circle since it is the most familiar and shows the most uniformity. This is why we say that human affairs and other things which have a natural movement have a circular motion, because they seem to have a beginning and end periodically; time itself is said to "roll round," because time and circular motion seem to determine one another. This completes Aristotle's discussion of time.

BOOKS V TO VII

ORGANIZATION OF THE BOOKS:　In these books Aristotle develops the principles he has set forth in detail in the first four books. As has been noted, the first books were originally called *On Nature* and the last four *On Motion*. As the last books are mainly refinements and consequences of the first principles assigned to the study of nature in the first four books, it is not necessary to go into any of them in detail. Each book will be reviewed briefly.

BOOK V
THE TERMS OF MOTION

CHANGE AND MOTION:　This book serves as an introduction to the analysis of motion which Aristotle takes up in his last three books. Chapter 1 deals with the difference between change and movement. Change is the more general phenomenon, one aspect of which is motion. There are four ways in which a body may be said to change. 1) From one opposite to its "extreme," for example, from hot to cold. 2) From a contradictory to its negative. Movement from a contradictory to its negative means moving from being to non-being or death. 3) From a contradictory to its positive, i.e., from non-being to being or coming into being. And 4) from a negative to a negative, i.e., from non-being to non-being. The word movement only applies to the first way things change. The second, third, and fourth ways refer only to change. For something to be moved it both has to be in existence and to stay in existence. Second, it has to pass from something *to* something. Thus, Aristotle considers coming into being and going out of being change but not movement. The last way that things are said to change is not movement because nothing is moved. Movement is therefore the passing from one "positive" term to its opposite. The term must be positive because it must actually *be*. Movement is when something cold becomes its opposite, hot. Note that the two opposite terms are not "moved" in the process. There must always be something which is moved. In this case the subject is water.

KINDS OF MOVEMENT:　Chapter 2 proves that there are only three kinds of movement: 1) change of quality (white to black), 2) change of quantity, growing and shrinking, getting fat, getting thin, and 3) change of place, i.e., locomotion. Change of place includes the movement of the stars in their orbits. Coming into being and going out of being as stated above cannot be considered movement. For substance, that which actually exists, has no opposite, only a contradictory—namely, not being substance, or not existing. Thus, if substance changes, it ceases to be, and this is contrary to the conditions of movement.

CONTINUITY AND RELATED TERMS: In Chapter 3, Aristotle defines the basic terms which he will use for his discussion of continuity, or the state of being without interruption to be reviewed in Book VI. Things are *together in place* when they are in the same immediate place. Things touch when their ends are in the same immediate place, as a chair touches the floor. A thing is *consecutive* to another body when that body comes immediately after it and there is nothing else between the two. Two men sit consecutively to each other at the table. If a body immediately follows another body and touches it, it is said to be *contiguous*. The wing of the house is contiguous to the central part. *Continuous* is when those things which are contiguous to one another have their ends either fused together or bound together so that they are one. A line is continuous. Of the last three definitions consecutive, or following after, is included in the definition of contiguous, which is included in the definition of continuous. Continuous, therefore, according to Aristotle, comes last in the order of classification.

WAYS IN WHICH A CHANGE CAN BE ONE: In Chapter 4, Aristotle lists the five ways in which a movement can have unity. 1) A change is *generically* one, when it takes place in the same category; for example, change of quality or change of quantity. 2) Changes are *specifically* one when the category involved in the change and the particular modification of that category are the same; for example, acquiring knowledge by learning or becoming white. 3) Change can be *absolutely* and *individually* one, as when Socrates changes. 4) A change is said to be one when the *change process* is whole and *complete*. 5) Finally, a change is considered one when it is *uniform*. Changes which take place at the same rate of speed, at the same time, and for the same distance fall in this category.

CONTRARY MOVEMENTS: Chapter 5 points out how one movement is contrary to another. This problem has been considered already in our discussion of the difference between change and movement, contradictories and opposites. Aristotle defines contrary movements as "those which pass, the one from this opposite to that, and the other from that to this." Example: white becoming black, while black becomes white. If either becomes gray, this is not a contrary movement, for gray is intermediate or halfway between white and black.

REST AND MOTION: Chapter 6 analyzes in what way rest is contrary to motion. It can only be said to be contrary when it involves a body which can be moved. When that which cannot be moved is at rest, it is said to be unchanging.

BOOK VI
CONTINUITY OF SPACE, TIME, AND MOTION

INTRODUCTION: This book shows how space, time, and motion are continuous. The proof is based on the demonstration that every finite space, time, or motion can be subdivided an infinite number of times. In Chapter 1 Aristotle redefines what he means by consecutive, contiguous, and continuous, and shows by these definitions that indivisibles such as a point or a "now" cannot form anything continuous.

TIME, SPACE, AND INFINITY: In Chapter 2 Aristotle turns to the question of whether time and space are infinite. First he distinguishes between that which can be extended without limit and that which can be divided without end. From his argument, it is clear that Aristotle considers space, time, and motion finite for the reason that motion is a function of substances, of things which actually exist. That which exists has to be finite, because its matter is structured and, therefore, limited by a definite form. Space and time are dimensions of motion, which has been shown to depend on substance. Therefore, space, time, and motion are finite. Aristotle believes that experience proves that the kind of a world in which we live is an orderly system composed of finite, physical things related to one another in terms of space and time. Space, time, and motion are phenomena of this world, which only become intelligible when we study the behavior of each individual object in relation to the whole system. If space and time exist as observation show us they do, and if they are knowable, then they have to be finite. Space and time can be said to be infinite, however, in the sense that both are potentially divisible an infinite number of times. Aristotle proves this point again by demonstrating that it is impossible to take an infinite time to travel a finite distance, or to travel an infinite distance in a finite time. But it is possible to travel an infinitely divisible distance in a finite time, and to travel a finite distance in an infinitely divisible amount of time. Both space and time are wholes which are limited in extent but infinitely divisible.

MOTION AND REST IN A MOMENT: In Chapter 3, Aristotle proves that there can be neither motion nor rest in indivisible now.

THE LAST FIVE CHAPTERS OF BOOK VI: These concluding five chapters discuss the relationship between the various factors of change and the time in which change takes place. They prove that change like time is divisible. Chapter 4 discusses how motion may be divided with respect to its parts. Every motion is composed of the following factors: 1) the time in which the change takes place; 2) the movements of the individual parts of the object which is moved; and 3) whatever forms the field of change, for example, distance, quantity, and quality. Chapter 5 shows that the end of a movement is not a divisible part of the process of motion, but the limit of the process. The exact time or instant, the "now" when a thing has actually changed, is indivisible and therefore outside the continuum of motion, as the point which forms the end of a line is not part of that line. The beginning of a change process, however, is a divisible part because there is no indivisible "now" when you can say the process actually begins. "Now," like the point on a line, is outside of, and therefore not part of, continuous time. For example, you cannot put a "now" to the moment when a car moves away from the street corner. You can only observe that it has begun to move.

CHANGE IS CONTINUOUS: Chapter 6 examines what is meant by the exact time of a change process. The time in which a change occurs covers the time when any part of the change process takes place. The time in which a change occurs must be understood in the same way as the place in which an object is found. For example, the Japanese attack on Pearl Harbor took place on December 7, 1941, in December, 1941, in 1941 and in the second quarter of the twentieth century. Now the immediate time when Pearl Harbor took place was December 7, 1941. When you supply the hours during which the attack occurred you have the exact time. The immediate time of a change is the time meant from the beginning of the change to the end of the process. From this reasoning, it follows that change must be going on throughout every part of the change process. Thus anything which is in change must have been changing previously; anything which has completed a change must have completed a lesser change or a part of that change previously; that which is changing must have completed a lesser change or part of the change previously and that which has completed a change must have been previously changing. In other words, change is continuous. There is no way of separating from the entire process the first instance of change which started motion. The same is true with the process of coming into being and going out of being. Change is a continuous succession of things changing and having changed.

THE RELATION OF CHANGE TO TIME: In Chapter 7, Aristotle proves that a limited movement cannot take place in an unlimited time. Similarly, unlimited movement cannot take place in a finite time. The same is true of coming into being and passing out of being. In other words, when one is born, he is part of the process of generation, of a finite change in a finite time.

REST AND TIME: In Chapter 8, Aristotle proves that there is no "first stage" of rest, for the same reason that there is no earliest instant of change. There is no indivisible moment when you can say rest started. As there is no exact *place* where a thing is when it is in motion, so there is no exact time when a thing is at rest. When an object is moving, you can trace its path, but you can only say where it is if you interrupt its motion. Similarly, you can only say when a thing is at rest if you interrupt the time during which the thing is not in motion. "Nows" measure rest as points measure motion. This chapter thus shows a further interaction between time, space, and motion.

THE REALITY OF TIME: In Chapter 9, Aristotle refutes the arguments of a disciple of Parmenides, called Zeno (born 489 B.C.), who held that time does not exist. In Chapter 10, Aristotle proves that an indivisible thing such as a "now" or a point cannot move. This means that no change is unlimited except the circular motion of the heavens. Every natural motion is a definite, individual, describable process. On the basis of the knowledge of the astronomy of his day, Aristotle concludes that the motion of the "first heaven" is unlimited because it is the only change which has been going on through an infinite amount of time.

BOOK VII
MOTION CONSIDERED FURTHER

INTRODUCTION: Many early critics of Aristotle thought that Book VII was not necessary to an understanding of Aristotle's physics and left it out of their commentaries. Apparently, it was an early work which Aristotle included in his study on nature as an introduction to Book VIII, The Theory of the First Mover.

NO SERIES OF INDIVIDUAL CHANGES IS INFINITE: Chapter 1 goes through the well-known argument that whatever is in motion must be kept in motion by something. The moved, which is in motion, must have a mover to move it, which in turn must be moved by another mover, which in turn must be moved by another mover, and so on. You cannot have an infinite series of movers however, because then the thing which is now moved would never be able to be moved. Aristotle has already proved that an infinite motion cannot take place in a finite time and vice versa. In order for motion to exist, there must of necessity be some First Mover who started the whole process.

OTHER PROBLEMS RELATED TO MOTION: In Chapter 2, Aristotle proves that the cause of movement must be in contact with the thing moved. Again he shows his ignorance of the laws of inertia, which explain how an arrow, for example, can move through the air for a certain distance without being kept in motion by the bow. Aristotle says that contact also plays a role in changes of quantity and quality. We are moved to see by the contact of our eyes with the objects. When the object is not there, we can no longer be said to see it. Chapter 3 examines the problems involved in processes which are similar to, but not the same as, changes in quality; for example, loss of sight or hearing, or making a statue out of bronze. Chapter 4 answers the questions, What does it mean to compare two motions? How are they equal, greater, or less than each other? Chapter 5 discusses a few fundamental principles of mechanics. For example, Aristotle shows how a force that can move a certain load a certain distance in a certain time, can move half the load in either twice the distance in the same time or the same distance in half the time. As can be seen from this brief outline Book VII does not contribute much to Aristotle's general philosophy of nature.

BOOK VIII
THE UNMOVED MOVER

INTRODUCTION: In Book VIII, Aristotle discusses the physical basis for his theory of a First Mover for the universe. This means that Aristotle deduces the necessity of a First Mover as the logical explanation for the existence of motion. In the *Metaphysics*, he considers the First Mover from the standpoint of being. Can a

First Mover, in the form of a super-sensible being, be said to exist? Although in Book VIII of the *Physics* Aristotle does not go into the metaphysical aspects of the problem, this book does shed some light on his work on the nature of being. He derives his argument for the existence of a First Mover from his understanding of the nature of motion. He argues in favor of a supernatural world from the nature of the natural world itself. He does not first make up some theory about what God is. He looks at the world about him, and then says that the nature of this world makes it necessary for some being outside the world, yet related to the world as its first cause, to exist. Something has to keep the world in motion.

MOTION IS ETERNAL: In Chapter 1, Aristotle states that motion is eternal. Anaxagoras had argued that there was a time before motion began; and Empedocles believed that there are alternating periods when the world is in motion and when it is not moving at all. Aristotle replies that motion is the moving of the movable; it is making the potentially movable actual. 1) We cannot say that something which can be moved existed for a time before it actually was moved. It must have either come into being before or it always was in being. If it came into being before, this means there was a change before it was moved for the first time. If it always was in being, some change must have taken place earlier to enable it to be moved. In both cases, we have to assume some change before the first act of motion. 2) There can never be a time when there is no motion, as time is the "number" or measure of motion. But there has always been time. A period of time has been shown to be that which passes between two "nows." No matter how far back you go you will always find a "now," and "now" is the link between the past and the future. You can thus never go back to a first "now." 3) We cannot imagine motion ceasing, for then we will have to imagine a change will take place after the last motion ends; namely, the change from being able to be moved to being unmovable. To be unmoving is not the same thing as to be unable to be moved. Therefore motion is eternal.

COMMENT: The idea that the world was created, that something was created out of nothing, is a Judeo-Christian concept and exists only in that tradition. The Scholastics, for instance, argued that the world had to be created because if time were eternal, there would never be a "now." If the train to Boston were traveling from all eternity to Boston, it would never reach Boston. Aristotle, however, considers the general process of motion eternal, although individual acts of motion can only take place within a definite period of time. The problem for the student resides in the meaning of the word, eternal. The Greek *aidios* means "everlasting," in the sense of "time which has no set end." Understood in this sense, eternal motion can have a place in the finite world. *Aidios* does not mean eternal, in the sense of "beyond time" "without the existence of time." This concept of eternal cannot be applied to a finite world, as the great medieval philosopher, Thomas Aquinas, rightly argued.

OBJECTIONS TO THIS VIEW: In Chapter 2 Aristotle replies to three objections against the eternity of motion. 1) No change can be everlasting, since it takes place between two contraries which limit it. Aristotle answers that a single movement cannot go on forever, but this does not mean that there cannot be some kind of motion, not from opposites to opposites, but continuous and the same, which goes on forever. 2) You can see that motion has a beginning from the motion of inanimate objects. These start from a state of rest. They are set in motion by some eternal mover. Aristotle passes over the problem that the motion of inanimate objects is started by a mover outside them. A more serious question, he says, is why some things that are at rest are not always at rest, and why those that are in motion are not always in motion. 3) It seems that animals can start movement inside themselves. Why cannot the universe also be self-moving? Aristotle replies that animals can only start local movement. They thus have control only over a limited kind of motion. But animals are never completely at rest. Some movement is always going on. The heart is always running, for example. Over such movements, animals have no control.

CLASSIFICATION OF NATURAL OBJECTS: In Chapter 3 Aristotle examines his observation that some things that can be in motion are sometimes at rest, and asks why this is so. He concludes that some things are always in motion, some things are always at rest and some things are of a nature to move sometimes and sometimes not to move.

NATURAL AND UNNATURAL MOTION: In Chapters 4-7 Aristotle tries to prove this conclusion. In Chapter 4 he starts by saying that in every act of motion there is the *active* mover and the *passive* moved. Whatever is moved is moved by something. That which moves *by nature* is different from that which moves by force, or unnaturally, in the sense that the natural mover is that which is actually a particular "such" acting on that which is potentially this particular "such." For example, the potentiality of fire to move upward is made actual when the natural agent (its tendency to move up) actually makes fire move up. An acorn naturally grows into an oak. When it is eaten by a squirrel, it is destroyed unnaturally by violence. To do violence to something is to force it from its natural direction.

THE FIRST MOVER MUST BE UNMOVED: Chapter 5 reviews the argument of Book VII that there cannot be an infinite series of movers and that therefore there has to be a First Mover which is unmoved. Aristotle proves this point in two ways. 1) In inanimate things we have already proved that what is moved is moved by something else. As you cannot take the series back to infinity, there must be a First Mover. 2) HE must be either self-moved or un-moved. In the case of animate things, which move themselves, no animal moves its whole self, but always a part. Either the senses or the mind moves the other part. Thus in self-moving creatures there are two factors; that which is moved and the unmoved part which moves. It follows that the First Mover of all motion must be un-moved.

UNMOVED MOVER IS ETERNAL: In Chapter 6 Aristotle argues that if motion is eternal, the First Unmoved Mover must be eternal. There are many unmoved movers in the universe, but these are not eternal. They die and are followed by other unmoved movers. The First Unmoved Mover is eternal in the following ways: 1) nothing which is the cause of eternal motion can have size, since that which is composed of matter and form will be subject to decay; 2) that which is eternal must be changeless. Aristotle concludes that there must be some unmoving First Mover above change and decay.

ONE UNMOVED MOVER: It follows that there is only one Unmoved Mover. First, nature does "nothing in vain," and second, eternal movement must be continuous and unbroken. Motion which is interrupted and followed by a new motion is not continuous. Therefore, it is not eternal. For motion to be eternal, it must be unified; consequently, it must be produced by only one mover.

THE UNMOVED MOVER IS ABSOLUTELY UNMOVED: The third characteristic of the First Mover is that he cannot be moved even incidentally. Animals and human beings are said to move in-cidentally in the sense that the unmoved part of the organism, the soul, is carried from place to place. The soul, for example, moves with the man. Moreover, we have seen that the unmoved part of animals is the cause of only one kind of motion, namely, locomo-tion. But even locomotion depends on external causes, such as growth and environment, and thus cannot be eternally maintained by the animal. The First Unmoved Mover must not be able to be moved in either of these ways.

THE TWO KINDS OF MOTION: Aristotle says that we find two kinds of motion in the natural world: 1) the eternal motion of the heavens whose mover is the Unmoved Mover, and 2) the motion which stops and starts of earthly objects. The second kind of motion is kept in being by a chain of motion moving from the stars and planets down through intermediate bodies to earthly things.

THE MOST ELEMENTARY: In Chapter 7 Aristotle proves that the motion caused by the First Mover must be the most basic form of movement, as it must be able to go on forever. He has shown earlier that locomotion or change in place is the most elementary kind of movement. In Chapters 7 and 9 he proves 1) that no change is continuous and therefore eternal except locomotion; and 2) that no locomotion can be continuous and infinite except circular motion. Chapter 8 proves that only circular movement can go on continuously forever. Chapter 9 states that circular movement is the prototype or first type of all motion. Aristotle illustrates his view of circular motion by describing a circle and its diameter, AB. Non-circular motion goes from point "A" on one side of the circle along the diameter to point "B" on the other side. If the movement of an object were to continue after it had reached point "B," it would have to reverse its direction and go back toward point "A." Aristotle thinks that this reversal could not take place instantaneously, but that there would be a minute period of time when all motion between "A" and "B" stopped completely. He concludes that it is impossible for motion in a straight line, such as that between points "A" and "B," to be continuous. Motion around the circumference of a circle, however, involves no such difficulties. Circular motion, Aristotle says, can be continuous (i.e., not interrupted), because it is always in the same direction. A further advantage of circular motion, in his view, is that it admits of the least possibility of change. Because it does not have to change direction, it can continue at a fixed rate, and it can continue forever. This means that a body which moves in a circular path can change only with respect to its position along its path.

WHERE THE UNMOVED MOVER IS: In Chapter 10 Aristotle uses rather lengthy arguments to prove again that the First Unmoved Mover has no size, or dimensions, that it has no parts and is indivisible. The question now arises as to where in the universe the Unmoved First Mover lives. Aristotle says it either has to be at the center of the universe or at the very edge of its circumference, because that is where "beginnings" take place. He decides for the circumference because the First Mover must be able to give the fastest motion to the universe. The fixed stars, in Aristotle's opinion, have to move fastest of all natural bodies because, as we have seen, they are found in the first heaven, which is the outer limit of the universe. If we remember our mathematics and think of the universe in Aristotle's terms as a revolving circle containing a series of rotating spheres, one inside the other, we will realize that that sphere that is at the circumference of the circle of the universe must revolve faster than any of the other inner spheres. Consequently, the fixed stars have to have the fastest motion of all the physical bodies in the universe.

HOW THE UNMOVED MOVER MOVES: Aristotle does not tell us how an Unmoved Mover who has no body or shape whatsoever can *be* in some place on the circumference of the world, nor how it keeps the universe in motion. It must be remembered that he believes that the mover must keep in physical contact with what it is moving. Perhaps, then, the First Mover gives the wheel of the universe a couple of good pushes a day to keep it going. If he did so, however, it would mean that he himself is moved by some other mover. Apparently, Aristotle's view of the Unmoved Mover living on the edge of the universe was one of his early theories. In the *Metaphysics* he attempts to solve the problem of how something which has no body, but is simply some kind of force, can actually impart movement to something else without itself being moved.

THE METAPHYSICS

INTRODUCTION: The *Metaphysics* is the most important of all Aristotle's philosophical works, for it contains the philosopher's theory of being. At the same time, it is the most difficult of Aristotle's books to understand. The great Arabian philosopher of the eleventh century A.D., Avicenna, is said to have read the work forty times without understanding a word. Research has indicated that the book is a selection of notes, written during various periods of Aristotle's career. Most of Book Lambda, for instance, seems to be an expression of Aristotle's early thinking when he was still very much under Plato's influence. Other parts are evidently the result of Aristotle's later reflections on the same subject. For this reason, the *Metaphysics* does not form one well-organized whole. Aristotle seems to have changed his opinion regarding many matters during the course of his intellectual development. In the *Metaphysics,* Aristotle seems at different times to have held opposing views on the two most important questions in the book, namely, the nature of primary being, and the possibility of having scientific knowledge of this kind of being.

> **COMMENT:** The word "metaphysics" comes from the Greek words: *"meta"* meaning "after" and *"phusika"* meaning "physical things." Aristotle never called his science of being "metaphysics" or "after physical things." Scholars attribute this name to the editorial work of early commentators on Aristotle, and in particular to the work of a certain Andronicus of Rhodes (early first century B.C.) who is credited with having unearthed the manuscript. As Aristotle's treatise on the nature of being was customarily placed after his treatment of "physical things," it was referred to as "the metaphysics."

THE CHALLENGE OF PLATO: As regards a theory of being, the biggest challenge confronting Aristotle was Plato's theory of Ideas. Plato held that what a thing is, is essentially the idea of the thing. Houseness, the universal concept of a house, is what makes a house really a house. The bricks and stones are of secondary importance in determining what makes a house "housy." Aristotle could not develop any theory of being without taking his great teacher's theory into serious consideration. He agrees with Plato that universals are objectively real (that is, that they are present in the natural world, and not just abstractions in our minds). But he does not agree that universals exist *choristos* or separated from matter, as self-existing forms. The *Metaphysics* is consequently concerned with the two problems related to Plato's theory of Ideas. Aristotle's early formulation of these problems was as follows: "Do super-sensible forms really exist? And is a science which has such forms as its subject matter possible?" Later in his career, Aristotle changed the form of the questions, as he saw more clearly that the forms of physical bodies cannot exist apart from their matter. The question, "Do universals exist as super-sensible forms?" became "What do we mean when we say, 'Something is'?" What does it mean "to be"?

THE SIGNIFICANCE OF THE *METAPHYSICS*: It is evident from the foregoing that the *Metaphysics* will present many problems to the reader. Scholars of every age have worked long and hard trying to resolve the apparent contradictions contained in the book. Their solutions form the basis of our Western concept of being. The *Metaphysics* thus plays an important role in the history of ideas. We are all heirs to Aristotle's concepts of actuality and potentiality; the doctrine of immanent form; his theory of being as activity; and his idea of the First Cause of the world, the Unmoved Mover.

ORGANIZATION OF THE *METAPHYSICS*: The first three books are an introduction to the problem of metaphysics or, as we would call it, philosophy. In the first book, Aristotle states his view of the origin and development of thought and the place of theoretical knowledge in his philosophical system. In the second book, Book Alpha the Less, Aristotle makes some remarks on the philosophical method of inquiry. Book Beta lists the problems connected with philosophy in general. As elsewhere, Aristotle does not present these difficulties in a dogmatic fashion. Books Gamma, Epsilon, Zeta, Eta, Theta, Iota, Mu, and Nu attempt to examine these problems in an effort to arrive at the truth in the "science of first philosophy," as Aristotle calls it. Books Mu and Nu contain some of the best criticism we have from classical times of the ideas of Plato and the Pythagoreans. Book Lambda, one of the most controversial of the books, presents Aristotle's conflicting views on the First Unmoved Mover. Book Delta, the fifth book, reviews Aristotle's system of terms as a preparation for a definition of being which follows in the next books. Only Book Kappa, the eleventh book, cannot be fitted into the general pattern of the work easily. It repeats concepts already known to us in the *Physics* and other works. Its chief value is that it serves as a prologue to the theory of the Unmoved Mover in Book Lambda. In trying to piece together the essential parts of Aristotle's metaphysics, the reader will find most of the material in six of the twelve books listed above, and should look at these most important books in detail. They are Book Gamma, Books Epsilon, Zeta, Eta, Theta, and Book Lambda.

COMMENT: The names of the books in the *Metaphysics* follow the letters of the Greek alphabet: A, in Greek, is "Alpha," B is "Beta," etc. The first letter of the Greek word represents the letter in the alphabet.

BOOKS ALPHA, ALPHA THE LESS, AND BETA
AN INTRODUCTION TO FIRST PHILOSOPHY

INTRODUCTION: Before going into the main part of his theory of being, Aristotle, as is his habit, tries to find out just what "the science which we are seeking" is. In order to find this out, Aristotle first reviews his theory of how we know anything at all; second, he defines what wisdom is and whether metaphysics can rightly be considered wisdom; and third, he briefly outlines the progress made in the science of wisdom by philosophers before him.

HOW WE KNOW: Aristotle opens the *Metaphysics* with the optimistic statement, "All men by nature desire to know." We value our senses because they bring us knowledge of the world outside ourselves. Knowledge is thus rooted in sense impression. Some animals are only capable of sense perception. Others possess with human beings the capacity for memory (i.e., for storing each individual sense impression). Man, the highest of the animals, gains what we call experience from his use of his memory. For example, by associating the same memory image with different sense impressions, man acquires what Aristotle calls unified or general experience. Facts are no longer separated from one another in the memory and therefore without meaning, but are joined together under some general pattern of recall, according to the kind of facts they are. For example, a child touches a hot stove and quickly draws his finger away. This is one sense impression. After he has touched the hot stove many times and stores these impressions away in his memory, he begins to connect each individual impression to a general fact. "I burn my finger every time I touch a hot stove."

EXPERIENCE, ART, AND KNOWLEDGE: Many people stop at this point in their intellectual development; but this generalized experience is not yet art, and is still far from scientific knowledge. Art is born, says Aristotle, "when out of the many bits of information derived from experience there emerges a grasp of those similarities in view of which they are a unified whole." The key words which explain the nature of art, or skill, are "similarities" and "unified whole." Art grasps the reason why certain facts have something in common. For example, the mother will give her child a certain medicine when he is ill, because she knows *from experience* that this medicine has helped her child in the past. The doctor, the man of art, will prescribe a certain medicine because he has diagnosed the *reason why* the child is ill and knows that this medicine usually cures that particular illness. Although art grasps the reason why, it is still concerned mainly with sense-experience, with the production of an effect upon a physical body. Science is born when an examination of many related facts leads to an inquiry into their cause, purely for the sake of finding out the cause. Men of experience, says Aristotle, perceive the fact "that." The scientist knows the reason "why," which is the main object of his interest. Scientific knowledge is thus based upon sense-knowledge but is removed from, and independent of, sense perception. For example, I know from experience that two chairs plus two chairs equal four chairs. The axiom, 2 plus 2 equals 4, is scientific knowledge, a universal truth that is both independent of any physical object and yet can be found in all material objects. Art and knowledge are similar in that they both can be taught, whereas experience cannot be taught. In the order of time, however, art comes before science. The first artist appeared long before the first scientist. Aristotle thinks the first artist must have seemed a miracle to his fellow men, because he knew the "why," which enabled him to produce a calculated effect.

FIRST SCIENCE: It follows from this theory of knowledge that any science is abstract, in the sense that it is removed from the concrete individual fact. Some sciences, however, are more removed from fact than others. The science which is farthest from direct perception but which understands the primary causes governing every fact is what Aristotle calls "first science."

THE NATURE OF WISDOM: First science is not a productive science like art. It is not able to change the universe nor does it have any practical use. Yet, Aristotle says, we value this type of knowledge the most. The basic reason we value the scientist more than the building constructor is that "all men naturally desire to know." Knowing is the function of *homo sapiens*. Men first started to philosophize out of curiosity. Their wonder and amazement at simple phenomena such as the eclipse of the moon made them realize they were ignorant. Aristotle tells us man learns to escape ignorance, and he learns for the sake of knowledge, not for some practical reason. According to Aristotle, in the course of human development, man first acquired knowledge for useful ends. It was not until the basic requirements of existence had been satisfied that science first appeared. In his opinion, the appearance and cultivation of science presupposes leisure. Mathematics in Egypt, he says, first appeared among the priests, because of all the population, they alone had their basic needs taken care of and thus had enough free time to speculate.

WISDOM IS PERFECT FREEDOM: We pursue knowledge for its own sake and not for the sake of some practical purpose. In so doing, we are freeing ourselves from the limitations of the physical world. Now, the less dependent upon concrete fact a science is, the more free it will be. Wisdom or theoretical knowledge, therefore, is the only science that is completely free, since it is farthest removed from concrete fact. Consequently, the free man will be he who possesses the knowledge of freedom: wisdom. It may be argued that it is not good for man to have such knowledge and that it should belong to the gods alone. Aristotle gives an encouraging answer. That theoretical knowledge is divine, he does not doubt. The gods are thought to be the causes of all things, and thus the science of First Causes is the most likely one for them to have. If wisdom is divine, there is all the more reason for man to pursue it, for in so doing he will be striving toward the most valuable thing in the world.

THE SUBJECT MATTER OF WISDOM: In the Physics, Aristotle said that there were four things you had to know about a thing corresponding to four questions you could ask about it, if you wanted to explain its existence. These were the four causes: 1) "what a thing was meant to be" or the formal cause, 2) the "out of what" or the material cause, 3) "by what means it was brought into being" or the efficient cause, and 4) "the for the sake of what it exists" or the final cause. First science, Aristotle tells us, must be a science of the highest and therefore "most first," or primary, causes of the universe.

A REVIEW OF THE DEVELOPMENT OF PHILOSOPHY: In order for Aristotle to define his own position with respect to the first causes of the universe, he devotes the rest of Book Alpha to a review of what has been said and thought on the subject before him. Aristotle was a firm believer that knowledge was derived from experience—both social and physical. He also may be said to be the first philosopher who was conscious of himself as one link in the chain of human experience. We have seen from the *Physics* that it is Aristotle's habit to trace the history of the idea under consideration before he develops his own views on the subject. Although Aristotle's awareness of his relative role in history is an advance over the past, it must be admitted that he uses his predecessors in a way that suggests that every thought that was thought before him was but a prelude to his own brilliant theories. If Aristotle can be said to have seen himself as a link in the philosophical chain, he most probably saw himself as the culminating link in the chain. The review of philosophy which we find in the *Metaphysics* reads much like a modern textbook on early scientific thought. The impression left with the reader is that the early philosophers were groping for something, but did not know quite what it was they were seeking nor how to go about their search. Some understood some of the causes, but others gave other explanations. Later, a few philosophers grasped a portion of the truth, but none of them saw the whole truth of the four causes. Aristotle compares them to "untrained swordsmen in a duel" who rush about and occasionally make fine strokes but do so without scientific expertise.

ATTACK ON PLATO: At the end of Book Alpha, Aristotle launches the first of his many attacks on Plato in the *Metaphysics*. As these attacks are scattered throughout the work, we shall list them briefly here. The attacks are generally aimed at Plato's theory of Ideas, but we find many arguments refuting another view which Plato held apparently late in his life, namely, that numbers are also separately existing forms.

ARGUMENTS AGAINST THE THEORY OF IDEAS: Aristotle agrees with Plato that a theory of universal concepts is necessary to explain and make possible scientific knowledge. Knowledge, Aristotle never tires of saying, is of universals. On the other hand, Aristotle does not think that universals exist apart from their objects as pure existing forms for the following reasons. 1) The Ideas are useless because they mean that we have to posit two substances instead of one, for every physical object. In the case of Socrates, we would have to admit both his being as Socrates and his being as man. There would thus be two Socrates instead of one, which is false. Again, the Ideas do not explain how we know individual things. They cannot really be part of the substance of things or else they would exist in them. The Ideal Man is not present in Socrates. According to Plato, Socrates participates in the Ideal Man, as the image participates in that of which it is the image. Third, the Ideas are useless because they do not explain why and how things move. They are themselves eternally immovable and thus cannot be the cause of motion, as Plato describes them. Finally, the Ideas are useless because they are super-sensible forms used to explain sensible things. If they are to explain the sensible world, however, they should have something of the sensible in them. If they do, this means that they are really only projections of sensible things. The Ideal Man, for example, would be the image of Socrates instead of the other way around. 2) The theory of Ideas is logically indefensible. How can the essential reality of something exist apart from that whose reality it is supposed to be? Aristotle says that to say that sensible things are merely "patterns" of the Ideal Reality is "to use empty words and poetic metaphor." Second, what does Plato mean when he says that all sensible things come from the Ideas? In what way do they come from the Ideas? Certainly, sensible things are not produced by the Ideas, nor do they follow *from* the Ideas. Of what then are the Forms forms? Third, if the Ideas are self-existing forms, they will be individual substances in the same way as things composed of matter and form are individual. We will thus have to posit another form which will explain what the individual nature of the Ideal Form and the nature of the physical object have in common. This reasoning leads us to what might be called Aristotle's "third man theme." Both the individual Ideal Man and Socrates will have something in common—namely, human nature. Consequently, their common human nature will be the third man which will explain the similarity of the other two.

ATTACK ON PLATO'S THEORY OF NUMBERS: Aristotle's attack on Plato's view that numbers are like the Ideas follows the arguments against the theory of Ideas. First, how can numbers be the cause of anything? Second, how can there be both the number which is an Idea and a number which is the object of mathematics. It is clear that we deal with only one kind of number, the number of mathematics. Third, even if you say that only one kind of number exists, the number which is the object of mathematics, you still are wrong in saying that numbers exist separately from things. If you say that they do, you must admit that every object of mathematics—lines, points, circles, etc.— also exist independently of physical things. Such a view reduces mathematics to an absurdity. For example, we would have as many separately existing lines as there are possible lines that one can draw. In this case, which line would be the real object of mathematics? Fourth, if the essential reality of things is numbers, or mathematical objects, what makes individual objects in the physical world move? Numbers are unable to explain motion. A detailed analysis of Aristotle's attack on Plato's unfortunate trip into the world of Ideal Numbers will be found in Books Mu and Nu.

CONCLUSIONS OF THE ATTACK ON PLATO: In conclusion, it must be admitted that many of Aristotle's criticisms of Plato are in many ways a deliberate misreading of what Plato had to say. Moreover, his attack on the theory of Ideal Numbers is directed at a very insignificant aspect of Plato's whole philosophy. Finally, when it comes to explaining the cause of motion in the world, Aristotle is compelled to use a revised version of Plato's theory. The Unmoved Mover is, in actual fact, nothing but a self-subsisting form similar to, although not the same as, Plato's Idea of Absolute Goodness.

THE PHILOSOPHIC METHOD: In his short book, Alpha the Less, Aristotle gives his idea of the "right" approach to philosophic inquiry. Truth is hard to discover he tells us. "It is easy to hit a door," he says, "but to hit the door and be unable to hit the keyhole illustrates the difficulty of reaching the truth." He thus urges that we pay attention not only to those opinions agreeing with our own, but also to those opinions which we think are not worth very much. In the last chapter of this book, he emphasizes the importance of training and habit in any scientific undertaking. "The more familiar a thing the more intelligible it seems." But we should not confuse familiarity with the method used in a science with knowledge of that science's subject matter. For example, mathematical preciseness is important in those subjects which deal with nonmaterial things, but is not as necessary in the study of the natural world. We have to adjust the method of inquiry to the principles of the relevant science. In the second chapter, Aristotle repeats his proof that you cannot have an infinite series of causes. Every casual chain must have a beginning somewhere. This proof, as we have seen, plays an important part in his theory of the First Unmoved Mover.

THE PROBLEMS INVOLVED IN THE STUDY OF PHILOSOPHY: In Book Beta, Aristotle lists all the possible difficulties related to the problem of whether there is such a thing as a super-sensible being. "We must investigate very carefully," he says, "whether or not something besides the material of things has its own being; whether this exists separately or not; and whether it is numerically one, or more than one."

FIRST SCIENCE AND ITS SUBJECT MATTER: The problem which concerns Aristotle most is whether there can be one unified science whose scope includes all the first principles governing the lesser sciences. Aristotle investigates this and related problems in Chapters 2 and 3 of Book Beta. He sees part of the difficulty in the fact that "being" means different things. How are we to define fundamental or primary being, namely, that type of being which cannot be attributed to anything else? Is primary being a substance or a first principle? What is the subject matter of metaphysics? Is it the study of substance or of first principles? If the subject matter of metaphysics is substance, there can be no science of it, and we must look for another science which will study first principles. You cannot demonstrate the individual "what" of a concrete existing thing. Perhaps there is a science between that of universals and that of sensible things. Plato believed that the objects of mathematics were midway between forms and concrete things. Aristotle, as we have seen, does not believe that numbers can exist apart from matter. He thus dismisses the possibility of a science based on mathematical objects.

FIRST PRINCIPLES AS GENERA: If first science is of first principles, what kind of existence are we to attribute to them? Do they exist as genera or as some other type of universal? Man, for instance, is known as *homo sapiens. Homo* is the *genus* or kind of animal man is. *Sapiens* denotes the particular *species* to which man, as we know him, belongs. Now, if first principles are genera, are we to say that the genus, *homo,* is the first principle of man, (i.e., what makes a man a man)? If we say that first principles are genera, we must admit that unity and being are the highest genera, as they are characteristics common to the entire natural world. When we say, for example, that something *is,* we are also saying that it is *one.* Everything that exists, exists as a unified whole. Unity and being, however, cannot be genera. If they were, you would be unable to account for the other genera which exist and are the source of difference in the world. If being is a genus, then everything in the world must belong to one single genus. This is obviously false. It follows, therefore, that primary being exists only in individual things. Universals must be relegated to the status of "secondary being," dependent on individuals for their existence.

FIRST PRINCIPLES AS UNIVERSAL CONCEPTS: In Chapter 4 Aristotle lists the difficulties connected with the problems of form as a first principle. Knowledge, he says, is of universals. We can never know a concrete, individual thing. Consequently, universals must exist as forms or definitions of individuals, otherwise we could not know individuals. For example, we could not know what man is, if human nature did not exist in the objective world as the universal form of man. If, however, the form of man is his primary being, does it follow that the primary being of all men is one and the same, or does each have his own particular being? In saying that the universal concept is a first principle, we have gone no further in finding out what makes everything that exists an individual thing.

OTHER PROBLEMS RELATED TO THE EXISTENCE OF FIRST PRINCIPLES: 1) If first principles exist, are they perishable or eternal? They cannot be perishable or else they would not be first principles. But if they are imperishable, how are we to explain the fact that they produce things which perish? 2) Do the first principles of unity and being exist as substances or as attributes? If they are not substances, no other universal can properly be said to exist. If they are substances, then Parmenides was right when he said all things are one, and unity is being.

MATHEMATICAL OBJECTS AS PRIMARY BEING: In Chapter 5, Aristotle demonstrates that numbers, points, and circles cannot be primary being. If an invisible point which has no size or shape is a primary being, to what kind of body does it belong? For we cannot consider a point as part of the sensible world. Therefore, whether we say that the objects of mathematics are or are not primary being, we have proceeded no further in knowing what the primary being of our world is.

THE EXISTENCE OF FIRST PRINCIPLES RECONSIDERED: In Chapter 6, Aristotle again raises the difficulties connected with the way first principles exist. 1) Perhaps, he says, first principles exist potentially, waiting to be brought into actual existence. But if first principles are only potentially real, then there must be some other set of first principles which are actually real behind the first set of first principles. If there are not, then nothing exists. 2) If first principles actually exist as universals, they cannot exist independently, or else Socrates would be Socrates, man and animal, all at the same time. 3) If first principles exist as individuals, we can never know them, for knowledge is only of universals. Book Beta leaves the reader still in doubt as to whether first science exists, and whether it has a subject matter that is knowable.

BOOK GAMMA
THE SUBJECT MATTER OF FIRST PHILOSOPHY

INTRODUCTION: In Book Gamma, we begin to reach the core of Aristotle's metaphysics. In Book Beta, Aristotle listed all the difficulties connected with a science of being. In so doing, he demonstrated what the subject matter of philosophy is not. It is not, for instance, the study of universals or of the "intermediates": number and mathematical objects. At the opening of Book Gamma he says definitely that there is a science which studies "being as being and the properties of being *per se.*" In order to find out what this science is, we have to determine what "to be" means. Second, we have to find out how one science can cover all the many ways of being there actually are. The being of a tree, for example, is not the same as the being of a stone, the being of a star, or the being of a man. "To be" can refer to a natural process, such as motion. It can refer to a life process, such as the soul. And it can refer to the end term of a process, such as "to be a good man." Aristotle tells us that "to be" can also be used in a relative way, as when we say, "to be healthy."

SUBSTANTIAL BEING: There is, however, one thing which all existing things have in common. It is the "something" particular to each natural body which 1) imparts to it an independent existence, 2) is the ground or cause of its existence, and 3) determines its individuality. For example, when you talk of "being healthy," there must be something which is the subject of health. Movement requires *something* which can be moved. Life is the function of *something* which is able to have life. Life, motion, or quality cannot exist apart from "this something" which Aristotle calls *ousia,* or substantial being.

> **COMMENT:**   The Greek word *ousia* is usually translated "substance," but the English term is misleading. Perhaps a better translation would be fundamental, or independent, existence—the being of concrete, individual things. Aristotle calls air, water, and earth, *ousiai,* because they do not belong to other beings as their attributes, but are independent beings in their own right. In Book Zeta, he discusses the various meanings associated with the concept of *ousia,* and we shall see how difficult a concept it is.

Aristotle concludes that, as motion is the proper subject matter of physics, and life, the subject matter of biology, so *ousia,* or fundamental existence, is the subject matter of metaphysics. Moreover, as each science studies its subject matter from every angle, so first philosophy must study all the ways something can be said to exist as an independent, substantial being. In order to determine what things can be classified as *ousiai,* the philosopher must grasp the first principles and causes of fundamental existence.

UNITY: If the being of things is the principle subject matter of philosophy, it follows that unity must also be an object of study. "To be" and "to be one" mean the same thing, for the being of each *ousia,* or existing thing, is one undivided being. Socrates, for example, does not have one being as an existing thing, and another being as a particular man. Whatever is, is one, and what is one, is.

THE UNITY OF PHILOSOPHY: Metaphysics is the study of substantial being. This fact tells us nothing, as yet, of why philosophy is one science and not many. What is its unifying principle? For example, the unity of physics lies in its subject matter, motion. The unity of the science of health is found in its chief object of interest, namely, health. When you study health, however, you study the most varied subjects, such as medicine, surgery, anatomy, and even the opposite of health, the nature of disease. We should thus distinguish between the *primary* or major concern of the science of health, which is health itself, and the other related sciences which are its *secondary* concerns. These sciences are a part of the science of health, because they are directly relevant to understanding what health is. Now, if in the other sciences you must study not only the subject, but also its opposite, inasmuch as it is relevant to the subject, so in the study of being, you must study both the primary and secondary aspects of fundamental existence. 1) You must study the attributes of substantial being, quality, quantity, and relation, which do not exist apart from things. Whiteness, for example, does not exist independently; there are only white chairs. 2) You must study the contraries or opposites inherent in the concept of substantial being. (As we saw in the *Physics,* the first principles of natural philosophy are substance, and two contrary terms.) Now, the opposite of the "one," is the "many." The opposite of unity is plurality. Under plurality come other concepts, such as "otherness," "dissimilarity," and "difference"; thus, it is plain that one science can study both the unity of being and the diversity of being without ceasing to be one science. Everything, says Aristotle, can be reduced to being and non-being, unity and plurality. He concludes that it is most fitting for one science to study "the what" of being as its *primary* object of interest, and the attributes and contraries of being as its *second-*

ary concern. For these secondary subjects are relevant aspects of what it means "to be."

METAPHYSICS, THE HIGHEST SCIENCE: It is clear from the foregoing that philosophy as the study of being as being occupies the highest place in Aristotle's hierarchy of sciences. For this reason, it falls within the scope of philosophy to examine even the axioms of mathematics, because these are axioms which relate to being *qua* being. Other scientists study a limited aspect of being, but only the metaphysician investigates the whole of existence as such. The natural philosopher, for example, studies the being common to natural objects. The philosopher, on the other hand, studies the whole of reality in its essential nature. Because he is in this privileged position, the philosopher is the one scientist responsible for determining those principles which lie at the base of all reality. For we can only know the truth if we are certain that the principle upon which we base our understanding of reality is true. In Aristotle's opinion, there is only one such principle, the Law of Contradiction.

THE LAW OF CONTRADICTION; THE FIRST PRINCIPLE OF THE SCIENCE OF BEING: Aristotle devotes the rest of Book IV to demonstrating this "most certain of all the principles." Expressed in Aristotle's language, the law reads: "It is impossible for the same attribute at once to belong and not to belong to the same thing in the same relation." This means two things. 1) It is impossible for something to be and not to be at the same time, and in respect to the same thing. For example, a man is either alive or dead. He cannot be halfway between life and death, and he cannot be both dead *and* alive at the same time. 2) It is impossible for a substance to be a particular something and to be its opposite at the same time and in the same respect. For example, something is either a man or it is not a man. It cannot be both man and not-man at the same time, in the same respect. A man is a man and nothing else. He is not a walking corpse or a matured embryo. He once was an embryo, and he may become a corpse, but when he is a man, he can only be a man. Some people might argue that they can think that a man is both dead and alive at the same time. Aristotle says this is impossible. If you think this, then you are holding two contrary opinions simultaneously, and this you cannot do. You may change your mind the next instant, but while you are thinking one thing, you cannot think its opposite. You may think *of* a man being dead and alive at the same time. But you cannot at the same time think and not think a particular thought, such as, "A man is."

DEMONSTRATION OF THE LAW OF CONTRADICTION:
Aristotle thinks this principle is so self-evident that he considers it
the *arche,* or starting point, of all demonstration and all other
principles. Nevertheless, he realizes that many thinkers have denied
this principle and demand proof of its validity. He thus turns all
his energies to proving the truth of the Law of Contradiction with
an enthusiasm which may leave readers somewhat breathless.

NO REAL PROOF POSSIBLE: In the first place, Aristotle says
there is not and cannot be a really valid proof of this principle. If
we demand a proof for everything, we shall never have a starting
point for any proof, and we shall never be able to prove anything.
Something must be obviously true without our having to prove
it. Nevertheless, Aristotle says he will try to prove the unprovable
in two ways: 1) by showing that the Law of Contradiction is the
first principle of language, and 2) by showing that those who
deny it have an incorrect concept of the nature of reality.

PROOFS BASED ON THE STRUCTURE OF LANGUAGE:
Aristotle gives six proofs of the logical necessity for the Law of
Contradiction, three of which are given here. 1) If a man says
something can be and can not-be at the same time, in the same
respect, he is contradicting himself. He has no basis for argument
at all. 2) "Let a man just say 'man' to me," urges Aristotle, "let
him utter one word and try to deny the Law of Contradiction."
Clearly, when he says, "man," he is not referring to "not-man."
Conversation and argument would be impossible if you could not
define your terms. When someone says, "man," he is referring
to something definite and particular. No matter how many meanings you give for "man," the one meaning you *cannot* give is
"not-man." This does not mean that something which is not-man,
such as whiteness, cannot be included in the definition of a particular man. Attributes can exist and be defined in a subject. The
important thing is that you include in your definition only those
attributes which really are in the subject. If you include everything, the terms, essence and substance, will have no meaning,
and all attributes will become accidental. If all attributes are accidental, there will be no such thing as substance, for substance in
the sense of specific essence or "the what it is to be a particular
thing" is defined by attributes. For example, there are certain
things that can be said of Socrates that cannot be said of anybody
else. 3) If you affirm and deny anything of everything, all things
will be one, as Protagoras said. A boat will be a man will be a wall.
This is obviously untrue. When we speak of a man, we are speaking of a man, not a boat. Moreover, if you say a man is both a

man and a not-man, then he obviously is and is not a boat, at the same time. And if it is true that man is man and not-man at the same time, then it will also be true that he is *neither* man nor not-man at the same time. The consequences of such a position are absurd. If everything is equally everything else, there is no such thing as a determinate nature. If you deny the Law of Contradiction, you must deny it completely, and this leads to nonsense. In the last analysis, experience shows us that men do not really look on the world in this fashion. If men did, they would never do anything. If someone really thinks this way, says Aristotle, "why does he not walk early one morning into a well or a ditch, if he comes to one, instead of taking care not to fall in, thus showing that he does not think that it is equally good and not good to fall in."

PROOFS BASED ON THE CONCEPT OF REALITY: In Chapter 5 Aristotle takes up the argument from another point of view. What led men to think that all things could be true and not true at the same time in the same respect? He gives two reasons: one mistake lay in their view of what being really was. Early philosophers such as Anaxagoras and Democritus saw contraries generated by the same thing, as when heat and cold come from water. Consequently, they assumed that *both* heat and cold were actually in the water. Neither of them understood that something can be *potentially* the opposite of what it *actually* is now, and that contraries exist together in a subject as potentials of actualizations. Second, people believe that what *appears* to be contraries existing in one subject actually *are* contraries. They mistake sense-perception for reality. If the same thing seems bitter to some people and sweet to others, they think it actually is bitter and sweet at the same time. If all the people of a community are crazy and there are only two who are not, these two will seem crazy to the others. The mistake is to say 1) that what *is,* is only what meets the eye, that is, the world of change, and 2) that the impressions we derive from sense-perception are concepts of the world about us. Thought, many people believe, is the same as sense-perception, which is the same as physical change. But, our senses merely report the physical world to us; our minds use this information to form concepts of understanding. Aristotle charges Empedocles, Democritus, Anaxagoras, and even the great Greek epic poet, Homer, with this mistaken opinion. They saw that all substance is in motion, and assumed it was impossible to make any definite statement about that which always changes. Aristotle refutes this view by saying that even when something is ceasing to be, there is always a something—a substance, which is continuing. There is no ceasing-to-be by itself. There is always some unchanging reality, which persists through every change.

THE DANGER IN TRUSTING SENSE IMPRESSIONS: Aristotle says that for three reasons reality must be more than what meets the eye: 1) The impressions that sense-data make on each individual varies. Colors, for example, do not look the same to a healthy person as to a sick person. 2) Our perception of those objects which are proper to a certain sense are infallible, but our perception by one sense of objects common to another sense can be mistaken. For example, something can "look sweet." But the object of sight is not flavor, and what looks sweet could actually be bitter. 3) It cannot be true that only that which can be perceived by the senses exists for the simple reason that if there were no animate beings, there could be no sense organs. All three of these reasons are based on the belief that that which can be perceived by the senses (such as color, sweetness, and sound) are not purely subjective impressions existing in ourselves. A tree, honey, and the song of a thrush exist independently of our senses. Bitterness and sweetness are definite qualities. Sense-perception—the perceivable perceived by the perceiver—is an objective activity. But sense-impression is a subjective activity dependent on the particular sensing individual. The concluson is that we should not accept sense-experience as an infallible source of knowledge.

NO MID-TERM BETWEEN BEING "A SUCH" AND BEING "NOT-A-SUCH": Chapter 7 discusses the second main reason why some people have had a mistaken view of reality. They look at natural things and see that the same thing produces contrary qualities. They thus assume that there must be some intermediary between the two contraries which gave birth to them. Gray, for example, would be the intermediary between black and white. Aristotle proves this cannot be so. It is correct to say that gray is halfway between black and white in one sense. But if something is said to be gray, it is neither white nor not-white. It is also not-black. And it is not some foggy midway point between not-white and not-black, but some definite color—namely, gray. Philosophers assumed that "intermediates" existed because their arguments started from the wrong premises.

LAW OF CONTRADICTION, CONCLUDED: In conclusion, Aristotle returns to his argument that those who say that the Law of Contradiction is false are simply contradicting themselves. If someone says his own view is true (since whatever it, is at the same time and in the same respect what it is not), he is admitting that his view is true, because it is true and not false. He is therefore saying that his own view is true and not-false at the same time and in the same respect. He cannot, on the other hand, maintain that his view is both true and false at the same time. He thus admits the Law of Contradiction.

BOOK DELTA
DEFINITIONS

INTRODUCTION: Having thus shown that definition is necessary because both the nature of language and thought, and the nature of being, require it, Aristotle is ready to give his own definitions in Book V. These definitions are important for they provide the key to his thought as it develops in the rest of the *Metaphysics*. Since most of these concepts, however, are either parts of his natural philosophy or are developed elsewhere in the *Metaphysics,* we shall not go into them in detail. In all, he gives over thirty definitions. The most important of them are "beginning," "cause," "element," "nature," "necessity," "one," "being," and "primary being." Then he considers "same" and "other," "different" and "alike," and the concepts of "opposite," "contrary," and "other in kind." After "before" and "after" (prior and subsequent) comes a definition of "potential": "the source of motion or change which is in something other than the thing changed and the ability to perform this change." From this, Aristotle turns to defining his categories: "quantity," "quality," "relation." The "complete" and the "limit" form the next pair. Then follows a definition of "in virtue of which" as opposed to "by itself." Some things exist in virtue of something else, and others exist by themselves. Next, the "disposition in space," or condition of a body, is distinguished from its "permanent condition," or actualized characteristic, which in turn is differentiated from its "passive condition," or potential characteristic. The next set of definitions concerns "privation"—"to have or possess," "to be in" a thing, "to come from" something. After this come definitions of "part," "whole," "mutilated," and "genus." The last set of definitions concerns "the false" and "the accidental." False can mean "false as a thing," when you cannot prove that that thing is. For example: it can be false to say that I am sitting when I am not. False can also refer to a "false statement," insofar as the statement itself is false. The definition of a circle is untrue of a triangle. To say that man is a four-legged creature is a false statement. Accidental means "not necessary" or "not usual." For example, it is "accidental" if a man is white—i.e., he does not necessarily have to be white. The meanings of being and unity have already been suggested in the preceeding book, and Aristotle of necessity discusses them in detail later. In Book Delta, Aristotle distinguishes between accidental being (in the sentence, "the man is white," to be white is accidental being) and absolute being (the man is) in an unqualified sense. Second, he distinguishes between actual being and being in potential. Water is actually cold when it is potentially hot. Finally, there is the being of conversation that denotes the truth or falseness of anything. "Socrates is cultured" means that it is true that Socrates is cultured. In the statement, "the sum of the opposite angles of a right triangle is not equal to 180 degrees," *is not* means that this is a false statement. Since Aristotle goes more deeply into the meaning of absolute or substantial being in Book Zeta, we will not give his short definition here.

THE SIGNIFICANCE OF BOOK DELTA: In general, scholars agree that Book Delta is one of the most remarkable pieces of Aristotle's writing. It shows the philosopher's amazing talent for orderly thought in the way he succeeds in presenting all the various meanings that can be found in one word. It also is illustrative of his conviction that it is necessary to draw fine distinctions in definition, if you want to develop a cohesive system of thought.

BOOK EPSILON
TYPES OF BEING WHICH ARE IRRELEVANT TO PHILOSOPHY

INTRODUCTION: Aristotle is now ready to determine what type of being is the primary concern of his "first science." "It is the principles and causes of things which are that we are seeking, and of the things which are, insofar as they actually are." We know that none of the other sciences is concerned with the nature of unqualified being. They all select some aspect or class of being and start with "being" as something given or as a hypothesis. But not one of them tries to demonstrate what substance or essence is. Moreover, they say nothing as to whether the class of things which is their object of interest actually exists or not.

THEORETICAL SCIENCES: Insofar as they are concerned with a class of being, Aristotle places physics and mathematics among what he calls the theoretical or contemplative sciences, which are not productive of anything nor lead to action. Each of them studies a different aspect of the problem of being as related to matter and form. Although physics is the study of that type of being which is form-in-matter, it is the duty of the philosopher, and not of the natural scientist, to show how essence and form exist, and how they are present in matter. Mathematics, on the other hand, is concerned with physical form as unchangeable and separated from matter. Aristotle expresses the relationship between the three theoretical sciences as follows. Physics deals with individuals, with changing things which exist separately; mathematics deals with universals, with things which are unchangeable but have no separate and independent existence. First science deals with eternals, with things which are both separately existing and unchangeable. Now, if all causes are eternal, the First Cause must be the most eternal. Hence, metaphysics is called theology, since if the divine is to be present anywhere, it must be some kind of separate and unchangeable substance. Aristotle concludes that the theoretical sciences are better than the productive and practical sciences. He also thinks that theology is to be preferred above the other theoretical sciences. If there is a substance which is unchangeable, it will be prior, that is, it will have existed before, the natural changeable substances with which physics is concerned.

> **COMMENT:** We have still not determined whether a separate and unchanging substantial form actually exists. Furthermore, the definition of metaphysics as theology, or the study of substantial form, contradicts the definition of metaphysics given in Book Gamma as the study of *ousia*, or substantial being, in *all* its forms. These contradictions are the result of Aristotle's change of opinion while he was working out his metaphysical philosophy. His problem was: is real being *only* that which is unchanging and unaffected by the natural world, or can we say that changing things also exhibit a kind of being in their very act of change? Is there only one kind of being or a hierarchical system of being?

CONCEPTS OF BEING WITH WHICH PHILOSOPHY IS NOT DIRECTLY CONCERNED: Aristotle has said that philosophy is the science of existence. Now he wants to eliminate two concepts of being which might bring confusion into the study. These are 1) accidental being and 2) being as truth.

ACCIDENTAL BEING: Science is not only an analysis of things. It is also a discipline which can be taught. In order to be taught, science must be concerned with things that can be taught. These are universals, and things "which are always or for the most part." The accidental is unteachable, for it is unpredictable. It is that which "sometimes is and sometimes is not." Since it is an attribute which belongs only to a particular individual object, it cannot be one of the essential characteristics common to all objects of one type of genus. It therefore admits of no definition, because definition is of the typical. Aristotle insists that because the accidental is individual, there can be no study of it. The man who builds a house does not build into the house all the possible modifications and gadgets which a house can have, for these are infinite in number. Some people will like the attributes of the house he has built; others will want a different house. But the actual act of building is not concerned with whether the house is accidentally pleasing or not. Building a house is concerned with what a house essentially is. The question we must ask is: is everything which exists either "always" or "for the most part"? The answer is no. We know there are accidental causes. Yet, it is clear that there can be no science of the unique and the exception to the rule. Science cannot state the exceptions. All scientific knowledge (and Aristotle is emphatic on this point) is only of that which is always or usually so. Metaphysics must therefore study those properties of being which stem from the nature of being, and are not incidental to it.

THE ACCIDENTAL IS REAL: In saying that the accidental can never become an object of science, Aristotle is not saying that it does not exist. He is only asserting that the accidental can never be really investigated because it cannot be determined. It is the task of science to remove at the outset anything which is irrelevant to its basic subject matter. Otherwise only confusion and chaos will result.

ACCIDENTAL CAUSATION: Aristotle also holds that there is such a thing as accidental causation. Causes exist which do not form a part of the causal chain of a natural process. If everything which exists can be accounted for in terms of the causes which govern its coming into being and decay, then everything would have to be of necessity—things could not be otherwise than they are. But we know that certain things can be otherwise than they are. For example, the fact that a man will die is *necessary;* death is the termination of the natural process of human growth. But the manner of a man's death is a matter of *accident,* for he can die in any number of ways. Whether a man dies a violent death or dies from some incurable disease is due to causal factors which cannot be predicted and are particular to his case alone. After he has died, we can go back in the series of causes which led to his death, and find that factor which does not refer back to any prior cause and which specifically accounts for his manner of death. Such a factor, in Aristotle's view, "is the starting point of the accidental, and nothing else is the cause of its coming into being." Needless to say, there can be no science that studies the causes of the accidental, since these causes are unique in each case, and therefore subject to no governing principle or law.

BEING AS TRUTH: Being as truth is the second type of being that does not fall within the province of philosophy. The reason is obvious. Being as truth is a question of logic, not a question of metaphysics. It depends on what Aristotle calls the "combination and separation" of words. How we combine or separate thought is a question which philosophy is not meant to handle. Falsity and truth are not *things* but *thoughts*. In one sense, both can be said to exist as things, in the form of an accurate perception of reality. The image of the relationships between various natural phenomena in the world of thought must correspond to what they actually are. But philosophy is not interested in perception, and the combination and separation of perceived objects in thought. It is concerned with the relationships between objects as they exist *apart* from thought. Philosophy's aim is to grasp the connection between cause and effect as it can be *objectively* known.

BOOK ZETA
THE NATURE OF PRIMARY BEING

INTRODUCTION: In Book Zeta, Aristotle attempts to answer the most important question of the *Metaphysics*: What is the nature of this being which is the basis of all other being? What does it mean "to be"? This book is perhaps the most difficult one in the *Metaphysics* to understand. Needless to say, there are many interpretations that could be offered as to what the philosopher meant by primary being, or *ousia,* but only one of them is given here. Although Aristotle's discussion of being does not follow a very orderly path, the book seems to fall into two main parts. The first discusses being as the subject of discourse; the second investigates it as the product of change.

PRIMARY BEING IS A "THIS SOMETHING": Being, says Aristotle, in the opening sentence of Book Zeta, can have a variety of meanings. For instance, it can mean what a thing is, or a "this something," and it can mean that a thing is a "such." It is clear that primary being (*ousia*) must refer to a "this something," because when we say what a thing is we say it is a man or a god, we do not say that it is long or yellow or is of some other quality.

PRIMARY BEING—THE SUBJECT OF DISCOURSE: It is obvious that the categories cannot constitute the real being of anything, in the sense of stating what that being "is." "To be tall," for example, is not essential to our understanding what a man is. Likewise, "to walk" or "to sit" adds nothing to the being of an object, for there is always *something* which walks or sits. The "this something" exists independently of walking and sitting, and does not owe its existence to its walking or sitting. When we point to a "what," we point to individual things—to this man, or to this horse. A man "is" in some way more than sitting or walking ever can be, because when we talk about him we can say something definite about him and about him alone. We can only talk about "sitting" by referring to something which sits. But we can talk about this man, as this man, without having to refer his "being" to another subject. "Hence," says Aristotle, "that which *is* primarily not in a qualified sense . . . is what we mean by *ousia*," or primary being.

THE MEANING OF PRIMARY: We cannot know what primary is, unless we define what "primary" means. In Aristotle's opinion, "primary" (which is derived from the Latin word for "first") has several meanings. A thing can be primary in definition, in knowledge, and in time; Aristotle says that primary being is "first" in all these ways. It is "first" in definition, because to define a quality, you must define it in relation to substance, to something which *is* essentially. It is "first" in knowledge, because you know something better when you can say precisely "what it is" than when you can merely list its characteristics, such as tallness or smallness. Finally, primary being is "first" in time. None of the other categories can exist apart from the being of individual objects. Because a "this something" is "first" in all the above described ways, Aristotle rephrases the philosophical question, "What is being?" He asks, "What is primary being? What is *ousia?*"

THE FOUR USES OF OUSIA: There have been many theories as to what primary being is, Aristotle tells us. Some say it is matter, and others say it is the form of a thing. But it seems to belong most evidently to bodies. In conversation, we use *ousia* in at least four different ways. The primary being of anything can refer 1) to its essence, or its "what." 2) It can mean the universal concept of that thing. For example, in the sentence, "man is mortal," "man" refers to the universal concept of man. 3) It can refer to the genus. In the sentence, "man is a rational animal," "animal" designates the genus to which man belongs. 4) It can mean that which underlies all these things, namely, matter. Aristotle looks at the last of these meanings of *ousia* first.

1. IS OUSIA MATTER?   When we ask, "what is this?" the answer is, "it is a chair; it is a man." But what *is* the chair? Some would say that basically a chair is wood. If you take away the other attributes of chair, such as its size, height, and color, you are left with the material from which it is made. Aristotle replies that if you say that the primary being of the chair is its matter, you have not really said what the *chair* is. Other things can be made of wood. Moreover, wood is just wood until it has been made into something, such as a chair. Matter cannot answer the question, "what a thing is," for it is indeterminate.

2.   IS OUSIA A THING'S ESSENCE OR FORM?   Is primary being the essential character of a thing, the "what it means to be that thing," or its intelligible structure? Is the primary being of chair "what it means to be a chair" (i.e., something to sit on)? The only way we can know "what it means to be a thing," or its essence, is to express this "what" in words. Thus, Aristotle turns to investigating the value of a definition's stating the essential character of the objects to which it applies. In Book Delta, he defined definition as the concept of that in which the identity of a given thing, (the "what it means to be a given thing") consists. In one way, the essence of anything would seem to be that thing, and in another way it would not. "What anything is," he says, "does not denote the *whole* of its being, but only its essential characteristics." For example, "what you are," primarily does not consist in your being cultured. The "essential you" does not depend on any accident such as culture. It depends on what you are of yourself, and in accordance with your nature.

ESSENCE BELONGS ONLY TO SPECIES OF GENUS: It is important to Aristotle's theory of substance to understand the relation of essence, or "the what a thing is," to its *logos,* or what can be said about it. Essence is the intelligible structure, the knowable aspect of an object. But what we know about anything is primarily what we can say about it, what we can *define* it to be. Definition, therefore, in Aristotle's view, is the formulation into words of the essence of anything. Essence, in consequence, only belongs to those things of which there can be a definition, to those things whose character is a definite "what." This means that there is no essence of a compound subject such as "white man." Does the essence of "white man" lie in "whiteness" or in "man"? Strictly speaking, it lies in neither concept. There can be no definition of such a being. Essence can only belong to a species or genus whose forms of being are subordinate one to the other and whose dependent characteristics are essential to the notion of "what it means to be" that thing. For example, in the definition, "Man is a rational animal," the genus, "animal," and the species, "rational," are essential parts of the concept of what man is.

THERE IS NO ESSENCE OF DEPENDENT QUALITIES: It follows that a definition, in Aristotle's view, cannot properly be made of dependent attributes, such as the categories: quality, relation, position, etc. "White" and "tall" in one sense have no essence. They have no independent existence, but always exist in a subject. Thus, they never express the essential character of anything. Nevertheless, says Aristotle, we do assign definite meanings to qualities, and in this sense, they may be said to have an essence. "Medical," for example, implies a very specific concept. Yet, we do not say "medical" of a particular thing, but in relation to many things. There are medical instruments, medical men, and medical plants. But there is no "medical" *per se*. "Medical" is thus a term of reference and cannot be the essential being of anything. For this reason, when we define "medical man," we do not define the dependent concept "medical" and the concept "man," but we consider the two together under the unified concept "medical man." As was the case with "white man," however, the compound subject, "medical man," strictly speaking has no specific essence, in the same ways as the subject "man" has.

DO SOME COMPOUNDS ADMIT OF DEFINITION?   Although most compound subjects, in Aristotle's view, admit of no definition, there are a few that do. These would include such things as "snub nose." Aristotle says that there can be a definition in the strict sense of the word of "snub nose," because "snub" is a quality which belongs to "nose" essentially, not accidentally. "Snub" only refers to "nose" and has no meaning apart from "nose." Aristotle is careful to point out that "snub," taken by itself, is not a primary being, however, and thus can have no definition apart from "nose." Sometimes, he remarks, it appears to us that qualities like "snub" and "odd" exist independently, but in fact this is not true. Although you can talk about "the odd" independently of "number," "odd" only has being with reference to number. There is no "odd" without "number," just as there is no "snub" without "nose."

ESSENCE AND DEFINITION ONLY BELONG TO SUBSTANCES:
Aristotle sums up his discussion of essence and definition by repeating that "what it is to be" a particular thing, in the strict use of the word, belongs only to substance, since the "what it is to be" of the categories depends on the subject in which they inhere,

and thus has no specific character independent of the subject. Since definition is the formula, or *logos,* of the essence (i.e., its logical statement), it follows that it too belongs "either only to substances, or especially, and primarily, and simply to them." In making definitions, therefore, we must be careful to give those attributes of an object which constitute its essential nature. "Wet" adds nothing to the concept of what a log is, but "rational" is a quality essential to the formulation of what "man" is.

IS THE ESSENCE OF A PARTICULAR THING THE SAME AS THAT PARTICULAR THING?   In the section of Book Zeta which we have just discussed, Aristotle seems to be concerned with two things: what is the relation of essence to *ousia* and what is the relation of definition to *ousia?* He has said that the essence of anything, "the what it is," is the character of that thing which can be formulated into a definition. But is the essence of a particular thing the *same* as that particular thing? Is the intelligible structure of a thing what the thing really is? Aristotle's answer to this first question is "yes." Since the essence of anything is its primary being, and a particular thing is considered to be nothing else but its primary being, then the essence of a thing and the thing are one. "Each individual thing is one and the same with its intelligible structure, and not merely accidentally so, because to have knowledge of the individual is to have knowledge of its essence." It is absurd, he says, to separate a thing from its essence, for then "horse" would be different from "essence of horse" and the two would require a third essence to explain the similarity between them, which in turn would require another essence, and so on into infinity. If essence is primary being, why should not a thing be identified with its essence at the outset? The makeup of a thing, what we know and can state about it, is identical with the thing; it is *in* the thing as its *substantial form.*

IS THE ESSENCE OF A THING AS FORMULATED IN A DEFINITION THE SAME AS THE PARTICULAR THING?   This next question is harder to answer. What is the relation of the definition of a thing to that thing? On the one hand, a definition is the statement of the character or essence of a thing. It is what can be said about it. In this sense, the definition of a thing and its essence are one. The definition of "man," for example, is what man essentially is. On the other hand, the definition is obviously *not* the particular thing. It says what *kind* of being a thing is, but it is *not* the thing's being. It is a "such" not a "this something"; it is the formulation of what is knowable about a thing. "What it means to be a man" is clearly not the same as "this particular man." The problem which Aristotle is trying to solve here is that of the relation between concepts and the things these concepts denote, between what we can say about a thing in a scientific statement, and that thing of whose "statable aspect" the definition is the expression.

PRIMARY AND SECONDARY BEING: Aristotle insists that we can have certain knowledge of the real structure of things. What the scientific formula, or *logos,* states is the *ousia* of a thing. Things are what they can be said to be insofar as they can be known. But what can be known about anything is not the intrinsic being of that thing. It is just one aspect of its being. To put it in other words, what can be known about a thing is its *essence,* but not its *existence.* It is a thing's character, the form which it has in common with other beings like itself. The knowable aspect of things is "what always or for the most part is" with regard to a certain class of objects. This means that the essential "what" of any thing is not a principle of individuality but a principle of classification. All men possess similar characteristics, for example. This objective similarity is the knowable aspect of man, and provides the basis for the definition of "man." When essence is abstracted from concrete being, and formulated into words, it becomes a *universal concept* which denotes a specific essence or formal principle, which applies to all individuals of a given class indifferently and puts them in that class. "Man," for example, can be attributed to all men. But the "man" which is the subect of the sentence, "Man is mortal," is not the same kind of *ousia* as "this man in the street." It is universal *ousia* derived from particular *ousiai.* We have seen that Aristotle considers only individuals *ousiai,* in the strict sense of the word. Because the universal is also a kind of *ousia,* Aristotle makes a very important distinction between the two. 1) The concrete individual, such as "this plant" and "this man," Aristotle labels *primary substance.* 2) The second type of *ousia* is the universal concept which alone can become the subject of scientific predication. This type of *ousia* he calls *secondary substance,* because it is derived from primary substance. To state the difference between the two more clearly, when we say "this is a table," we are using table in its meaning of secondary substance. "This is a table" means "this has the essence of table." In the sentence, "this table is yellow," we are using table to denote a primary substance, a "this something."

COMMENT: Aristotle makes this distinction between primary and secondary substance in the *Categories,* and there is no reference to it in his discussion of substance in Book

Zeta. Nevertheless, since it is a distinction which is essential to the understanding of his theory of being, it has been included here.

ARISTOTLE'S ANSWER TO PLATO: In making the distinction between primary substance, which alone is true substance, and secondary or derivative substance, Aristotle is attacking the heart of Plato's theory of Ideas, which states that the universal concept or formal essence exists apart from, and independently of, the concrete individual. Aristotle, as we have seen, agrees with Plato that the universal is real. If it were not, there could be no knowledge of anything. The world is knowable precisely because everything possesses an intelligible structure, which, as its form, places it in its appropriate class. Aristotle insists, however, that this form does not exist apart from the individual. The universal, *qua* universal, does not exist in the objective world. What does exist are individual objects which possess a common essence or form. This form may be the same in terms of what we define it to be, but it is never the same in number. Socrates and Parmenides are both men; they both possess the specific essence of "what it is to be a man." But Socrates and Parmenides are two *different* men, possessing a similar form, but not numerically the same form. The existence of the universal as form separated from matter is a mental reality, not a physical reality. In the process of knowing, the mind identifies general similarities in instances of the particular. It abstracts essence from its existence and composes similarities into a definition, which has numerical identity in the mind, and can be attributed to all members of a class. There is no need, in Aristotle's view, to posit a separately existing universal, such as an Ideal Man, as the object of scientific inquiry, because the universal is present in the objective world as an element of the individual. He insists that only the individual, the concrete whole which is form-in-matter, can truly be said to be primarily and in its own right. Essence may be separated from individually existing things in thought, but never in reality. Universals can only be secondary substances.

IF THE OBJECT OF SCIENCE IS SUBSTANCE, SHOULD NOT SCIENCE STUDY INDIVIDUALS?   Aristotle has been accused of self-contradiction when he says that only individuals are substance in the true sense of the word, but that scientific knowledge is of universals. If the object of science is substance, should not its true object be that which exists primarily, namely, the individual? Yet, he seems to assign a higher reality to the secondary aspect of substance, to its formal principle and intelligible structure, rather than to the individual which really exists. Two things may be said about this accusation. 1) When Aristotle says that the individual is truly substance, he does not mean that the universal has no objective reality, as we have seen. But he does mean to reject Plato's view that the universal is a *separately existing* substance. The universal is real because it is that principle in a substance which makes that substance this or that kind of thing. It is an *indwelling principle* rather than a transcendent being. This means that the objects of science really exist, for they are the universal element in things. 2) The universal is properly the object of science because it is the *essential* element in things. Because it denotes what "always or for the most part is," it is in a certain way more real to us, than any particular instance of a "what," in that it is more intelligible. In this respect it should be pointed out that when Aristotle speaks of primary and secondary substance, he means primary and secondary relative to us, not in time or in nature. The point he wants to make clear is that the universal only exists *in* the particular. This means not that science has no real object, but that its object can only be known through the perception of individuals.

THE RELATION OF THE FORMAL PRINCIPLE OF SUBSTANCE TO THE INDIVIDUAL: This is a question which goes beyond purely linguistic analysis. If *ousia* is the identifiable "what" of an existing thing, of what does the particular character of that thing consist? The basic fact of our existence is that we live in a world of change. Particular things are always changing into other particular things: the acorn changes into an oak, the bronze into a statue, green plants into coal. If one wants to understand existence as it is, he must give some account of how things change. In the chapters which follow, Aristotle tries to pin down the precise difference between *ousia* as a functioning individual being, and *ousia* as "the what it is to be that thing."

B. PRIMARY BEING—THE PRODUCT OF CHANGE: There are two main kinds of change: absolute change, such as generation and decay; and relative change, such as change of place, and other kinds of motion. Aristotle chooses to discuss the process of change in relation to absolute change, probably because he feels it will provide more certain examples of the real nature of change. He begins his discussion by pointing out that everything which exists in the world has been produced at some time or other. Some things have been produced by *nature*, others by *art*, while some have been produced *spontaneously*. By spontaneous production, Aristotle is referring to those things to whose coming-into-being you cannot assign any definite cause. Spontaneous production is production by chance.

ARTISTIC CREATION: In keeping with his view that art imitates nature, Aristotle first turns to the process of artistic creation. He takes as an example the production of a bronze ring. As we know from the *Physics,* Aristotle considers four factors responsible for the coming-into-being of a thing. 1) Whatever is produced, is produced "out of" something—in this case, bronze; 2) whatever is produced is a "what"—in this case a ring; 3) it has to be produced "by some agent"—in this case, the artists; and 4) it has to serve some purpose. The problem which Aristotle wants to investigate here is the relation between the matter of the ring (the bronze) and its form (the ring). Whatever is produced is a product; it is something brought into being. The bronze ring is not just the bronze or just the ring. It is a "this particular something," "this bronze ring." Before it was made, there was just a lump of bronze. When we say that it was "made," we imply that shape or form was given to the bronze. If the bronze was "made" before, it also was shaped from some mass of material, which in turn was "made" by the quarry men as they brought it out of the earth. "Making," in Aristotle's view, means giving form to a material which does not have that particular form. In this case, the ring, *qua* ring, was not produced but was imposed upon the bronze so that the product was a composite of matter and form, the bronze ring.

THE PRODUCTION OF HEALTH: Aristotle gives another example of artistic creation, that of bringing a sick man back to health. In one sense, the doctor may be said "to produce" health, for he effects a cure. He knows what will bring about a cure, and he prescribes the proper medicine. But the doctor does not "make health" in the sense that he produces health where the condition of health never before existed. The doctor only produces health in those people who are *without* health. This example illustrates the fact that every artificial product is made from a definite material, which, as Aristotle demonstrated in the *Physics,* is not formless, but is without that particular form which the artist wants to give it. The sick man, for example, was without the "form" of health.

FORM AND MATTER IN THE NATURAL WORLD: Aristotle makes it clear that neither the form nor the matter of anything is produced in the process of "making." 1) You cannot produce pure form. You cannot, for example, make a ring out of nothing. Moreover, as Aristotle has repeatedly emphasized, forms without matter do not exist in the natural world. They only exist as abstract concepts in our minds. As concepts, they are a "such" and not a "this." We have seen that only a definite "this something" exists. 2) Likewise, matter itself is not produced in the process of making. Every material which is the subject of a change process is itself a combination of matter and form, which previously was produced, either by a natural or an artificial process, from some other informed material. In Aristotle's view, no unformed matter exists anywhere. Bodies have health, for example, and trees and stones have shapes. 3) The conclusion of this discussion is that only bodies composed of matter and form are subject to change. This means that only a "this individual something" composed of matter and form comes into being. Genera and species are not, properly speaking, "produced." In the process of natural "production," Socrates fills the same role as "this bronze sphere" did in artistic creation, while the genus, "man," is analogous to the concept, "bronze sphere." From this example, it is clear that the typical ("man" and "bronze sphere") cannot be brought into being. What is produced is the particular, namely, Socrates and "this bronze sphere."

THE TYPICAL AND THE INDIVIDUAL: Aristotle again argues against Plato's theory of pure self-existing forms. In the natural process of reproduction, and in the process of artificial creation, a new individual combination of matter and form "always or for the most part" succeeds the old. Aristotle is impressed by the persistence of type in each individual process of natural reproduction. Plato had argued that the fact that man begets man means that there is an Ideal Man from which all men are modeled. Aristotle says this is not so, as we already know. He finds that always a particular man begets a particular man. The form may be the same in *kind* but never in *number*. The reproductive process involves two separate forms. The son is not his father. He is a different individual altogether. The similarity between individuals of a given class is the *basis* of the universal, but it is *not* the universal.

DOCTRINE OF IMMANENT FORM: How are we to explain the fact that men beget men and not elephants? What is the difference between the natural or artificial processes and accidental processes? Aristotle says that all natural things contain in their form the power to act in a certain definite way. The essence or the "what" of anything is also the *arche* or principle of its generation. For example, in artistic creation the artist has the plan of the house he is going to build in his mind. This blueprint may have much in common with plans of other houses, but the house which the architect builds will be built according to the particular plan he has "thought up" in his mind. In the natural world, according to Aristotle, "the seed produces in the same way as those things which are made by art." Each seed carries within itself a blueprint of what it will become; it will realize this plan and no other. Thus, even though we may see ten trees of the same kind together, we know they are all different. They have the same *kind* of form, but they are not *one and the same form*. As we saw in the *Physics,* the efficient cause of a natural body may be the same as the formal cause. But it is only the same in *kind,* never the same in number. Aristotle's theory that type or genus does not exist apart from physical bodies but is present in the individual as an aspect of its being, is known as the Doctrine of Immanent Form.

THE RELATION OF FORM TO MATTER: In Chapter 10 Aristotle returns to the problem of the relation of primary to secondary substance. 1) If *ousia* is the concrete individual thing which is the product of change, what is the relation of form to matter in the product? 2) What is the relation of the material elements to the concept of the specific essence of the product? In what way can a being composed of form and matter be said to be one? In what does the unity of its definition consist? Aristotle says the problem is difficult. Although the parts of primary being (i.e., of a concrete individual) are matter and form, the *sum* of these parts does not make one substantial being. You cannot add matter and form as you would add 2 and 2 and arrive at a concrete individual. The primary being of a concrete individual is to be found particularly in its "what it is," or essence, as it can be expressed in a definition.

IS THE DEFINITION OF ANYTHING THE SUM OF ITS MATERIAL PARTS?   In trying to specify the role of matter in a thing's primary being, Aristotle asks whether a thing's essence is made up of material parts. He proceeds to show that the parts which make up the definition of anything are different from the parts of which the physical object is composed. For example, the concept of an acute angle has as one of its parts the concept of a right angle. An acute angle is less than 90°. But the concept "man" does not have as its parts the material elements of bones and muscles, even though the physical man is so constructed.

MATTER SHOULD NOT BE ELIMINATED FROM THE ESSENTIAL NATURE OF THINGS ALTOGETHER: In one sense, says Aristotle, matter is part of the definition of the object, and therefore part of its essential being, as it is part of the concrete whole. He distinguishes between two kinds of matter: perceptible matter and intelligible matter. Perceptible matter is matter that you can see and feel. Intelligible matter is extension in space, such as a circle or a line. When one is defining perceptible concrete beings such as "an animal," Aristotle feels no definition would be possible without some reference to movement. This reference to movement would necessitate some account of the organization of the animal's material parts. The problem is more difficult when it comes to intellectual matter. Nevertheless, Aristotle thinks that even the concept of a circle has a material element in it. You cannot define "circle" without reference to extension in space. It would be a mistake to eliminate matter from the concept of things. "Man" is "body" and "soul," just as Socrates is "this body" and "this soul." Aristotle concludes that matter is a part of a concept, where that concept refers to a concrete object.

PRIMARY BEING RE-EXAMINED: A little reflection will show us that it is not easy to separate matter from form in the definition of concrete objects and to decide what parts belong to the form and what parts to the concrete whole. But, Aristotle says, if this is not clear, then the definition will also not be clear, because strictly speaking the definition is only the formula (*logos*) of the essence, not of the material element. To Aristotle, matter cannot become the subject of definition, because it is in itself indeterminate. At this point, Aristotle makes a clear distinction between *ousia* as essence, and *ousia* as concrete substance. Matter, he says, cannot be present in the formula of substance, but only in a concrete substance. There is no formula involving matter, "but there is a formula in accordance with the primary substance, because substance is indwelling form of which together with matter the so-called concrete substance is composed." This indwelling form, as is the soul of man, is the principle in virtue of which matter is a definite concrete thing.

THE INDIVIDUAL IS UNKNOWABLE: Aristotle's conclusion that the primary being of anything really lies in its essence, as expressed in a formula (*logos*), leads to the further conclusion that no individual can be known in its individuality. Form, as we know, is the principle of a body's conformity to type. It follows that matter must be the principle of a body's individuality. Because matter is indeterminate, it is therefore unknowable. Consequently, the individual *qua* individual is unknowable. Strictly speaking, therefore, Aristotle holds that we can only have knowledge in the sense of scientific demonstration and definition of the typical in an individual. He does suggest, however, that it is possible to know the individual through sense-perception.

SIGNIFICANCE OF ARISTOTLE'S VIEW OF SUBSTANCE:
1) Although Aristotle assigns greater importance to form as the primary being of a concrete substance, matter also plays a role in the determination of what a concrete substance is to be, for it determines its individual characteristics. Just how matter individuates and whether it is the sole principle of individuality in a concrete substance, Aristotle never tells us. 2) In saying that primary being is essentially form, which is itself immaterial, Aristotle is saying that substance is really form. He is thus preparing the ground for his theory of pure form as that which is most truly substance. Aristotle discusses the being of pure form in his account of the Unmoved Mover in Book Lambda.

THE UNITY OF DEFINITION: Having determined that the principle of a concrete being's unity is to be found in its form, Aristotle considers the unity of the definition of that form. In the process of definition, he says, you always proceed from the general to the particular. First, you determine the genus of an object, then its species, and finally the various other traits which belong to it. For example, in the definition "man is a biped animal," "animal" is the genus, and "biped" is the species. The concept "animal" is assumed in the concept "biped," as only animals can be said to be two- or three-footed. Since the parts of the definition, therefore, can be subordinated to one another on the basis of the most general concept, namely "animal," the definition of "man" is said to be a unity.

UNIVERSALS ARE NOT PRIMARY BEINGS: Returning to his original statement that primary being can mean a thing's essence, a universal, a kind, and a subject matter, Aristotle now lists the reasons why primary being cannot be a universal or a genus. 1) Primary being is an individual, while a universal is common to a class. If a universal is primary being, it will have to be the primary being either of everything which is classified under it or of nothing. It obviously cannot be the primary being of everything, for each universal has different substances classified under it. Likewise, it cannot be the primary being of one of the objects, for then all the objects of the class would become one. 2) Universals are not primary beings because primary being is not an attribute of a subject; but what is universal is always attributed to a subject. Perhaps, however, a universal can inhere in a primary being, and appear as a subject. Thus, perhaps "animal-in-general" can appear in a man and in a horse. Aristotle says it cannot. The concept, "animal," is derived from our observation of men, horses, and cats, and is predicated of these primary beings. Moreover, if "animal-in-general" were primary being, then primary being would inhere in Socrates, who is himself a primary being, and thus he would be two individuals. 3) Primary being is single. If two primary beings were in the same thing, that object could not be one. Similarly, qualities and quantities cannot exist as primary beings in an object, for if they did, each object would be many things not one.

OUSIA AS DEFINITION AND REALITY: Aristotle sums up the discussion so far: Primary being as secondary substance (i.e., as essence defined) is different from concrete individual being in that it is without matter and is not a particular but a universal. The universal is outside the laws of change and decay. House as an intelligible form never comes into being at all, for instance. If, however, a definition is a universal, it is clear that there can never be a definition of a particular individual concrete something for two reasons. The principle of individuality states that matter is indeterminate. Second, the composite of form-in-matter is subject to change. What the senses cannot remember after a "this something" has passed away, the mind will never know. Science cannot apply definitions to the changing individual object. It can only demonstrate what is always or is usually so.

IF IDEAS EXIST INDEPENDENTLY WE CAN NEVER KNOW THEM: Since the individual alone is truly substance, it follows that unity-in-general and being-in-general, like the Ideal Man, cannot be the primary being of individual objects. Each individual thing exists as one whole particular being, not as part of being-in-general. Men, says Aristotle, who say that the Ideas exist as self-subsisting beings may be right if any such Ideas do, in fact, exist. Whether they do or not, we shall never know. If they exist, they will exist as individual forms, in the same way as forms-in-matter are individual substances, because everything that exists is a "this something." Because the Ideas are not forms-in-matter, we shall never be able to perceive them with the senses. Because they are not universals, they can never become the object of science or of definition. Pure form is more unknowable, therefore, than individual concrete forms-in-matter. Aristotle, on his part, is certain that pure forms exist. "Even if we had never seen the stars," he says, "there would, I suppose, be eternal beings beyond the range of our acquaintance." If there are primary beings which exist as pure form, although we shall never be able to say *what* these forms are, nevertheless, we can say *that* they are.

PRIMARY BEING IS THE SPECIFIC NATURE OF ANYTHING: Aristotle still has not answered to his satisfaction the question as to what primary being or *ousia* really is. In the last chapter of Book Zeta, he takes up the problem from a new angle. Let us not ask "what" a thing is, he suggests, but "why" it is. But we must ask the question in the right way. It is useless to tsk why a house is a house. The right way to put the question is, "why are these bricks and stones a house?" Similarly, "why does it thunder?" means "why is a noise produced in the clouds?" When we ask "why" in this fashion we are seeking for the cause (or essence) of a particular thing. When we ask, "why are the materials a house?" the answer is, "because the essence of house is present in them." In like manner, this body containing this particular form, or essence, is a man. Aristotle concludes once again that the cause in virtue of which matter is a definite thing is the substance of that thing. Form determines the material elements of all bodies composed of matter and form. Form is not an element, like bones and sinews. If it were, we would have to posit yet another principle in virtue of which, for example, this form, these bones, and these sinews were this man. Form is the "something else" in virtue of which a thing exists. If primary being is thus the principle of a thing's existence, it follows that the primary being of anything which exists "by nature" must be the very *nature* of that particular object.

CONCLUSION: By the end of Book Zeta, Aristotle seems to have reduced his four causes to two. The formal, efficient, and final causes have been fused into one formal principle, which is considered the fundamental nature of the concrete existing thing. Only the material cause has been left completely separate. In making this distinction between the functions of matter and form, Aristotle is preparing the ground for his theory of the unity of matter and form in Book Eta. In attributing primary being especially to form, Aristotle has cleared the way for his theory of the Unmoved Mover, who is pure Form.

BOOK ETA
MATTER AND FORM

INTRODUCTION: The inquiry into the nature of primary being continues in Book Eta. In this Book, Aristotle shows how an object composed of both matter and form is yet essentially one.

REVIEW OF BOOK ZETA: Aristotle begins by reviewing the discussion of Book Zeta and restating his conclusion. Although the primary being of an object can be expressed in, and thus can be said to be its definition, the actual existence of any object which our senses can perceive is made of both matter and form. Now every sensible object is subject to change. They may come into being and pass away. They move from place to place, or they may change their size or shape. In all these changes there is something that remains throughout the process. This something Aristotle has defined as matter. Matter, however, is not actually in existence until it has received some kind of form.

MATTER IS POTENTIALITY: The character of matter is to be now "this something" and then to change into "this new something." Matter thus possesses the ability to assume a formal existence. Aristotle says that this means that the indefinite material which underlies every change process has the quality of *potential* existence. Potential comes from the Latin word meaning *to be able*. We must not imagine matter as something definite and concrete. In fact, we should not imagine matter as anything at all. For anything which actually *is,* is already a combination of matter *and* form. Matter is that indefinable something which now possesses the form of a rough block of bronze and which is capable of assuming the form of a statue. But until matter *becomes* a block of bronze or a bronze statue, it is not *actually* in existence. It is only potentially existing. This is not to say that matter has no existence whatsoever. The seeable is that which is potentially seen; a tree has a shape, for instance. The sensible is that which can be sensed; honey, for example, has a taste all its own. But the tree is not actually seen nor the honey actually tasted, until some one sees and tastes. Matter is related to form as the seeable is related to the seen. It is that which has the possibility of actual existence by assuming a definite form.

THE SEARCH FOR ACTUAL EXISTENCE: If matter is that sort of being which potentially exists, what is the actual being of sensible things? There have been many views on this question, Aristotle informs us. The Atomist, Democritus, for instance, believed that individual actual existence could be explained in only three ways. All matter had the same nature but could change according to shape, position, and arrangement of parts. Aristotle believes that things differ from one another in more ways than that. 1) For example, there is a difference in the way materials are put together. Some things are blended, such as food; some things are bound together, such as bundles; and some are glued, such as books. 2) Some things differ in their position. The difference between a threshold and a lintel is basically one of place. 3) Some things differ in time, for example, breakfast and dinner. 4) Some things differ in direction, like the four winds. 5) Finally, some things differ in quality, like wet and dry. It is obvious that many variable characteristics go to make up the individual "what" of the concrete object. Although they cannot be said to be its essential being, they nevertheless are necessary to understanding what that essential being is.

FORM AND FUNCTION: Actual existence does not depend on a combination of characteristics. It also does not depend on a synthesis of various material elements. Aristotle says that existence is understandable only in terms of what a particular thing actually does. We define something by reference to its function, to what it is meant to do. Matter and its characteristics are dependent upon the type of function a natural body is meant to perform. Wood and stone are only potentially a "this something." But a threshold is wood and stone placed in a certain way for a certain purpose. Those who define a house as timbers and stone are speaking of the potential house. Those who say a house is something which shelters men and possessions are speaking of the function or purpose of the house. Those who include both these definitions in their concept of a house are saying what a house actually is. In the *Physics,* Aristotle suggested that the function of an existing thing determines its form. In this passage, he equates form with function and shows how form and function can be the same through an analysis of a few definitions. "Calm weather," for instance, means "absence of motion in the air." "Air" is the material. "Absence of motion" refers to the behavior of the air, to its formal being. In the concept, "a calm sea," sea is the material, while "calm" refers to the action of the sea. In both cases the behavior of the material is decisive in telling us what that particular thing is.

THE RELATION OF MATTER TO FORM: In Book Zeta, Aristotle concluded that the unity of a definition depended upon the unity of the object, but he had not yet determined the reason why. Substance as definition, he says, presents the same kind of problem as numbers do. Indeed, definition seems to be a kind of number for several reasons. 1) You can divide both definition and number into indivisible parts. 2) When you add or subtract parts of a number, the result is not the same number; when you add or substract parts of a definition, you end with a different object. 3) Number is an integral whole and so is definition, says Aristotle. "Five" is one number, not many numbers together. Similarly, "man" is one concept, not a combination of concepts. 4) Both numbers and definition have precise meanings denoting specific things. Neither can vary in form and remain the same. Unfortunately, however, this comparison of number and definition is not helpful in telling us why *ousia* as definition has to be a unity.

ESSENTIAL BEING AS ACTIVITY: Aristotle concludes that the logical answer to why the definition of anything is a unity is only to be found in the function that a thing performs in a change process. He has come to the heart of his philosophy. In Book Zeta, Aristotle discussed *ousia* from the standpoint of definition and the natural process. He explained the product of change in terms of matter and form, and stated that only the formal aspect of anything was contained in its definition. In Book Eta, he shifts his inquiry from the concrete object as the *product* of change to the actual existence of the object in the *process* of change. In other words, he has changed the focus of his interest from the nature of existence as a noun to its function as a verb. For example, man's being, as a noun, refers to an organism composed of body and soul. Man's being, as a verb, denotes the particular way the human organism actually exists. Being in this sense is not a thing, but an activity. There are, of course, different kinds of fundamental activities, but it is clear that the being of natural bodies is the activity of change. For this reason, we must look for the answer to what makes a natural body one body in the activity of change. To explain the nature of actual sensible being, Aristotle develops the concepts of potentiality and actuality.

POTENTIALITY AND ACTUALITY: To understand the importance of potentiality and actuality to the concept of change, we must look at the words which Aristotle uses throughout this discussion. *Dunamis* is the Greek word for power, or the capacity to do something, from which we get our word "dynamic." The word is usually translated as potentiality, but when we talk about the dynamics of a particular situation, we are close to Aristotle's meaning. *Ergon* is the Greek word for "work." Aristotle uses it to refer to the proper function or type of work an individual thing is supposed to do. *Energeia,* from which we get our word "energy," denotes the actual performance of the function a particular thing is meant to perform. *Energeia* has been translated variously as activity, actuality, and functioning. Actual primary, sensible being is defined as the *energeia* (or functioning) of the *ergon* (or function), which is the *dunamis* (characteristic or specific capability) of a given body.

FORM IS FUNCTION: In the earlier chapters of Book Eta, Aristotle equated matter with potentiality. Bricks and stone are potential to a house, a threshold, or a wall. They actually become the house, threshold, or wall, when these objects are standing and functioning as they are supposed to do. Aristotle now goes so far as to say that matter *is* potentiality and form *is* function, the "wherefore" of a natural body. When the power to do something actually functions, we have an existing physical object; we have change.

POTENTIALITY AND ACTUALITY IN THE PROCESS OF CHANGE: Matter, however, should not be considered potentiality in general. Every object has a particular matter out of which it came. Change is not a chance linking of chance combinations of matter and form, nor is one object related to another haphazardly. There are different forms of matter, different potentialities, different capacities, and different characteristics. Something cannot come from anything. There are certain definite factors which enter into every change, and those factors are particular to that particular change. In this way Aristotle explains how the continuity between objects is maintained. Every actually existing object is potentially some other existing object, but it cannot become just any existing object. Every actual existence has its four distinctive causes. What is the material cause of man? The menstrual fluid. What is the efficient cause? The semen. What is the formal factor? "What it means to be a man." What is the "wherefore" or end of man? The complete man. The formal and final cause together denote the *function* of man. The point Aristotle stresses is that every change from potentiality to actuality has a specific result.

USEFULNESS OF THE CONCEPTS OF CHANGE: The unity of objects in the natural world may be explained by these twin concepts of change. For example, if we look at a physical object potentially, it is matter. Bronze is potentially a statue. If we look at it as it actually is, it is form. This account explains objects that are subject to change, but can it explain the existence of unchangeable beings? In the case of natural substances, which are eternal, such as Aristotle thought the sun and moon were, their unity must be somewhat differently conceived. Aristotle assumes that the matter of the sun and moon is not the same kind of matter which comes into being and perishes. He calls their matters the matter of "locomotion." The sun and moon, as individual existing substances, have unity as they have being. There is no reason to look for another cause of their unity.

OTHER PROBLEMS CONNECTED WITH POTENTIALITY AND ACTUALITY: One problem which concerns Aristotle is that the concepts of potentiality and actuality do not seem to be adequate to explain things like points and whiteness. He concludes that these concepts have unity but doubts that they have an independent existence. Whiteness, for example, is a quality, and we know that qualities have at best a secondary form of existence. A greater challenge to the usefulness of the concept of potentiality and actuality in explaining change is whether a body can be potentially two contrary things at once. Is the human body both potentially healthy and potentially sick? Is water potentially both wine and vinegar? Aristotle says no. The human body changes from being healthy to being sick. It is never both sick and healthy. Similarly, you cannot make vinegar from water. Water turns into wine and wine becomes vinegar. This explanation raises the question of natural and unnatural change. Sickness is a form of bodily corruption, as vinegar is the corruption of wine. But sickness is an accidental and unnatural change, whereas the change from wine to vinegar is a natural change. The reason is that the function of man is to be healthy; sickness is the absence of health. It is not necessary to the function of man to be sick. It is contrary to his function. Dying or the change of wine into vinegar are natural processes of decay, however. One follows the other, as night follows day.

THE UNITY OF NATURAL BODIES: From the foregoing, it is clear that the unity of natural bodies is not brought about by linking part to part, like an epic poem. It does not consist in a combination of parts nor a participation of one part in another part, nor by "a communion" of parts with each other. The conclusion is that there is no unifying principle or formula that explains *why* objects are one. Potentiality and actuality are not two different parts which must be made one in some way. "Matter and form are but two different aspects of the same reality, the one with respect to a thing's capacities, and the other with respect to its actual functioning." To ask why they are united is to ask why one is one. In the words of one student of Aristotle, the actually existing object is "the awakened potency of matter, which . . . is the promise of form to be realized." The only other factor necessary to explain change is the moving power which effects the change from "a power to function" to "an actual functioning."

DOCTRINE OF IMMANENT FORM RESTATED: In Book Zeta Aristotle developed his theory of immanent form in terms of the conceptual definition. Here he restates his theory in terms of the factors which explain change. Neither matter nor form exists separately in the natural world. Matter apart from form is a useful concept for thought, but it simply does not have an existence in the world as we know it. Likewise, there is no self-existing form in our world. There is only form-in-matter, or actualized potency.

SIGNIFICANCE OF ARISTOTLE'S CONCEPTS OF POTENTIALITY AND ACTUALITY: Aristotle's account of change is perhaps his most significant contribution both to his own philosophy and to the development of thought after him for the following reasons. 1) Aristotle sees the whole of reality as the stage for the drama of change and motion. The concepts of potentiality and actuality enable him to answer Parmenides without a shadow of a doubt that change is both real and intelligible. 2) The concepts of potentiality and actuality lead him to the conclusion that being is an activity. It is not something static, but is present in every natural process in the form of dynamic, purposeful activity. In fact, potentiality and actuality constitute being as we know it in the natural world. 3) The distinction between potency and act accounts not only for one particular change, but also for the continuity of change in a world of seemingly different and unrelated types of beings. The product of one natural process is a particular individual whose specific way of functioning makes it the subject of a new change cycle. Every kind of informed matter is potentially another specific kind of informed matter. Thus, the eternal interaction between potentiality and actuality unites the lowest form of natural existence to the highest form in a continuous upward spiral of change. Aristotle's reasons why one change takes place lead him to the theory of a hierarchical scale of existence, on which everything is related to the being above it as matter is to form. This theory, however, should not be seen as a theory of evolution. Forms are not produced *from* matter; they are imposed *upon* matter. Consequently, a higher form of being cannot evolve out of a lower form. There has to be some efficient agent to produce the higher type of form-in-matter, namely, the higher being itself.

BOOK THETA
POTENTIALITY AND ACTUALITY

INTRODUCTION: In Book Eta Aristotle demonstrated that changing existence is impossible without the possibility of existence (without unformed matter capable of taking a form). In Book Theta he goes more deeply into the nature of potency and act.

POTENTIALITY: Aristotle tells us we are to understand potentiality as the source of change in anything. He distinguishes between two kinds of potentialities or powers: the power of being acted upon, or *passive* power; and the power of acting upon something else, or *active* power. The potential exists in both inanimate and animate objects. The difference between the two is that the potential in bodies which have no reason can only produce a specific effect, while man has the power to produce contrary effects. Aristotle thinks that the potential in man is specially evident in his power to make things. Thus, he considers the arts and sciences powers, since they can produce change. The potential, then, differs according to the degree in which its subject has reason. Aristotle calls man's capacities rational, and those of inanimate beings, non-rational. The difference between conscious and unconscious behavior can be understood by the following example. In the inanimate world, warmth can only be produced by what is warm. The science of medicine, however, can produce both disease and health.

IMPORTANCE OF POTENTIALITY: Aristotle remarks that some philosophers have not understood the significance of potentiality in the explanation of change. A well-known philosophic school of his own times, the Megarian School, for instance, taught that there was no such thing as a power—there was only act. This position led them to absurdities. To be a builder means to be able to build a house. If you have never built a house, you cannot be a builder. On the other hand, if you are a builder only when you are actually building, you would be spending most of the time being not-a-builder. Does that mean that every time you start to build you learn your art all over again? Of course not. Furthermore, if honey is only sweet when it is tasted, it would not be anything at all when it is not being tasted. Protagoras would be right that all things are one. The final absurdity is in the case of seeing and hearing. If you do not admit that we have the ability to see and hear even when we are not exercising these functions, then a person will be blind and deaf many times a day. The Megarian view leads to the conclusion that nothing can come into being. For if something does not have the *power* to come into being, it obviously cannot exist ever. The Megarians are unable to explain our world of change.

RELATION OF POTENTIALITY AND ACTUALITY: Aristotle next explains the relation of potentiality to actuality. Actuality or fulfillment seems above all to be related to motion. For example, we do not say that things which do not exist are beings in motion. Things that "are not" may be thoughts or desires, but they may not be moved. Among things that are not, some can be said to exist potentially, but they are not in being because they are not completely actual. You can imagine or conceive of the impossible, but what is really not capable of existence can never be.

HUMAN ACTION: Turning to human activity, Aristotle says that all our powers are either born with us (such as the power of sensing or knowing), or acquired, (such as flute playing). We are also capable of acting in one way at one time and in another way at another time. Thus, in rational activity there is another factor which enters into the picture, namely deliberate choice. We can choose whether to exercise our power of sight or of flute playing or not. The relation between choice and human action is the basis of Aristotle's ethics.

ACTUALITY: Having defined potentiality, Aristotle turns to consider actuality, as distinct from the former. Potentially, the statue is *in* the block of wood because it can be produced *from* wood. The opposite of the potential statue, the actual wooden statue (Aristotle finds it hard to define actuality precisely because of the nature of potentiality), is itself indefinable. You can only point to an example. He explains that the actual is related to the potential, as waking is to sleeping, and the process of building is to the ability to build. Actuality is the opposite pole of potentiality. Actuality, however, is not always the contrary of potentiality. We have seen that some things are only potential, not in the sense of potential to existence, but potential to knowledge, such as the concepts of the infinite, the impossible, and empty space.

ACTIVITIES OF PROCESS AND ACT: There are some kinds of activities which are processes and others which are called acts. The difference between the two lies in the end or product of the activity. The product of change is not part of the actual change process, but is outside it. Man, for example, begets another man, but not himself. An act such as seeing, on the other hand, has no other end than the act of seeing. He who is thinking *has* thought. The object or end of the action lies in doing the action itself. These complete actions Aristotle calls *entelechies,* or those things which have their end in themselves. Incomplete actions or processes are similar to house building. While the house is "a-building," the action is incomplete. The motion is only completed when the house actually stands. In a complete action, however, which has no other end than the activity itself, there cannot properly be said to be motion. Motion, we learned from the *Physics,* implies a mover and a moved. The moved is that which moves from one condition to its opposite. But in the case of knowing, there is no movement from one state to another. There is only the power to know functioning. Knowing has no other product than the activity of knowing. Aristotle thus concludes that complete actions like knowing are more perfect than incomplete ones. It follows from this reasoning that that which never needs to be made actual or pure activity complete in itself should be the highest form of existence. Aristotle thus assigns the character of pure activity to the source of all motion, the Unmoved Mover.

THE ACTUAL IS PRIOR TO THE POTENTIAL: An important aspect of Aristotle's theory is that the actual must be prior to the potential, both in thought and in reality. It is clear that we can only have knowledge of the potential by knowing what the actual is. The power of sight is only known through the act of seeing. The visible is explained in terms of the seen. You must know what seeing is before you can define sight and the seen.

THE ACTUAL IS PRIOR IN TIME: The actual man comes before the embryo which becomes the man. There has to be the mustard plant in order for there to be the seed. Every natural process must have an efficient cause which must be actually existing. The same is true in the case of knowledge. The Sophists argued that learning was having knowledge of what you did not know. Aristotle replies that all knowledge is built on previously learned knowledge.

THE ACTUAL IS PRIOR TO THE POTENTIAL IN BEING: Man comes before the embryo because he has the actual form of a man, while the embryo does not. Aristotle restates his theory of biological teleology. Everything that comes into being does so for some functional purpose, for some end which determines the kind of existence that thing is to have. For example, animals do not see in order that they may acquire the faculty of sight. They have sight in order that they may perform the function of seeing. In this case, the function of seeing is the activity of the power of sight. Aristotle thought that he was the first thinker to pay attention to the idea of a final cause. It is important to realize that he did not consider the final cause of anything as *outside* that thing, but as *present* in it as the perfection of its function. The acorn does not exist so that squirrels may grow; it exists in order to grow up into an oak. The growing into an oak is the functional purpose for the sake of which the acorn came into being. It is interesting that Aristotle considers this striving for self-perfection natural, when at the same time he insists that it is purposeful. Apparently, he viewed purpose, the actual in nature, as an immanent force of attraction toward which all things were unconsciously drawn.

THE ACTUAL IS PRIOR TO THE POTENTIAL BECAUSE IT IS ETERNAL: The final proof that actuality is prior to potentiality is based on the fact that eternal beings are by their nature prior to those that perish. Aristotle shows that nothing eternal is potential in the following way. Whatever potentially is not, may also cease to be. Whatever ceases to be is perishable. Eternal beings, by definition, cannot cease to be. Therefore, they are always actual. For the same reason eternal movement is also always actual. The potentiality which belongs to the sun and moon is potentiality only with relation to movement from place to place. Since the stars do not seem to be subject to the potentialities of coming into being and ceasing to be, Aristotle thinks they are the only type of eternal material motion we know.

THE QUESTION OF EVIL IN THE WORLD: Aristotle's view that the actual is prior to the potential leads him to conclude that there is no first principle of evil as some philosophers had thought. 1) That which is actually good cannot be otherwise than good. But that which has only the power to be good can be either good or *bad*. 2) Actual evil must be worse than potential evil. It follows, therefore, that evil, by nature, is as interior to potential good as potential good is inferior to actual good. Consequently, evil cannot exist as a principle apart from concrete individual things. 3) Evil cannot exist in anything which is eternal, because eternal beings possess no potentiality, and therefore are not subject to error or corruption.

CONCLUSION OF BOOK THETA: With this demonstration that actuality is prior to potentiality in logic, time, being, and value, Aristotle has set the stage for his theory of eternal being. The rest of Book Theta discusses questions which have little relevance to his theory of God. Chapter 9 shows the relation of actuality to potentiality in geometric figures. Chapter 10 deals with that other aspect of being mentioned in Book Delta, being as truth. Aristotle concludes that it is not possible to be in error about actual being. You either know it or you do not.

BOOKS IOTA, KAPPA. MU, AND NU
ON UNITY, NUMBER, AND THE EXISTENCE OF THE IDEAS

BOOKS IOTA AND KAPPA: These do not seem to belong to the main body of the *Metaphysics*. Some scholars think that Book Iota should be put at the very end, but it probably belongs where it is. It discusses the characteristics and attributes of *ousia*: the nature of unity; the relation of the many and the one; concepts derived from the "many," such as otherness, dissimilarity, and difference; and the nature of contraries and intermediates such as gray. In the last chapter, Aristotle prepares the ground for his description of eternal being by discussing the difference between that which can perish and that which is imperishable. Perishable and imperishable, he says, are not the same kind of contraries as hot and cold, or black and white. Black and white are accidental qualities, which are not essential to the concept of any object. A man can be either black or white, but he cannot be either perishable or imperishable.

"Imperishable" denotes a different kind of being than "perishable." It therefore forms part of the essential concept of what it means to be a particular thing. The fact that perishable and imperishable are essentially opposed to one another is one more reason why Aristotle thinks that there can be no separately existing Ideal Forms. If there is both man who exists in the natural world, and the Idea of a man which exists in another world, we must suppose that there exists both perishable and imperishable man. This, of course, is absurd.

BOOK KAPPA: This seems to be completely out of context. The first half of the work mainly repeats much of what Aristotle has discussed earlier: the unity of wisdom, the nature of first principles (are they form or matter?), the unity of philosophy, the relation of mathematics to metaphysics, the Law of Contradiction and criticisms of it, the position of theology among the sciences, and being as accident and truth. In the next half, he reviews problems which are familiar to us from the *Physics:* the nature of chance, potentiality, actuality and movement, the nature of the infinite, types of change and motion. He ends the book with four proofs that motion can never be the subject of motion. There is no motion of motion.

BOOKS MU AND NU: Here Aristotle takes up the problem of whether Ideas and Ideal Numbers can exist separately from matter in great detail. The substance of his arguments against Plato's doctrine has already been given in an earlier part of this outline of the *Metaphysics.*

BOOK LAMBDA
THE UNMOVED MOVER

INTRODUCTION: It will be remembered that Aristotle said at the opening of the *Metaphysics* that his purpose was to determine whether substances other than those which we perceive with our senses actually exist or not. If they do, can these substances be the object of any science? In the course of the *Metaphysics,* he has shown us what "to be" means, and what aspect of sensible primary being can be known, namely, its form as expressed in definition. But he has cast some doubts on whether a substance which we cannot perceive with the senses is knowable. In Book Zeta, for instance, he suggested that such a substance cannot be known. The universal is the knowable. Primary being, however, is individual and particular. Consequently, unless we can use our senses, primary being is not knowable at all. It follows that non-sensible substance is unknowable. Thus, in order to derive a workable definition of being, Aristotle turned from the pursuit of non-sensible being to the study of the activity of sensible things.

THE NECESSITY OF THE EXISTENCE OF A NON-SENSIBLE SUBSTANCE: It will be remembered that there is considerable evidence that Book Lambda was one of Aristotle's earlier works, written under the influence of Plato. Nevertheless, it cannot simply be considered one of the philosopher's youthful theories. Aristotle has said that if a science of being exists, then it must study all kinds of being, sensible and nonsensible, perishable and nonperishable. Furthermore, elsewhere in his philosophy he has argued that a First Mover must exist, witness the last book of the *Physics*. Finally, in Book Zeta, he stressed the fact that although we cannot say *what* eternal being is, we must say *that* it is, for actuality must be prior to potentiality. Book Lambda thus constitutes the crowning achievement of Aristotle's metaphysics. In it, the philosopher restates his reasons why eternal being has to exist, and gives his description of the kind of being the First Mover is.

THAT THE FIRST CAUSE IS: Actual individual being or substance has been shown to be the most fundamental of all existing things. Aristotle has also demonstrated that all sensible substance is subject to change. Trees, stones, man, and beast are all perishable. Now if all substances are perishable, then everything is perishable, including change itself. But Aristotle has proved that although natural bodies come into being and go out of being, the process of change is eternal. Motion always has been and always will be. Since time is the measure of motion, time has also of necessity always existed together with motion. We have seen that most motion is individual; it has a beginning and an end. But there is one motion which Aristotle considers eternal, namely, circular motion. Nevertheless, although the process of change and circular motion are eternal, we cannot say that there is no uncaused movement. Consequently, we cannot escape the question, "what causes the first heaven to move?" In this respect, Plato's Ideas are seen to be useless, for they are not the cause of anything. That which causes the first motion of the heavens must not only have the power to cause movement, it must *actually* cause movement. We have seen that what can function, can also not function. If the first principle of movement was not wholly actual, change would not be eternal. It follows that this first cause must not be composed of matter, for matter is potentiality. Aristotle concludes that the existence of the sensible world of changing substances necessitates the existence of a first substantial being which is pure act. Aristotle realizes that some may argue that potentiality is prior to actuality, because some things, such as the infinite, exist potentially, but never actually. His answer is that, if potentiality is the First Cause, there would never be actual existence as we know it.

WHAT THE FIRST CAUSE IS: It is not enough to say with Plato and the Atomists that motion is eternal, if you cannot explain why it is eternal. Aristotle firmly believes that the world is not run by chance. There is *always* a reason, a cause, for every motion. Primary circular motion must have its cause too. If you explain circular motion by saying that time also goes in cycles, you will still have to admit that there is some permanently active principle behind the recurring cycles of the years. There must also be something permanent behind generation and decay. Indeed, our own eyes prove to us that the outer starry reaches of the heavens move in an eternal circular motion. If they move, something must move them. 1) This something must be a substance, because substance is the basic unit of existence. 2) It must not move itself, or else something else would move it and so on into infinity. 3) It must be entirely actual. It cannot function one day and not the next, or else the universe would not ever be.

HOW THE FIRST MOVER CAUSES MOTION: It is clear that the First Mover cannot move the world as its efficient cause for several reasons. First, all efficient causes have been shown to be made of matter. They therefore cannot ever be entirely actual. Aristotle and the Greeks never accepted the view that the world was created. Creation means that *something* was created out of *nothing*. Every Greek philosopher believed that *something* had to be there in the beginning, because being could not possibly come from non-being. Second, the First Mover cannot move by physical contact, for it is, and must be, immaterial. Now, there is only one way which something can be the cause of motion and not move itself. Objects of thought and desire, Aristotle tells us, move without being moved. The objects of thought, concepts and ideas, cause us to think. Yet we cannot say that they are "moved" by our thought. We can desire the good: prestige, wealth, social position, virtue; but the good does not move nearer to us no matter how much we want it. It does not move at all. Rather, *we* move toward that which seems good to us. The good is thus the cause and the end of human action, as that outside our actions which draws us to itself. The First Mover is related to the universe in the same way. The First Mover is reality's final cause.

THE FIRST CAUSE IS INTELLIGIBLE: The First Mover moves the world as its ultimate good, in the same way that the desirable attracts the desire. But what kind of good is the First Cause to be? Aristotle derives what type of good the First Cause must be from his theory of the scale of existence. We have seen that he believes that every natural body has a striving to be in a certain place. In the lower forms of natural existence (i.e., in inanimate beings), this striving is simply an unconscious tendency to be oriented in a certain way. Aristotle would explain the activity of a compass needle by saying that it had a tendency to be drawn toward its final cause, the magnetic north pole. On the second rung of the ladder of existence are sensible beings. Their natural striving toward self-perfection is found in their instinct. Although the instinct of dogs, for instance, permits them to discriminate between what is good for them and what is not, it still is a non-rational principle of movement. Human beings, of course, are the highest form of natural existence we know. And man, alone of all the creatures, possesses that form of striving which is the rational desire toward the actual good. Man also has a non-rational impulse toward things which appear good, but the truly good is the real object of the will, which is desire ruled by reason. Human striving toward this good is what Aristotle calls *love*. If the truly good is the object of the rational will, then that which is really good is obviously something determined by reason, and therefore something intelligible. The truly good must be pure form. Now, the First Mover is an even higher form of being than man: it *is* pure form. Therefore, the First Mover of the universe must be an intelligible principle, for it is the ultimate actual good for the sake of which all things move in response to their natural inclinations. Aristotle concludes that the First Mover "causes motion, as being an object of love."

THE LIFE OF THE FIRST MOVER: The life of the First Mover must be the best ever enjoyed. Furthermore, this life must be *always* the best, for its very activity is pleasure. What kind of life is this best life? It is evident that if the actually good is intelligible, it must have its existence in intelligence. The First Mover must therefore exist intelligently. Now, since the First Mover is wholly actual, he cannot sometimes know and sometimes not. He knows eternally, now and forever. The activity of the First Mover is, therefore, pure knowing. For this reason, the First Mover or God not only has life but *is* life. "The activity of mind is life," says Aristotle, "and God is that activity. The fundamental activity of God is eternal and perfect life . . . . We hold then, that God is a living being, eternal and most good; and therefore life and a continuous eternal existence belong to God; for that is what God *is*." From his limited experience, man can only dimly imagine what happiness a life of perpetual knowing is. Occasionally, there comes that moment of clarity when we suddenly understand what life is all about. Aristotle says that the life of God must be much more wonderful than this.

THE NUMBER OF THE UNMOVED MOVERS: In Chapter 8 Aristotle tries to determine how many Unmoved Movers there actually are. He finds that the First Unmoved Mover explains the necessary existence of the first type of motion, which is one and eternal. But He does not explain the great diversity of motion that exists in the world. Now the heavenly bodies can only be eternal, if they are a kind of substance. Are there, then, other movers which are also unmoved who cause the motion of the planets and the stars? Chapter 8 has caused many problems among students of Aristotle. After discussing the possible number of Unmoved Movers, Aristotle suggests in this chapter that there must be some forty-nine eternal substances which move the heavens. Later in Book Lambda, however, he repeats that there is only one Unmoved Mover, Who is divine. Some scholars insist that this theory of many Unmoved Movers is not an essential part of Aristotle's philosophy. Many of Aristotle's own pupils, for instance, maintained their belief in one First Cause, because they did not see how the world could be one and yet have many First Movers. The late classical philosopher, Plotinus, who lived from 204-250 A.D., said that he found the relation between the First Mover and the other Unmoved Movers unclear. The Medieval philosophers found support for their belief that angels moved the spheres in Aristotle's theory of many First Movers. They solved the problem of the many and the one (i.e. the relation of phenomena to being), by saying that the lesser First Movers were subordinated to the First Mover, Who was God. Scholars today are inclined to believe that Chapter 8 was a later addition to the *Metaphysics*. They think that Aristotle had become much impressed with the research of a contemporary astronomer of his time, named Callippus. They say the chapter was inserted into the book, because Aristotle revised his opinion that there could be only one First Cause. They believe that late in his life, he was more and more attracted to explaining natural phenomena by natural causes rather than supernatural causes. What Aristotle himself thought we shall never know. At the end of Chapter 8, he seems to find support for his theory of a plurality of First Substances in the popular Greek belief in many gods—a belief, he says, which has outlasted many generations. Being a Greek himself and heir to the Greek religious tradition, Aristotle probably did believe in many gods. His argument for many Unmoved Movers would seem to support this view. It must be remembered, however, that Greek philosophy never identified itself with religion as Christian philosophy has done. Until Christian times, religion and philosophy were separate spheres, each with its own traditions and subject matter. In fact, religion and philosophy came together only for a brief time once in the history of the Western World, in the Middle Ages. Thus, it does not seem too inconsistent for Aristotle to defend the existence of many gods in one chapter of his *Metaphysics*, and in the next breath to insist that the philosophical First Mover is both one in definition and in number, as the universe is one. Nevertheless, it would be interesting to know how Aristotle thought his First Movers were related to one another.

GOD'S ACTIVITY IS MIND KNOWING ITSELF: In Chapter 9 Aristotle returns to the question of the nature of the divine life. If God is pure understanding, what does He understand? For if He does not have any object for His understanding, He is no better than a man asleep. He will only be potential understanding, not actual understanding. Clearly, God will not choose just anything as the object of His thought; He must have the best object. He must therefore understand that which is most divine and most valued. Now, that which is most good is God Himself. Therefore, God as pure Mind must understand Himself, as the best possible object of His thought. God's act of understanding is thus "the Thought of Thought." It is self-knowledge.

THREE OBJECTIONS TO THE CONCEPT OF GOD AS SELF-KNOWLEDGE: Aristotle replies to three possible objections to his theory. The first objection is that knowledge is always of other things and only incidentally of itself. The second objection is that the act of knowing is not the same as the knowable. Aristotle answers these objections by referring to his own view of how we know anything. When we think, he says, our act of thought is the same as the object of our thought. In the act of knowing, our mind actually becomes what it is thinking, for "mind is potentially all things." Formless, immaterial mind becomes its contents which is form abstracted from matter. Now, when we know anything, we really are knowing mind as it knows the object. This is why we acquire self-knowledge through the act of thought. Thus, since God is pure Thought, it follows that His thought is perpetual self-knowing. The third objection is whether the object of knowledge is an indivisible whole or a composite. Aristotle says that it must be indivisible because the object of knowledge is form, which is indivisible. Since God is the highest form, He is the object of his own thought, and therefore indivisible. It follows that God's knowing of Himself is outside time and space and goes on throughout eternity.

THE GOOD AS A SEPARATE SUBSTANCE AND AS THE ORDER OF THE UNIVERSE: The last question which Aristotle considers is a most difficult one. Does God, as the Good, exist as the orderly arrangement of the parts of the universe (i.e., as its intelligible structure)? Or does the Good exist as something separate from, and independent of, the world? Aristotle thinks that the Good exists "probably in both ways." In one of his most famous examples, he says that the efficiency of the army "lies partly in its battle order and partly in its general; but chiefly in its general." The battle order depends upon the general; the general does not depend upon the battle order. Once again, Aristotle insists that the world is not a result of chance. It is a system of complex relationships, which seem to him to be ordered toward one end, which probably exists independently of the world. He likens the world order to the household, "where free persons have the liberty to act as they please, but whose activities are more or less predetermined" by their choices in favor of the common good. Slaves and animals, however, have no responsibility toward the common good and act as fancy moves them. By this example Aristotle shows that he realizes the importance of chance as a causal factor in the world. Each class of existence has its own functional principle which determines its continued survival. But within the classes there is room for chance to produce the uncommon and the unusual.

OTHER THEORIES OF CAUSATION: Aristotle ends Book Lambda with a brief review of other theories of causation. Plato and the Pythagoreans said that there was not just one first principle, the Good, but two: Good and Evil, the two primary contraries. Other philosophers said that neither Good nor Evil were really principles; they were just relations. Empedocles went so far as to equate the Good with Love, thereby confusing the formal principle of the Good with Love, which is both matter and form. Anaxagoras said that the Good was an efficient cause. His theory necessitates our finding another Good as the final cause. In general, Aristotle feels that none of the previous philosophers said why there should be contraries, or really explained generation and decay. Those who said there were two first principles would have to accept a third which would be higher than the other two. All the others would have to admit that their systems required the existence of something which is contrary to the highest knowledge or Wisdom, namely ignorance.

THERE IS ONE FIRST CAUSE: Aristotle concludes that his view is the best. 1) The Good exists as an individual self-existing Being which is outside the natural order of being, yet is related to it as its Final Cause. 2) This cause is not the intelligible structure of the universe, but the active principle for the sake of which the universe is ordered. It is like the general who draws up his troops for his strategic purposes. Aristotle concludes Book Lambda with a now famous quotation from the Greek epic poet, Homer. "The rule of many is not good; let there be one ruler."

WEAKNESS OF ARISTOTLE'S THEORY OF CAUSATION:

There are several parts of Aristotle's view of the First Cause of the universe which are not satisfactory. 1) He never decides whether the Good is in the world, as its order, or outside it, as its end. It seems most probable, however, that he places the Good outside. 2) He has not given a full account of how there can be diversity in the world if there is only one eternally active principle. His discussion of this subject indicates that he feels that matter and form are to explain diversity, but they do not appear to be really adequate. If the First Cause is pure form, how do you explain the existence of matter? Does it follow that because there is actual existence there must also be potential existence? Aristotle says not. What *can* be may also *not* be. Yet he offers no theory as to why the potential exists at all. He takes the world as given. 3) Finally, he does not give a very satisfactory account of the nature of God. Does God only understand Himself, or can He understand all things indirectly? Aristotle indicates that the First Cause is completely detached from the world. Yet, how can He be completely detached and still be the chief reason for its being? It is clear that Aristotle did not consider the First Mover an object of religious devotion. He is simply a useful philosophical explanation of the universe. Perhaps, Aristotle himself was never able to discover the reason why the universe exists, although he was convinced that it has to have some purpose in being. As he himself says elsewhere, we can *know* that an eternal individual perfect being exists. (Book Lambda proves why there must be one.) But we can never *know* what it is. Therein lies the mystery of the universe.

THE *ETHICS*

INTRODUCTION: Ethics belongs to the second main classification of science in Aristotle's system, practical science. The word "practical" is derived from the Greek word *praxis,* meaning doing, or action. Ethics belongs to that branch of philosophy which has to do with human action. The word *ethics* comes from the Greek word *ethos,* whose primary meaning is custom, manners, habit. Aristotle uses the word chiefly in its secondary meaning of character, that which reveals what a man really is. Aristotle thinks that to ask what a man really is, is not to ask whether he is intelligent or talented. Such qualities are accidental to what it means to be a man. He thinks that a man reveals what he is through what he does, through how he performs his function of being a man. In the *Metaphysics,* Aristotle showed how the Good (that is, excellence) is the Final Cause of man, and how the will informed by reason provides the motivation for human progress toward self-perfection. He made it clear that the Good is the standard of measurement of all human action. For this reason, any judgment of character must be made in terms of moral values. Ethics, therefore, is the study of character, of the moral element in human nature. It is the study of action in terms of self-perfection.

PLATO'S APPROACH TO ETHICS: Plato was highly conscious of the moral aspect of human nature. In his more intuitive perception of the fundamental unity of human existence, he made no hard and fast distinction between the *morally good* and the *scientifically true.* He considered the world of action and the world of knowledge interdependent. A man could only become good by knowing the truth, and he could not know the truth without being good. Plato believed that to know what something really *is,* is to understand its significance; it is to realize what its intrinsic value is in relation to us. Consequently, he identified perfect truth with perfect value in his concept of the Ideal Good, as the light which makes the world intelligible. Since the Ideal Good was a form which existed separately from matter, absolute value was an objective and unchanging standard. It was not a product of man's reasoning, nor dependent upon man's knowledge for its existence. Plato taught that the discovery of the real meaning of things was not a simple intellectual exercise. Knowledge could only be acquired by experience, by leading a life whose actions were in harmony with the Ideal Good. Something of Plato's idea of what "meaning" really means is found in our expression "true to life." When we say a picture is true to life, we are not merely making a factual observation. We are saying that somehow the painting has caught what is significant in life, in the sense of what we think has value for us in understanding what life is all about. Plato believed that knowing was the experience of the meaningful in terms of its value.

ARISTOTLE'S APPROACH TO ETHICS: Aristotle's approach to ethics is more analytic and consequently more practical than Plato's. Aristotle is the first philosopher to make the definitive distinction between the Science of the Good, and the Science of the True. He breaks up Plato's unity of knowing and acting into two independent philosophical categories: the theoretical sciences and the practical sciences. Each of these has its own subject matter, and its own method. The theoretical sciences study what always, or usually, is. Their first principles are thus rooted in experience, or in reality. Consequently, the theoretical sciences can arrive at the truth. The practical sciences, however, have human action as their subject matter. This, we know, is unpredictable, for it concerns what sometimes is and what sometimes is not. Thus, there is no way we can discover sure and certain principles for these sciences; we are forced to base our study on opinion rather than on experience. There can be no absolute moral standard which will serve as the principle governing every action, because every action is individual and unique. For this reason, the good of any action is relative to the kind of action it is. It follows that the practical sciences can never have as their goal absolute truth. Their truth can only be relative. Because moral truth, consequently, is a lesser kind of truth than the scientific truth, Aristotle subordinates the life of acting to the life of knowing. With Aristotle, ethics descends from the world of eternal being to the world of becoming.

ARISTOTLE'S WRITINGS ON ETHICS: Of the three works said to have been written by Aristotle, only one is generally said to have come from his pen. This is the *Nicomachean Ethics*. Many scholars say that the *Eudemean Ethics* is an earlier version of Aristotle's ethical theory, but since we are not completely sure, it seems more fitting to turn to the *Nicomachean Ethics* for an understanding of Aristotle's ethical system. As was the case with the *Physics* and the *Metaphysics,* we shall take up the main points of Aristotle's ethics, trusting the reader will read the details for himself.

BOOK I
HAPPINESS: THE CHIEF END OF MAN

THE FIRST PRINCIPLE OF THE PRACTICAL SCIENCES—THE GOOD: As we have seen, ethics is not a theoretical science; it is rooted in action, in human experience. Thus, since everything we do is for some purpose, the first principle of ethics must be the cause or purpose of action, namely, the good. Now, there must be some chief good at which all action aims, or else we shall have to go back indefinitely with the explanation, "this is done for the sake of this good." There must be some good which is not done for the sake of another good, but for the sake of itself. For example, we drink to quench our thirst in order to keep healthy in order to keep on working in order to become rich in order to live well. Aristotle tells us that our study of the practical sciences must begin with finding out what man's chief end is, and of what science it is the first principle.

POLITICS—THE MASTER PRACTICAL SCIENCE: Aristotle thinks the master science of human affairs is that which includes both individual and community behavior. This science is politics; its first principle is "the general good for man." Politics is the major practical science, because the good of the state is more perfect and "more noble" than the individual good of an individual man. What is the general good of the state? Aristotle tells us that it is hard to know for certain, because we are dealing with a principle which only holds good as a general rule. A man can be ruined as well by having too much money, as by a lack of courage, for instance. There are no certain principles and rules for the science of the good. For this reason, experience is the best teacher of the student of politics. The young man should be kept from politics, because he has not had enough experience of human action and the demands of life, both of which form the subject matter of this science.

HAPPINESS—THE FIRST PRINCIPLE OF POLITICS: In determining the first principles of politics and ethics, therefore, we must fall back on human experience, that is, on the opinions of "the many and the wise." Aristotle does not offer his own opinion of what the good of the state is, but relies on what "the many" have thought it is. The common run of people, he says, think that the highest good attainable by action is *happiness,* by which they mean "living well." Aristotle accepts the general belief that happiness or human welfare is the first principle of the practical sciences.

WHAT KIND OF A GOOD IS HAPPINESS: It is easy to say that happiness is the chief end of man, and the first principle of politics, but it is harder to say what happiness is. There are many views on the subject. Each person tends to form his idea of happiness from his personal experience of life. Most people, for example, think that wealth, possessions, honor, or health constitute the happiness of mankind. Aristotle says they cannot, for each one can be shown to be "for the sake" of another good. He suggests we turn to "the wise" for an answer, and look at what various philosophers have said the good means.

THE GOOD IS NOT AN ABSOLUTE VALUE: Aristotle dismisses Plato's concept of an Idea of the Good or absolute value for several reasons. 1) Good can mean many things, such as useful, excellent, and enough. 2) If we think the good is a self-existing substance, we should have a science for it. As it is, we have different sciences for different subjects, all of which have their particular quality of goodness. 3) A good man and a good horse are good in different ways. Therefore, goodness seems to be a sort of quality. 4) Even if the good exists as something divine and eternal, it is not therefore more good than if it should exist only one day. 5) The good might be some kind of a principle which expresses the relation of the goodness of individual things to one another, such as the good of the man to the good of the horse. This subject, however, does not belong to the study of politics and ethics. We are looking for a good which is within human reach. The Idea of an absolute value is useless in human affairs. Knowing the Ideal Good will not help a carpenter make better houses, nor a physician heal. Knowing carpentry and medicine will. Similarly, the student of politics must study the good which is the principle of statecraft.

HAPPINESS IS FINAL AND SELF-SUFFICIENT HUMAN GOOD: Aristotle has said that the good means something different in different actions and different arts. But it can be seen that in every case the good is that "for the sake of which everything else is done." The doctor heals for the sake of health, for instance. Now the highest good of human society must also be that for the sake of which everything else is done. It must be something final. Second, it must be self-sufficient; that is, it must be something which taken by itself makes life worth living. Happiness fits these two conditions.

HAPPINESS AND VIRTUE: But in saying that happiness is the highest human good, Aristotle points out, we have not said very much. What *is* happiness? As usual, Aristotle gives his answer in terms of function. Every creature has its special good, relative to the kind of nature it has. The nature of anything, as we have seen, is understood in terms of its function. Now, the function of man is to live as a rational being, to act intelligently. But to be a good man, it is not enough simply to act intelligently. A good pianist, for example, does not just play the piano; he plays the piano *well*. This means that he plays it in accordance with certain standards of excellence which are considered proper to piano playing, such as good technique, sensitivity to the melody line, and so forth. When a man performs *well* his function of acting intelligently, he is said to be *virtuous*. Virtue implies acting intelligently by using your mind according to a standard "best" use of the mind.

DEFINITION OF HAPPINESS: Aristotle thus defines happiness as follows: it is 1) "the active exercise of the faculties of the soul, 2) in conformity with excellence or virtue, 3) if there are several virtues, in conformity with the best, and most perfect among them, 4) during a complete lifetime." Aristotle warns us that this definition of the good is only a general first principle, for the good differs in different situations. Ethics, he repeats, is a practical not a theoretical science.

THE THREE KINDS OF HUMAN GOODS: Aristotle thinks his definition is a pertinent one, because it includes all three of those goods generally thought to be a part of happiness: worldly goods, the goods of the body, and the goods of the soul. 1) Aristotle believes that happiness requires certain external conditions. A man must have wealth, friends, and political power. This last is especially important, for his function in the state is one of the essential conditions of his happiness. The state provides the stage on which he can perform good and noble actions. 2) He must have the goods of the body. He must be wellborn, of noble family. He should have a handsome appearance, long life, and many children. 3) Aristotle thinks a man cannot properly be called happy unless he has these first two goods, which alone make possible the cultivation of the highest type of human goods, the goods of the soul, such as justice and temperance.

HAPPINESS IS A LIFE IN SOCIETY: It is clear that Aristotle believes that happiness is not the result of chance, but is acquired gradually by living in a community that will give its citizens the kind of character that will make them good and eager to do noble actions. Happiness, therefore, is only possible in a community, or *polis*. A man cannot acquire happiness if he is a hermit. The political community is the only type of environment in which man can function as a rational being. For this reason, you cannot call a dog or horse, or even a child, happy, for none of these is able to take part in the activity which is peculiar to the community, and therefore proper to the nature of man.

> **COMMENT:**   For those of us who have a more romantic view of happiness, Aristotle's definition would seem to exclude most of the human race from even the chance of ever being happy. Aristotle thinks of happiness as a very particular thing. People who work just to stay alive, he says, cannot be happy. They are too busy and do not have the time to pit their minds against others in the game of politics. People who live in slums cannot be happy because they are so depressed by their surroundings that they cannot be expected to find the initiative to acquire knowledge. People who have a physical handicap or come from low social origins tend to direct all their energies towards compensating for this one defect. There is much truth in Aristotle's view of human happiness. On the other hand, one could well argue that most rich, politically active, and good-looking people seem to be the very opposite of happy. Aristotle would answer that they are unhappy because they have neglected to cultivate the goods of the soul. In general, Aristotle's view of happiness is based upon the context of the Greek world in which he lived. A slave-owning society is essentially aristocratic. Of its three classes—slaves, freemen, and noblemen—the one which has the obvious prerequisites for happiness is, of course, the aristocracy.

CAN YOU CALL NO MAN HAPPY UNTIL HE HAS DIED?

From the foregoing definition of happiness, the question naturally comes up as to whether you can ever call a man happy during his lifetime. Aristotle says that people do not like to call the living happy because their fortunes might be reversed. He argues however that fortune is not what really makes a man happy but "activity according to virtue," and there is no type of activity more stable and sure than virtuous activity. Men who are supremely happy, says Aristotle, spend their lives doing virtuous actions. Thus, even when their fortunes change, "nobility shines through . . . when a man bears many great misfortunes with good grace, not because he is insensitive to pain, but because he is noble and highminded." This example makes it clear that Aristotle's view of happiness is not merely a question of economics. No truly happy man, he says, can ever become miserable, for he will never do an action which is hateful or wicked, and he will bear "with dignity" whatever fortune may bring. As a general uses his troops the best way he can, so the good and happy man will use whatever befalls him as best he can, taking the good with the bad.

DO OUR MISFORTUNES AFFECT THE DEAD?   Aristotle says they do, in the way similar to the way the misfortunes of our friends affect us. But they can never make the happy dead unhappy.

HAPPINESS—THE SUPREME VALUE: Finally, Aristotle turns to consider happiness from the standpoint of the value we attach to it. In the hierarchal of values he places happiness above all other things we praise—such as courage, honor, excellence—because it is not a *relative good* (a good for the sake of another good) or a potential good, but the final and actual good of man. As the source and cause of all good things, says Aristotle, happiness should be considered worthy of honor and divine.

THE FOUNDATION OF VIRTUE—THE SOUL: Now that we know what happiness is, we have to find out what virtue is, since happiness has been defined as an activity of the soul in conformity with virtue. Obviously, the virtue or excellence of which we are talking is human virtue, and refers to excellence of soul. The student of politics and of ethics must therefore have some knowledge of what the soul is if he is to talk intelligently of virtue.

THE RATIONAL AND NON-RATIONAL SOUL: The human soul is composed of rational and non-rational elements. Of the non-rational, the vegetative faculty (the ability to eat, sleep, and reproduce) is common to all animals. The other non-rational element is the seat of desire, the appetite. This faculty can be persuaded to obey the second element of the soul, the reason. The fact that the desiring faculty can be persuaded to obey means that it has reason of a sort. The rational faculty of the soul, the part which is able to understand and to know, is also composed of two parts. One has the ability to reason about things within itself, and can understand mathematics and other theoretical sciences. The other listens to reason "as one would listen to a father."

THE VIRTUES OF THE TWO PARTS OF THE SOUL: Each part of the soul has its proper excellence or virtue. *Intellectual* virtues are those which belong to the rational element of the soul, to understanding and wisdom. The *moral* virtues belong to the non-rational element, and are related to the world of action, such as self-control and generosity. The moral virtues are the virtues of character.

ORGANIZATION OF THE ETHICS: The distinction between the moral and intellectual virtues forms the basis for the organization of the rest of the *Ethics*. Books II and III discuss the nature of good character. Books IV and V discuss the moral virtues, Book VI discusses the intellectual virtues. Book VII takes up the problem of what it means to be morally weak or morally strong. Books VIII and IX discuss the advantages and disadvantages of friendship. Finally, Book X looks at the problem of happiness from the standpoint of pleasure, and decides whether true happiness is the result of activity in conformity with the intellectual or the moral virtues.

BOOK II
WHAT IS GOOD CHARACTER?

THE ORIGIN OF THE VIRTUES: How are the virtues formed and from what do they come? Aristotle tells us that whereas intellectual virtues are the result of teaching, moral virtues are the result of habit (the Greek is *ethos,* from which word comes the word, *ethics,* or the things of habit). Moral virtues are not natural to us in the sense that we are born with them. We have them from birth only as a capacity which habit develops.

> **COMMENT:**   In this sense Aristotle holds the view that men are born neither good nor bad, but with a capacity to become either one or the other. As we develop our sense organs, so we develop virtue. We learn both by doing, as the builder learns building by actually building a house. For this reason, Aristotle feels it is terribly important what habits are formed in us when we are young, because different traits of character develop from different kinds of action. "It is by action that some become just and others unjust, and by acting in the face of danger . . . that some become brave men and others cowards." Habit and training are of prime importance in the development of moral virtue. Why else should a good lawgiver seek to make his citizens form good habits through the laws he makes?

THE METHOD OF ACQUIRING VIRTUE: Aristotle says that one studies ethics not to know what virtue is, but to become good oneself. Thus, we have to study different kinds of actions, and learn how they are to be done. Again, he cautions the student that the whole field of ethics is relative. One cannot be precise and give fixed rules, because every action or event is different. Nevertheless, he thinks there are some general rules which can be laid down. 1) Moral virtues are destroyed by too much or too little of one kind of action. In the case of health, too much food or too little food makes us sick. In developing the moral virtues, too much or too little of some action keeps us from developing the corresponding virtue. We know we are on the right path when we take the middle road between too much and too little. This is the road of moderation. 2) Pleasure and pain are a test of virtue. Aristotle tells us to trust our reactions. For instance, if a man takes pleasure in facing danger, he is courageous. If he finds the experience painful, he is a coward.

THE RELATION OF PLEASURE TO VIRTUE: Aristotle points out that since virtue is related to action, it also must be related to emotion. Now, pleasure and pain are a result of every action and every emotion. Thus, virtue must be related in some way to the two. It does not follow, however, that every virtuous action is a pleasant one. Other factors are involved. For example, Aristotle believes that when a man goes after a certain pleasure at the wrong time or in the wrong way, he becomes corrupt. This association of emotion with bad actions has led many people to say that virtue is a state free from all emotion. Aristotle feels that this is not entirely true. He takes a more relative position. "Virtue makes us act in the best way in matters involving pleasure and pain." Vice makes us act the opposite way. It all depends on your attitude. But if pleasure is not the criterion by which we can evaluate the rightness of our actions, what does determine whether we act virtuously or not?

THE THREE FACTORS OF CHOICE: Aristotle gives three factors involved in making the right choice: 1) the noble, 2) the beneficial, and 3) the pleasurable. Choosing the wrong course of action also involves three factors: 1) the base, 2) the harmful, and 3) the painful. Of all these, the pleasurable has the greatest attraction for us. For this reason, it is important that we are trained to feel pleasure and pain in the right way. If we are trained in the wrong way, we shall never be able to resist the lure of the wrong pleasure. "It is harder to fight against pleasure," observes Aristotle, "than to fight against anger." Thus, in one sense, virtue is victory over the wrong sort of pleasure. Aristotle concludes by saying that ethics and politics must deal with pleasure and pain, for the right attitude toward pleasure makes a man good; the wrong attitude makes a man bad.

PLEASURE AND PAIN: These are the materials of virtue which must be molded into the right form by training and habit.

BECOMING VIRTUOUS BY VIRTUOUS ACTION: Aristotle has said that virtue is developed by habit. He has now to answer the possible objection that it is impossible for a man *to become* virtuous by performing virtuous actions, since, if he does a virtuous action, he must be already virtuous, as a man who reads and writes is already literate. Aristotle's solution to this problem of how one can become something he is not, by acting the way he is not, is one of his many valuable insights into moral action. A virtuous action, he says, is not the same as a good work of art. In art, virtue or excellence is *in the result achieved by action*. For example, the virtue of music lies in the excellence of the music composed. But, in the case of a virtuous action, the *value* of the action lies *in the doer* of the action. There is no result which carries over from the action into some other thing.

TO ACT VIRTUOUSLY IS A QUESTION OF MOTIVE: The distinction just made is very important. By making it, Aristotle is saying that whether a man acts virtuously or not depends not on the action itself, but upon how he is motivated. For a man to act virtuously, he must be of a certain disposition: 1) he must know what it is he is doing; 2) he must choose to act the way he does, and he must choose to do so for the sake of the act itself; 3) the action must come from a "firm and unchangeable character." For example, to give money to charity is generally considered a virtuous action. But if I want to act virtuously by giving money to charity, I must satisfy the three conditions just given. I must know that I am giving my money to charity. I must choose to give that money to charity, not in order to make a profit, and not because such donations are tax deductible, but purely for the sake of the action itself. Finally, I must not give my money to charity today and tomorrow decide that it was a foolish thing to do. When virtue is understood in terms of personal motivation, Aristotle says, the paradox of how a man can *become* just by doing just deeds disappears. A virtuous action is that kind of action a virtuous man would perform. This kind of action *creates* a virtuous person. But only a man who actually *is* virtuous can act virtuously. By telling the truth, a child learns to be honest. But he is truly honest only when he knows he is telling the truth; he tells the truth because telling the truth is a good thing, and he has the habit of always telling the truth. In other words, a man is really honest when the virtue of honesty has become "second nature" to him. Aristotle concludes that the *really good* action is that action which springs from a good motive, and is the right thing to do in the particular circumstance. Most men, he observes matter-of-factly, do not perform such acts.

WHAT VIRTUE IS NOT: Since virtue is a matter of personal motivation, it must be one of three things in the soul: 1) an emotion, such as anger and fear; 2) a capacity or faculty; or 3) a disposition, the habit by which we acquire the correct attitude toward our emotions. Virtue is obviously not an emotion, for we do not praise or blame people for feeling pleasure, or anger, or pain. Moreover, the emotions are not directly concerned with the matter of choice, for we are said to be "moved" by emotion, but "disposed" toward virtue. The emotions are purely passive faculties of the soul. Virtue is also not a capacity or power. We are not praised or blamed for our capacity to indulge our emotion. It is even more clear that virtue cannot be a capacity from the fact that we are not born with a capacity for goodness or badness by nature. Virtue is something that is *acquired*. Virtue must therefore be a disposition or attitude of mind.

DEFINITION OF VIRTUE—A DISPOSITION TOWARD THE MEAN: What kind of an attitude is virtue? In a rather complicated passage, Aristotle states that every science and every art aims at finding the mean between "excess," or "too much," and "deficiency," or "too little." In everything which is without distinct parts and is divisible, he says, there is an arithmetical mid-point between the two extremes. For example, if 10 is too many and 2 is too few, 6 is the mid-point between the two. Aristotle thinks that virtue is also some kind of mid-point between too much and too little in both feeling and action. Nevertheless, it is clear that there is no mid-point in feeling and action which can be determined by arithmetic. How much food one should eat, for instance, if he wants to eat the "right" amount, depends upon the person involved. Similarly, the mean in matters of virtue is also relative. Aristotle, therefore, defines virtue as 1) a disposition to choose, 2) "consisting essentially of the mean relative to us, 3) which is determined by a rule, 4) that is, by the rule by which a wise man would determine it." The first thing to notice in this definition is that virtue concerns a choice mid-way between two opposing courses of action. The second point to notice is that choice is not a matter for our emotions, nor is it purely the product of our subjective reasoning. It is determined by a rule or principle such as would govern the actions of a wise man. This means that there is no excuse when we make a bad choice. If we do not have wisdom enough to make a choice, we should ask the opinion of the man who has. Right action is possible when we apply principles that are recognized by the prudent and the wise to be generally valid to a specific circumstance.

RIGHT ACTION IS RELATIVE: Since virtue is relative, right action is also relative. Every good action involves the right way to do it, the right time, and the right amount of doing. Aristotle insists that no emotion or impulse is naturally bad, but each has its own time and place. Nevertheless, he does not believe that every action and every emotion has its proper mean. Some actions and emotions are bad in themselves. In cases of adultery, envy, or murder, for example, Aristotle says there can be no question of right and wrong. These actions are inherently bad. But one can have too much or too little self-control at a particular time, just as he can have too much or too little courage.

VIRTUE—THE MEAN BETWEEN TWO VICES: Aristotle ends Book II with examples of what the mean is. As he goes more into detail in Book III, we shall pass over the examples here. The important thing to note in Aristotle's concept of virtue is that he sees virtue as the mean between two vices. These vices are even more opposed than the virtue is to either vice, although the mean virtue tends to be nearer one or the other of the two vices. For example, the virtue of generosity has the two opposing vices of miserliness and extravagance. If the generous man seems extravagant to the miser, the real spendthrift must appear the essence of liberality. Similarly, the spendthrift who thinks the generous man a miser must think the real miser a thousand times more miserly. Yet, if we look at the matter from the standpoint of the person's attitude toward the action, namely his attitude toward money, the virtue of generosity is more like the vice of extravagance than the vice of miserliness. A miser *never* gives his money away. The generous man gives it away in the *right amount,* while the spendthrift *throws* it away.

SIGNIFICANCE OF ARISTOTLE'S VIEW OF VIRTUE: We should not be misled by Aristotle's view of virtue into thinking that virtue is mediocrity, a kind of moral compromise between two evils. Rather we should think of the concept on two levels. 1) The Greek word for virtue is *arete,* meaning excellence. Insofar as virtue is excellence, thus, a positive value, goodness lies at the extreme opposite pole of badness. 2) Insofar as virtue is a "such," which must be defined in terms of something else, it is the midpoint between two vices. Virtue is not a combination of vices, however. It contains within itself the good which the two opposing

vices have in excess. For example, courage contains enough boldness to keep the courageous person from falling into cowardice; in
addition, it possesses enough foresight to prevent him from giving
way to foolhardiness. Courage is not a mixture of boldness and
cowardice, but the best of the two extremes. As "the best," it
obviously is directly opposed to its two "worst" vices. Virtue can be
compared to a set of scales. When we weigh ourselves, we move
the marker on the scale slowly over to the point where the arrow
delicately balances itself mid-way between the top and the bottom
of the scale. In one sense, virtue is the positive point on the scale
where the marker stops when the arrow finds its balance relative to
our weight. In another sense, virtue is the mid-point between top
and bottom where the arrow hangs in equilibrium.

ADVICE ON CHOOSING THE MEAN: How are we to choose
the mean if it is this delicate balance between two extremes?
Aristotle gives us two bits of advice. 1) Watch out for the vice
which is most opposed to its corresponding virtue. 2) Be on guard
against the vice which you yourself are most likely to choose.

CRITICISM OF ARISTOTLE'S CONCEPT OF VIRTUE: Aristotle
has been criticized for his view of virtue as a mid-point between
two vices. One criticism is that every virtue has only one opposite
vice, not two. It seems that when Aristotle tries to turn his idea
of moderation into a mathematical equation, his system breaks
down because even he is unable to apply the vice-virtue-vice
formula to every situation. Nevertheless, there is much sense in
Aristotle's feeling that any value can be dangerous when it is the
sole principle of a person's actions. There is a point beyond which
any value becomes tyrannical, if it is followed to the exclusion of
everything else. Men that live only by courage become rash. Men
who always "think twice" become timid in the face of decision.
For this reason, Aristotle believes that virtue is only possible when
two values are counter-balanced, so that neither one of them
destroys the other. A second criticism of Aristotle's idea of virtue
is that it is primarily an aesthetic view: it is based on a sense of
proportion and beauty, not upon moral standards. Right conduct,
in Aristotle's view, seems to be equated with aesthetic conduct.
In holding this opinion, the philosopher is merely following the
traditional Greek attitude toward virtue. The Greeks saw the
beautiful in terms of balance and proportion, and they carried
their aesthetic values over into the world of morality and right
action. Consequently, their maxim, "nothing in excess" was the
"golden mean," not only for the artistically pleasing but for the
morally right.

BOOK III
CHOICE

INTRODUCTION:　　In Book II, Aristotle defined the virtuous man as one who makes the right choice of his own free will, between two alternative courses of action. This definition raises the questions, "what does it mean to do something voluntarily, of your own free will? what does it mean to do something against your will?" Book III discusses the meaning of free choice, and how it is related to the practice of virtue.

INVOLUNTARY ACTIONS:　　In Book II, Aristotle says actions are involuntary, or against your will, when they are done because you have been *forced* to do them or because you do not know *not* to do them. Aristotle considers *compulsion* and *ignorance* the two sources of involuntary action.

MIXED ACTION:　　Not all forms of action, however, can be easily classified under the headings, voluntary and involuntary. The captain who throws off his cargo to save his ship in a storm is representative of what Aristotle calls a mixed action. On the one hand, the storm may be said to have compelled the captain to throw away property, for no one voluntarily gives up property without just cause. On the other hand, it was up to the captain to decide whether to risk the safety of the passengers and save the cargo, or to jettison the cargo and save the passengers. When he chose to throw away his cargo, he did so voluntarily for the sake of the immediate good which would result from the action: namely, the saving of the lives of the crew and passengers. Two things are clear from this example. 1) The mixed action is closer to a voluntary than an involuntary action. There is no doubt that the captain was responsible for his action, and liable to praise or blame from his superior upon his return to port. 2) The morality of an action (its goodness and badness) can only be determined from a knowledge of the particular circumstances which accompanied the action. Because the captain was in a situation of crisis, we cannot say that throwing away property that was not his own was a bad act. Once more, Aristotle insists that morality is relative, because ethics is concerned with particular concrete actions rather than with universal principles.

ACTING FROM COMPULSION:　　Aristotle realizes that some people can so rationalize a situation that they can say all acts are voluntary or all acts are involuntary. These who say that all acts are voluntary argue that the brain gives the command for the hand to move and the foot to walk. Without this voluntary action on the part of the brain, no one would act at all. Those who say that all acts are involuntary and done from compulsion, argue that every act is done either for the sake of pleasure or for a noble objective. Since the pleasing and the noble are outside of us, such persons hold that they "force" us to act. Aristotle says both views are untrue. The pleasure that we get out of doing anything is inside us, so we cannot say that it is an object external to us. To act under compulsion is to act when the cause of action is outside the actor, and he can do nothing against it.

INVOLUNTARY AND NON-VOLUNTARY ACTIONS: In his analysis of action, Aristotle makes a third distinction between involuntary actions and what he calls non-voluntary actions. This distinction is part of his concept of what it means to act from ignorance. For example, when a man criticizes his secretary but, seeing how upset she is, feels sorry for his action, he has done an *involuntary* act. This means that he did not realize what the results of his action would be, and if he had, he theoretically would not have done it. Thus, he is not really responsible for hurting his secretary, because he did not intend to hurt her. If, however, he criticizes his secretary, sees how hurt she is, and feels no pangs of conscience afterward, Aristotle says his action is *non-voluntary*. It is plain the girl's boss feels neither one way nor the other about his action. Therefore, the question of consent or non-consent to the action does not enter the picture.

INVOLUNTARY, NON-VOLUNTARY, AND IMMORAL: An action can be non-voluntary (that is, done neither with nor without the consent of the agent), but this does not mean it is outside the limits of the moral code. Aristotle tries to explain the relation between involuntary and nonvoluntary as they relate to a moral code by looking at examples of acts of ignorance. He distinguishes two kinds of ignorant acts: those due *to* ignorance, as was that of the executive who did not realize the consequences of his action; and those done *in* ignorance. For example, the actions of a drunk may be due to drunkenness and anger. But the man is actually acting *in* ignorance, because when he is drunk, he does not know what he is doing. This is the situation of every criminal, in Aristotle's opinion, since the criminal is really *in* ignorance of what he ought to do. Now, a crime cannot be called involuntary, if the doer does not know what is good for him, for it does not involve the conscious consent to, or rejection of, the act in terms of "what ought" to be done. But there is no doubt that crime is immoral. Aristotle says that not knowing *what* one ought to do makes men wicked. Thus, it is ignorance in *moral* choice and ignorance of general moral principles that make an act immoral, whereas ignorance of the particulars which surround an action and ignorance of the issues involved make an action *involuntary*. For example, "stealing [to take by stealth another person's property] is wrong" is a universal principle. "This horse is another person's property" is a particular circumstance. Therefore, to take this horse by stealth is stealing. Now, if you did not know that the horse belonged to another person and you took it away, your action would be involuntary. If you did know it belonged to someone else, but stole it anyway, your action would be immoral. Virtue is applying the right principle to the particular circumstance.

ACTS DUE TO IGNORANCE: Aristotle says that a man can be ignorant of the particular circumstance that surrounds an action in either one of six ways or in all of them. You may not know 1) who is doing the action. Some psychotics, for instance, do not know when they themselves do something. Normal people are, of course, seldom in doubt as to who is performing an action. 2) The doer may not know what he is doing, i.e., the kind of action it really is. 3) He may not know who or what will be affected by the action. 4) He may not know what kind of instrument or tool is used in the action. For example, a child may strike someone with his toy, not realizing that the edge is sharp. 5) He may not realize the consequence of the action; and 6) he may not know the manner in which the doer acts. For example, I can slam a door shut and break a pane of glass, not realizing the force of my action.

VOLUNTARY ACTION: All action which does not fall under the heading of "due to compulsion," or "due to ignorance," including non-voluntary action, is voluntary. The man who stole the horse, knowing that it was another person's property, committed both an immoral and a voluntary action. This means that Aristotle puts all actions which are either calculated or done in passion under the heading of voluntary actions. We can choose to restrain our emotions, he says. That is why we say children can act voluntarily. The irrational emotions are as much a part of man as his calculating reason. It is a man's duty to avoid all wrongdoing. One might argue that a man who commits a crime in a fit of passion does not know what he is doing at the moment of the crime. Such a problem frequently confronts our judges who have to decide whether a murderer is mentally sick or actually responsible for his act. Psychiatrists generally agree, however, that there is a difference between the legally responsible and the psychotically sick. Although most criminals are suffering from some psychosis, they are nevertheless aware of what they are doing. Aristotle might say that their actions are non-voluntary in the sense that the moral rightness or wrongness of the action does not enter their thinking. In conclusion, it would seem that Aristotle's inclusion of criminal acts and acts of passion under voluntary action was essentially a sound thing to do.

CRITICISM OF ARISTOTLE'S ANALYSIS OF ACTION: The chief criticism that has been aimed at Aristotle's classification of action is that it does not allow for a real moral struggle. A man can know that it is wrong to do some particular act. He can fight against doing this act, and yet end up doing it anyway. A man driven by hunger can engage in stealing with the full knowledge that it is wrong to steal. Again, he can do some act because he knows it is a good thing, although he dislikes doing it. In many respects, Aristotle still remains under the influence of Socrates' teaching, "Virtue is knowledge." He firmly believes that if you know what is good for you, you cannot want to do otherwise. Aristotle, and the Greeks in general, had little concept of duty, (doing something that is morally right, but personally unpleasant).

CHOICE: A discussion of voluntary and involuntary action leads Aristotle naturally to the problem of choice, for voluntary action is the result of deliberate choice.

CHOICE IS SIMILAR TO A WISH BUT NOT A WISH: Choice is not the same as voluntary action. On the other hand, it does not seem to be an emotion, an appetite, a particular kind of opinion, or a wish. Aristotle thinks it is nearest to being a wish, although it is not a wish for the following reasons. 1) We may wish for the moon (i.e., for the impossible), but we cannot *choose* to have the moon. Choice concerns that which it is possible to have. 2) We can wish that the Dodgers win the baseball pennant, but we cannot choose them to win. Their victory or defeat is not within our power to bring about. Choice therefore is about something which is in our power to do. 3) We can wish to be healthy, but we choose to take the medicines to bring us back to health. This example shows that wishing is of ends, choice is of means. Choice, therefore, involves the means of obtaining something possible which it is in our power to have.

CHOICE AND DELIBERATION: If choice is none of the foregoing, is it then a thought process; is it deliberation, or, as we might call it, decision-making? Aristotle thinks it is for the following reasons. 1) Deliberation is about what can be done, 2) about what it is in our power to do, and 3) about means rather than ends. An example of moral decision-making is the following. If I am deciding whether to go to college or not, I first have to consider whether it is possible for me to go to college. Then I have to decide whether a college education is within my power to acquire. Am I college material? Finally, I have to decide whether I have the means to go to college. Where am I to get the money for college? How am I to support myself? If my deliberations lead me to answer "yes" to all these questions, then I can say, "I choose to go to college," and make my choice accordingly. The practical result of my choice, my enrollment at the nearest university, is the end of my deliberation. Action is thus the result of choice, which is the result of deliberation.

DEFINITION OF CHOICE: In conclusion, Aristotle defines choice as "a deliberate desire for things that are within our power." He makes it clear that choice is about means, and not about ends. Wish is about ends, namely about the highest good for man, happiness. He observes that the more moral a man is, the more the truly good will be the object of his wishing. Most men, however, wish for anything that seems good or strikes their fancy. This does not mean that Aristotle thinks that there is an absolute standard of happiness by which the moral man may regulate his wishes. Rather, the good is a relative thing. The better the man, the better his wish. In this passage Aristotle extends his relative philosophy. In his earlier work, *On Philosophy,* he argued that where there is a better, there must be a best. This argument led to a relative best for each class of natural being. In the *Ethics,* however, it seems as if Aristotle had rejected the concept of a relative best in favor of a relative better.

> **COMMENT:**   Although in this passage Aristotle says choice is about means, not ends, elsewhere he identifies choice with purpose. It is clear that choice is not only about means; there can also be a choice of ends. Perhaps the realization of this fact led Aristotle to use *proairesis,* or choice, more and more in the sense of purpose.

A MAN IS RESPONSIBLE FOR HIS ACTS: Aristotle's definition of choice is his answer to Socrates' belief that no man is voluntarily bad or voluntarily unhappy. Since voluntary action is a result of choice and choice depends upon ourselves, virtue and vice are both within our power. Happiness, by definition, is a result of voluntary action, but a man can also be voluntarily bad.

Several examples will show why. 1) If we look at our laws, we can see that they do not say what we shall eat, for that is not within the power of the lawmakers. But the law does say that it will punish criminals and honor good men, thereby proving that virtue and vice are within our power. 2) When a criminal pleads ignorance, the jury is not impressed. The court merely answers: "you ought to have known," meaning that it is a man's duty, because it is within his power to know and obey the law. 3) A man becomes bad by habitually doing bad actions. Some try to rationalize their conduct by such an excuse as "I cannot do anything about my laziness. Laziness is part of my character." Aristotle's reply is, "yes, you are responsible. You became lazy by doing nothing, and by no other way. You were not born lazy." 4) A fourth and more subtle argument that a man is not responsible for his actions is the Sophistic one of appearances. The Sophists argue, "we did not mean to be unjust. We did what appeared to us to be the just thing to do." Aristotle's reply to this argument is that a man is responsible for the type of moral character he develops. We are all responsible for what things seem good to us, for our goals are determined by the kind of person we are. If this were not so, virtue would be less a product of man's free will than vice, and we have seen that a bad man willingly chooses to be bad. Furthermore, if everything was a matter of appearance, there would be no virtue and no vice. A man should pattern his idea of the good after that of a wise man. Aristotle is firm that the development of character is within our power and that we are responsible for developing it. We become the type of person we choose to become in the sense that we choose to get off to a good start. The actual change in our personality, however, comes bit by bit, as habit gradually forms our character. Moral development is within our power because we can control the beginning of character formation, even though we cannot control the actual change.

BOOKS III AND IV
THE MORAL VIRTUES

CLASSIFICATION OF THE VIRTUES: The end of Book III and the whole of Book IV are given over to a discussion of the moral virtues (the virtues of character) in the light of the definitions Aristotle has just made. Since the virtues have been seen to involve both feeling and action, Aristotle proceeds to classify them with their corresponding vices in the following manner. 1) There are three virtues concerned with the right attitude toward the three emotions of fear, pleasure, and anger. 2) There are four virtues concerned with man's right attitude toward his practical activity in society. These virtues involve man's attitude toward money and honor. 3) There are three virtues concerned with man's right attitude toward living in society, such as self-appraisal, wittiness, and friendliness. Finally, there are two "mid-points of feeling" which cannot strictly be called virtues, namely modesty and righteous indignation. The following table of Aristotle's virtues and vices has been adapted from a similar table by the well-known Aristotelian scholar, W. D. Ross.*

ARISTOTLE'S VIEW OF THE MORAL VIRTUES: Aristotle's discussion of the moral virtues is in many places full of common sense and perceptive observation. His treatment of courage, for example, carefully distinguishes the truly courageous man from the man who is merely pretending to be brave. His insight into the virtue of self-control is even more valuable, and forms the basis of the later Christian virtue of temperance. Aristotle viewed self-control as the fundamental virtue. He identified it with the most elementary of all the senses—the sense which every animal has in common, the sense of touch. Because of its animal origin, the vice of debauchery, or excessive self-indulgence, is the worst of all vices because it reduces the man who practices it to the level of animals. In this sense, it cannot really be considered a "human" vice at all. The control of this basic appetite is, in Aristotle's view, the first step to becoming a man, in the full sense of the word. Thus, he warns that the appetites must be checked at an early age and put under the control of reason, if a child is ever to become a mature individual. On the other hand, Aristotle makes it clear that self-control does not mean a puritan approach to life. Aristotle would probably have had little understanding of religious asceticism, for he felt that all men naturally enjoy the sensual pleasures of life. He says there is no name for the "creature, who takes no pleasure in such things" (non-indulgence in sex), since he "is scarcely to be found." In his view, self-control involves a healthy, moderate approach to the pleasures of wine, women, and good food.

LIMITATIONS OF ARISTOTLE'S VIEW OF THE VIRTUES: In other respects, Aristotle's discussion of the virtues seems to be somewhat limited. When Aristotle speaks of courage, he primarily means physical courage. The soldier who faces death on the battlefield is courageous, for example. But Aristotle never discusses the

*W. D. Ross, *Aristotle, a Complete Exposition of His Works and Thought* (New York: Meridian Books, 1962), p. 198.

FEELING	ACTION	EXCESS VICE	VIRTUE	DEFECT VICE
1. fear		cowardice	courage	none
confidence		rashness	courage	cowardice
2. pleasure, or bodily desire (mainly touch)		debauchery	self-control	insensibility
3. anger		short temper	gentleness	apathy
	1. giving of money	extravagance	generosity	stinginess
	taking of money	stinginess	generosity	extravagance
	2. spending of money on a grand scale	vulgarity	magnificence	niggardiness
Practical Activity	3. pursuit of honor on a grand scale	vanity	high-mindedness (self respect)	humility
	4. pursuit of honor on a small scale	ambition	none	lack of ambition
Life in Society	1. behavior in social relations	obsequiousness (flattery)	friendliness	grouchiness
	2. behavior for relaxation	buffoonery	wittiness / charm	boorishness
	3. self-appraisal	boastfulness	truthfulness	self-depreciation
Mean states of feeling	1. shame	bashfulness	modesty	shamelessness
	2. pain at others' good or bad fortune	envy	righteous indignation	ill will

courage it might take to be an inventor, a colonist, or a daring thinker. With twenty centuries of Judeo-Christian experience behind us, we have been accustomed to believe that there is a courage that is higher than purely physical courage in the face of death—namely, moral courage.

THE GREAT-SOULED MAN: Similarly, there is something about Aristotle's discussion of the "crown of the virtues," high-mindedness, that is not very appealing. The main reason for our lack of sympathy with this virtue is that it is largely determined by the Greek taste of Aristotle's times. There is no doubt that his high-minded man is a man of principle and integrity. He also is a man of property and high station. "Principle" and "property" combine to make a somewhat stuffy individual, "slow in step," and "deep in voice." He also seems to be rather self-centered; for example, he is ashamed to receive favors from people, because he feels this will put him in an inferior position. Nevertheless, he will always pay back favors that he has received with even greater ones, so that he will put everyone in his debt. Again, he will try to win the respect of good men, but will not cater to the common mass of men. He has more admirable qualities, however: he will not act rashly, but only when something needs to be done. He will not seek public office out of pure ambition. He bears no grudges, speaks the truth, and is unassuming toward the common man. Finally, he is steadfast in the face of misfortune and will not complain or ask for help, no matter what befalls him. Aristotle's view of the Ideal Man can be better understood when we realize that, like his entire approach to morals, it is essentially an aesthetic one. The high-minded man is one who does everything with a sense of proportion. Even his slow step and deep voice are aesthetic qualities. We may wish that he had a little less of the statuesque about him and a little more humanity; but in so wishing, we are judging good character from our point of view, not from that of the Greeks.

BOOK V
JUSTICE

JUSTICE—THE HIGHEST SOCIAL VALUE: In the analysis of the virtues given in Books II and III, justice was not discussed, mainly, because it is somewhat different from the other virtues. In one sense, justice is the virtue of all the virtues. The just man is necessarily the virtuous man *par excellence*. But in another sense, justice really forms part of a social, not an individual, ethic. As the highest social value, it regulates all human activity in society. It is at once 1) the prevailing "disposition toward choice" in a given society, and 2) the standard regulating individual social behavior for the citizens of that society.

GENERAL AND PARTICULAR JUSTICE: In the opening chapter of Book V, Aristotle carefully develops these two meanings of justice. "Just," he says, can mean what is *lawful*. And it can mean what is *fair* and *equal*. Aristotle assigns the first definition of "just" to the exercise of justice "in relation to the whole." This kind of justice he calls general or universal justice. General justice, or what is lawful, is the type of justice which can be identified with virtue. A man is virtuous when he obeys the law, which itself is based on an understanding of what virtue is. Justice is different from virtue, however, in that it refers to the social aspect of virtuous behavior, an aspect which the word *virtue*, by itself, does not cover. The second meaning of justice is based on "what is fair and equal." Aristotle calls this kind of justice, *particular justice*—justice as it relates to the individual. Since the concept of justice as the social virtue really belongs to the study of politics, Aristotle confines his inquiry into the nature of justice in the *Ethics* to particular justice.

PARTICULAR JUSTICE: Aristotle defines particular justice on the basis of its corresponding vice, *particular injustice*. Particular injustice, he says, is taking more than one's share. Consequently, particular justice must be taking one's proper share. As with all the virtues, justice is a mean between taking too much and taking too little, but it is nearer to taking too little. Aristotle distinguishes two kinds of particular justice. 1) The first kind of particular justice relates to the fair and equal distribution of common goods (i.e., of honors and wealth) in society. It regulates who gets what public office, and defines the economic composition of society. This Aristotle calls *distributive justice*. 2) The second kind of particular justice regulates returning what is one's due in relations between man and man. Justice in this sense corrects injustices in private deals. Aristotle says that private deals are of two kinds: *voluntary deals,* such as buying, selling, and lending money at interest, and *involuntary deals*, such as theft, poisoning, murder, and bearing false witness.

JUSTICE AS THE FAIR DISTRIBUTION OF COMMON GOODS: The Greek word for "fair" is *isos*, which also means "equal." Aristotle readily admits that justice is only possible if it is based on some kind of equality. The problem is, what kind of equality will be really just? In order to understand what Aristotle means by "distributive justice," or the fair and equal distribution of common goods, we must remember that the Greeks thought of government posts as common goods, which were to be distributed among the citizens of a given society. The way in which you could become a government official, such as a magistrate or a city councilman, was based on the way in which offices were distributed. Whether an office was elective or acquired by appointment was incidental, in their view, to the principle of distribution, which said what kind of citizen could hold office. Now, different societies are founded on different principles. The democrats, maintains Aristotle, say the basis of distribution is free birth. Oligarchs say it is wealth, and aristocrats say it is excellence. Whatever basis you choose, that basis determines the form of your state, whether it is a democracy, an aristocracy, or an oligarchy.

DISTRIBUTIVE JUSTICE AS A DISCRETE PROPORTION: Fair distribution, according to Aristotle, involves two people and two things to be distributed. There are two shares (i.e., honor or wealth) and two individuals who want the shares. It stands to reason that the two people concerned are not equal in birth, wealth, or virtue. Similarly the two shares involved are also not equal either in merit or in monetary value. Justice is, in this case, the matching of people to shares, so that the relative position of the two people to each other remains the same as it was before. Just distribution matches the right person to the right share. Aristotle puts it in the form of a ratio. A and B are two people; c and d are two jobs. Now, A:B as c:d at the beginning of the transaction. This means that A:c as B:d. It therefore follows that (A plus c): (B plus d) as A:B. The last proportion expresses a "just" distribution.

> **COMMENT:**   Aristotle's use of words in his explanation of distributive justice throws light on the Greek view of the state. He talks about the state distributing "shares" in the government, just as we talk about shares on the stock market. In the sense that every Greek was a shareholder in the interests of his city, the Greek city state can be viewed as the "honest stock broker" making sure that the right stock goes to the right citizen. We will find this idea recurring in the *Politics*.

JUSTICE AS RETURNING WHAT IS DUE FOR INDIVIDUAL GOODS: Justice in this case is the mean point between the two extremes of gain or loss. Here, there is no question of the worth of the two people involved. The law does not ask whether a good man has stolen from a bad man; it looks only at the particular deed. If a judge is deciding a case of stealing, for instance, his aim is to restore the balance that existed before the stealing took place. In arriving at a just formula for what he calls *corrective* justice, Aristotle assumes in his example that the thief gained something by his stealing. Now, if A is the victim, B is the thief, and C that which was stolen (perhaps not the actual stolen object, but its value in money) the situation before the action happened may be expressed mathematically: (A plus C) equals (B minus C). After the stealing, B has become, (B plus C). A is now, (A minus C). To restore the balance, the judge has to return C to A. The last equation reads, (A minus C plus C) equals, (B plus C minus C). Justice has been achieved.[1]

JUSTICE AS RECIPROCITY IN ECONOMIC DEALINGS:

The Pythagoreans taught that justice was simple reciprocity; in their view, returning evil with evil and good for good was the whole of justice. Aristotle rejects this view as being too simple. We have already seen that distributive and corrective justice are not based on mere reciprocity. Aristotle says that we can find a more complex kind of reciprocal justice in transactions between private businessmen. This type of justice is based on what he calls proportionate reciprocity, whose mathematical expression is a diagonal combination of terms. For example, A is a builder; B a shoemaker; c, a house; and d, a pair of shoes. To effect a fair deal between these four, we must establish 1) *proportionate* equality between the goods,

---

[1] Aristotle's concept of corrective justice is usually diagrammed in the following fashion:

```
      A          E                      A'
      /          /                      /
      ——————————————————————————————————
      B                                 B'
      /                                 /
      —————————————————————————————
  D   C          F                      C'
  /   /          /                      /
  ——————————————————————————————————————
```

Before the theft took place, the line AA' was equal to CC'. But CC' took away what properly belonged to AA', namely, AE. Thus, after the theft, AA' was less than CC' by the amount AE, and CC' was more than AA' by the amount DC. In the new situation, therefore, AA' is reduced to EA', while CC' has been increased to DC'. The judge only sees the new unequal relation of EA' to DC'. It is consequently up to him to decide what the value of AE is, as expressed in terms of CF, so that he can take DC, an amount equal to CF, away from DC' and give it to EA' in order to restore equality. The judge's just decision is represented by BB', in terms of which AA' is made equal to CC'.

by 2) establishing *reciprocity* in value between the goods.[2] This means that we have to find some common denominator in terms of which to express the value of both the house and the shoes. The problem is: in terms of what can we express the value of the house (c), so that we can find out whether it is more or less than the value of the shoes (d). The obvious answer is that we can express both in terms of money, for, in Aristotle's own words, "money measures all things." But our problems are not yet over. How do we determine the *real* value of the product? Aristotle says that we can measure the real value of the product in terms of demand. We can only make a deal with those who need what we have to sell. It may happen that A does not want to buy B's shoes. The absence of A's demand for shoes will leave B with nothing to exchange. There may be another man, C, however, who is in need of shoes, and who will sell B food in exchange for B's shoes. But B does not want to buy C's food. If we can express the demand-value of A's house, B's shoes, and C's food in terms of money, our troubles are over; B can buy A's house with the proper amount of money, and C can buy B's shoes, and all three will have some guarantee that they will be able to exchange their products again in the future, because there is a durable medium of exchange, namely, money. When you have money, you can buy what you need at the moment for a just price, and not be forced to sell your product, which others at that time may not need, at its lowest demand-value. For this reason, Aristotle calls money, "the great measurer, and the proportionate equalizer of goods."

JUSTICE DIFFERS FROM THE OTHER VIRTUES: Aristotle has covered all the meanings of justice in the economic, social, and public sphere. In conclusion, he aptly points out that justice cannot be considered the same kind of virtue as the other virtues for several reasons. 1) It is not a mean (relative to us) between two opposing "unjust' vices, but is something which is realized in a mean amount. 2) Justice is the quality in terms of which we can say a man is just, because he practices by choice what is just. If a man gives his

---

[2] Aristotle's concept of a fair exchange, or diagonal reciprocal justice, is usually drawn like this:

In a fair exchange, the product (c) of the builder (A) goes to the shoe-maker (B), while x amount of product (d) of the shoemaker (B) goes to the builder (A), where (c) is equal in value to (xd).

neighbor neither more nor less than his due amount, we say he is just. If he never desires more nor less than what is his due share, we also say he is just. 3) Injustice is related to vice in the same way. It itself is not an excess nor a deficiency, but it is a quality which tends toward excess and deficiency. Aristotle concludes that injustice is a "violating of proportion." Justice, therefore, is both the external and objective *observance* of proportion and the internal and subjective *sense* of proportion.

POLITICAL AND NON-POLITICAL JUSTICE: Aristotle now turns to refinements in the meaning of justice. The first distinction is between political and non-political justice. 1) Political justice is only possible "among men who share a common life in order that their association bring them self-sufficiency, and who are free." Political justice is between free citizens in an independent state. 2) Political justice exists only among men "whose relationship is regulated by law." Where a dictator rules, there is no justice, because the dictator takes what he wants (the "lion's share") and is not satisfied with receiving what he deserves. 3) Political justice cannot properly be said to exist in a household, because reciprocity is only possible between two equal persons. A slave, however, is inferior to his master, a son is less than his father, and a wife is unequal to her husband. Thus, Aristotle believes that only citizens can act justly toward one another in the complete sense of the word. He thinks justice in the home a lesser kind of justice. What is just toward one's wife is what is just in the management of the household, since the husband and wife share the household as equals. But this relationship is a degree lower than that between citizens. It follows that the relationship of father to son is lower yet, and that between master and slave the lowest of all.

NATURAL AND CONVENTIONAL JUSTICE: This particular distinction formed the basis of Roman legal theory. Aristotle's concept of general justice became the Roman, *ius gentium*. This is the law of nations, which holds good for all times and all places. Conventional justice, the Roman *ius civile,* is law which governs a given society, and is a product of that society. Aristotle believes that there are certain general principles of justice which are the same everywhere, such as the commandment, "Thou shalt not kill." Conventional justice is that justice which is established by a law or decree to regulate a certain social problem, such as the law of capital punishment for murder. Aristotle has difficulty, however, making a clear distinction between the two kinds of justice, because the Greek word for "law" and the word for "custom" are the same: *nomos.* What he seems to be trying to say is that every law is a convention because it is man-made. But it is based on universal standards of what is just, which are the same everywhere.

RESPONSIBILITY FOR UNJUST ACTIONS: The last section of Book V is divided into three parts; in it Aristotle discusses 1) the extent of personal responsibility for a just or unjust action on the part of the individual, 2) involuntary injustice, and 3) injustice towards oneself.

INDIVIDUAL RESPONSIBILITY: When we look at justice objectively, it seems to be some kind of mean, or proportion. But when viewed from the standpoint of the man who acts justly, it takes on all the characteristics of a virtue. Justice for the individual is an attitude of mind toward choice. As in the case of a virtuous action, Aristotle makes the distinction between the unjust act and the man who acts unjustly. For example, a man can return a loan (a just action) for fear of the consequences. In doing this, he is not acting justly of his own free choice, but under compulsion. His action is thus another of those mixed actions which lie halfway between voluntary and involuntary acts. What factors, therefore, should determine our decision as to whether a man who acts unjustly is to be held responsible or not? As usual, Aristotle says he can only lay down a few general rules. He gives what he considers the four possible kinds of injury, and the varying degrees of responsibility which should be assigned to each one. 1) When an injury is committed in ignorance, it is not an unjust act at all, but an accident. The agent is not responsible. 2) When an injury occurs contrary to all reasonable expectation, it is not an unjust act, but a mishap. The agent is not responsible. On the other hand, when the injury is a result of reasonable expectation, but was not done "with malice of forethought," it is still not considered an unjust act, but is called a mistake, Aristotle says that the agent is to be held responsible. This kind of injury is similar to our definition of negligence. For example, if you leave the water boiling in a saucepan on the stove, and it boils away with the result that the saucepan is ruined, you have committed an act of negligence. 3) When the injury is done in full knowledge, but is not premeditated, this is an unjust act and the agent is responsible. Nevertheless, this does not mean that the man who committed the injury is necessarily unjust himself. For example, to injure someone in a fit of anger is an unjust act for which you are responsible, but the jury will not view your case as severely as that of a hardened criminal. 4) When a man harms another by deliberate and premeditated choice, he not only acts unjustly, but his unjust act is the action of an unjust man, for which he should be duly punished.

INVOLUNTARY INJUSTICE AND UNJUST TREATMENT: Aristotle then turns to consider involuntary injustice and unjust treatment. After looking at the problem from all sides, he decides that no one suffers unjust treatment voluntarily, of his own free will. The problem of doing an injustice *involuntarily* is more complex. Take a situation where a judge is supposed to award a piece of land in an inheritance case. 1) It is possible that the judge will be misinformed or that he will not have all the necessary information given him. Nevertheless, he makes his decision on the basis of law. Is his act just or unjust? Aristotle makes a fine distinction. He rules that the judge's decision is a just one in the sense that it is in accordance with the law, but it is unjust in the real meaning of the word. For it is not in accordance with a principle of universal justice, but with principles of conventional law. 2) A second possibility is that the judge knows all the facts but makes his decision for personal reasons of favoritism or revenge. Aristotle says that in doing this, the judge is not only acting unjustly, in the sense of going against the law, but he is also acting contrary to the universal principles of justice, as a proportion. He is receiving "more than his share" in the transaction, insofar as he expects to gain more than is due him. For example, he might rule in favor of the wrong man because he has been bribed to do so or because he has been promised a higher office if he so rules. The question in both cases is: is the judge's decision an involuntary, unjust act? Aristotle seems to think that in the first case the judge's decision is definitely an act of involuntary justice. In the second case, it is a mixed action. The Judge is not acting unjustly for the sake of acting unjustly, but for some other reason. It is not easy, Aristotle says, to act really justly or unjustly. To do so, you have to be consistently just or unjust, on principle. Both kinds of action require a habit of mind firmly disposed to act in that way. For this reason, he says realistically, most people only indirectly act justly or unjustly. They seldom act out of full knowledge or from a pure motive. Usually, they resort to unjust acts for the sake of some larger gain. Thus, it is hard for the large majority to believe that the truly just man cannot act unjustly. They think that the just man is no less capable of committing unjust acts than the unjust man, because they do not understand that he has acquired a basic habit of mind that prevents his choice of an unjust act.

INJUSTICE TOWARD ONESELF: After another legal excursion which concerns nice distinctions between the just and the equitable, Aristotle turns to the last problem relating to his concept of justice. Is it possible to be unjust to one's self? He concludes that a man cannot act unjustly toward himself in the strict sense of the word.

Justice and injustice are social virtues. In their performance, they require some one other than the agent as their subject. To act unjustly, you have to act unjustly toward someone outside yourself. Second, although acting unjustly and suffering unjustly are both evils, suffering unjust treatment is less bad than inflicting it. Consequently, a man will never willingly harm himself, if he knows he is doing it. Aristotle thinks there is one sense, however, in which a man can be said to act unjustly toward himself. Referring to Plato's thesis in the *Republic* that the justice of the soul is when each part of the soul is performing its proper function, Aristotle says that it is possible to consider the relationship between the irrational and rational parts of the soul a matter of justice. Thus, when the irrational part of the soul governs the rational soul, its action could be considered an act of injustice, because it is the function of the rational soul to rule, and the duty of the irrational soul to obey.

BOOK VI
THE INTELLECTUAL VIRTUES

CHOICE—INTELLIGENCE MOTIVATED BY DESIRE: After discussing the moral virtues, Aristotle turns to the intellectual virtues. These are the virtues which relate to excellence of thought. Choice has been seen to be the efficient cause of action, but what is the efficient cause of choice? Many philosophers since Aristotle have said that our emotions determine choice. Aristotle states categorically that the starting point of choice is *thought and desire combined*. Reason determines the "right rule" of virtuous action, what we *should* do. Desire motivates us to act. Thus, Aristotle defines choice as intelligence motivated by desire, or as desire operating through reason. Nevertheless, although reason and desire are both factors which determine our choices, reason seems to be the most important one. In order to choose correctly, we must know the "right rule." Choice, therefore, depends on the intellectual virtues.

THE INTELLECTUAL VIRTUES: The function of the intellectual faculties of the soul is to know the truth. Those habits and attitudes of mind which help the soul reach the truth are what Aristotle calls the intellectual virtues. It was shown earlier that Aristotle believes that there are two rational faculties of the soul. The first is the scientific faculty by which we understand first principles, and the nature of things which are necessary and certain. The second is the deliberative faculty, the faculty of opinion. This faculty has as its object things which "may or may not be," such as chance and the unpredictable. It is obviously this faculty which is most directly concerned with moral action. Each of these faculties has its corresponding virtues. Aristotle lists five qualities, or virtues, by which the mind attains the truth. These are scientific knowledge, art, practical wisdom, intuitive reason, and theoretical wisdom. Of these, the virtues of the scientific faculty are scientific knowledge, intuitive reason, and the theoretical wisdom. The virtues of the deliberative faculty are art, and practical wisdom.

THE VIRTUES OF THE SCIENTIFIC FACULTY: 1) Scientific knowledge is "the disposition by which we demonstrate." It is the capacity for demonstration and proof. It is the habit of thinking rationally, according to fixed rules. 2) Intuitive reason or native intelligence is that which enables us to grasp fundamental principles. Aristotle has repeatedly told us that science does not discover first principles. This is the function of *noûs,* or the intuitive reason. After experiencing a certain number of given instances, our intelligence suddenly "catches on" to the truth, which is present in those examples, and sees this truth as self-evident. 3) The combination of scientific knowledge and intuitive intelligence produces wisdom. Theoretical wisdom, or *sophia,* is directed at "those things which by their nature are most valued and most prized." It has as its object not only the truths of metaphysics but also those of mathematics and natural science. Since theoretical wisdom is aimed at the "noblest objects in creation," it follows that this is the highest type of knowledge there is. For this reason, Aristotle considers a life given over to the contemplation of "the most precious things, which have the crown of perfection upon them" the most perfect life a man can have.

THE VIRTUES OF THE DELIBERATIVE FACULTY: The faculty which governs opinion has two virtues: art and practical wisdom. 1) Art, or applied science, is the capacity or trained ability of making things according "to a true rule." The virtue of art has two aspects. a) You must know the rules governing the creation of the art object; b) you must understand the purpose, or function, the object is to serve. For example, when you make a design for a house, you should not only think of structure and building materials. You must also take into consideration whether the building is to be used as a home, a garage, an office, or a church. 2) Practical wisdom, or prudence, is the "capacity or habit of deliberating well about what is good and advantageous to oneself." Practical wisdom is a true disposition toward acting in matters involving what is good for man. A combination of foresight and intelligence, it applies the scientific knowledge of the structure of things as a means of solving particular problems in particular situations. It is concerned with the relative goods which are the object of desire and intelligent conduct. Since it is oriented toward action, Aristotle considers the possibility of practical wisdom being distorted by pleasure or pain. Although pleasure and pain cannot destroy scientific conviction, nor artistic principles, he thinks it can destroy the right disposition towards action. Practical wisdom has three aspects: a) It is the quality of seeing what is good for oneself and thus is directed at the good of the individual. b) It is the quality of seeing what is good in the household management, or *oikumenia*. c) It is directed at the good of mankind, and in this capacity, is called politics, or political wisdom.

THE RELATION OF PRACTICAL WISDOM TO THE OTHER IN-TELLECTUAL VIRTUES: In the next chapters Aristotle develops his concept of practical wisdom.

PRACTICAL WISDOM AND POLITICAL WISDOM: Aristotle says that practical wisdom and political wisdom have similar characteristics, but they differ in their object. The former is primarily active in the life of the individual, and the latter operates chiefly in the life of the state. Aristotle says there are two kinds of political wisdom. 1) The first is the "supreme and comprehensive" form of political wisdom, the ability to legislate well. Thus, we say that a workman "does" things, but a legislator "engages in politics." 2) The second aspect of political wisdom is the administrative faculty, which Aristotle subdivides into the decision-making faculty and the judicial faculty. As political wisdom is not the proper subject of the science of ethics, Aristotle leaves a full discussion of it to the *Politics*.

PRACTICAL WISDOM AND INTUITIVE INTELLIGENCE: Practical wisdom is not scientific knowledge because it is concerned with particulars, not universals. It is not theoretical wisdom because it is concerned with ultimate particulars, not ultimate universals. Aristotle calls actions "ultimate particulars." Is it then something like intuitive intelligence? Aristotle says it is a kind of perception directly opposed to intuitive reason. *Nous* grasps the universal in the particular, while practical wisdom aims to know only the particular fact. As the intuitive reason perceives universal principles, practical wisdom grasps individual facts. The two have this in common: 1) they are both a direct perception. But one grasps the essence of the individual; the other, the essence of the particular. 2) They both possess perception, not as the result of long deliberation or a thought process, but as an immediate understanding of "what the whole thing is all about."

PRACTICAL WISDOM AND DELIBERATION: Practical wisdom is not something that precedes deliberation, but is the capacity and habit of deliberating well. As scientific knowledge is concerned with the scientific syllogism, practical wisdom is concerned with deliberation, or the practical syllogism. For example, if A is the ends, and B, the means, then B should be done. It is the mark of the man of practical wisdom to deliberate well. Good deliberation, however, does not depend on a long process of reasoning. It is the product of applying general principles to particular circumstances. It is the habit of correctly sizing up a situation, of evaluating the problem at hand in terms of its general characteristics, and then deciding the way it is to be handled and the time it is to be done. Practical wisdom is the direct appraisal of a situation. It is thus the "first principle" of deliberation. As the intuitive reason gives conviction about the first principles of science, so practical wisdom gives conviction about the first principles of decision-making—namely the end of action, "for the sake of which" the action is undertaken. Aristotle realizes that some people may know from experience how to handle a situation without knowing the major premises which govern such situations. Consequently, he says that it is better to know the conclusion of the practical syllogism and not the major premise, than to know the major premise of the syllogism and not know the conclusion. In simple language, this means that he realizes it is better to know what to do in a certain situation without completely understanding the reason why, than to know the exact reason for doing something without knowing what to do.

PRACTICAL WISDOM AND UNDERSTANDING: These are not the same although both are concerned with matters about which "doubt and deliberation are possible." The difference between the two is that understanding passes judgment, while practical wisdom issues commands. For example, a judge first understands (i.e., forms an opinion) why a man committed the crime he did, and then his practical wisdom decides what kind of punishment the man will receive.

PRACTICAL WISDOM AND GOOD SENSE: Practical wisdom is not the same as good sense, because the former is acquired by experience and the latter is a natural endowment. Like intuitive intelligence, good sense is something people are said to be born with. A man of practical wisdom can develop from a man of good sense; but if you do not have good sense, you will never have practical wisdom. Aristotle realizes that every man is not capable of everything. He can only develop the abilities with which he was born. Thus, the fruit of native intelligence is theoretical wisdom. The cultivation of good sense over a lifetime results in practical wisdom. For this reason, Aristotle tells us, we should listen to the opinions of wise and experienced men, even though they cannot be demonstrated. "For experience has given such men an eye with which they can see correctly."

THE USE OF THEORETICAL AND PRACTICAL WISDOM: Aristotle goes on to review all the objections as to why we need both practical and theoretical wisdom. Three questions may well be asked. 1) Why do we need theoretical wisdom, which is only concerned with eternal unchangeable reality, and not with the day-to-day problems of our world of becoming? 2) If the aim of practical wisdom is to help men become good, what use is it to men who have already become good? 3) As for those who are not yet good, would it be better if they consult a wise man as they would consult a doctor and not try to acquire theoretical wisdom? Aristotle's answer is Plato's answer. You cannot have theoretical wisdom without practical wisdom. You cannot know what is good unless you have had the experience of doing the good, and *vice versa*. He develops his reasons why both theoretical wisdom and practical wisdom are necessary. First, both of them are desirable in themselves, for each is the virtue of a different part of the soul. Second, both are necessary, for both produce something. Practical wisdom is obviously the cause of right action; theoretical wisdom is also a cause. It is not an efficient cause, however, but a formal cause. As health is the formal cause of healthiness, so theoretical wisdom is the formal cause of happiness. For wisdom, in a sense, is what happiness is; it is the essence of being happy. Third, a man cannot act intelligently without the use of practical wisdom and the practice of virtue. Moral virtue trains us to aim at that which is really good for man, which is determined by theoretical wisdom; practical wisdom makes us use the right means to achieve that good. In this connection, Aristotle makes the important point that practical wisdom cannot exist without virtue. If it does, it degenerates into mere cleverness. Cleverness is using the right means for the wrong ends; it is knowing how to seize an opportunity to get what you want. Aristotle never tires of saying that a man may perform a just action and still not be acting justly. He may be acting from expediency. But a man cannot act like a good man without becoming good. And he cannot become good without knowing what a man's final good—happiness —is. His reasoning runs in an endless circle. "The eye of the soul," or the intelligence, cannot "acquire the characteristics of practical wisdom," which alone makes possible the development of theoretical wisdom without the practice of virtue. Vice distorts the first principles of action. Aristotle concludes that only a good man (i.e., a virtuous man) can judge correctly what the good end of man is, and that no man can have practical wisdom unless he is good.

PRACTICAL WISDOM AND VIRTUE: Thus practical wisdom depends on virtue and virtue on practical wisdom. Aristotle admits it is possible for a child to have a "natural" virtue. He may be naturally brave or naturally kind, for instance. But to act virtuously, without consciousness of what the right behavior is, is to act instinctively, "without vision," as one blind. The full development of moral virtue requires training in practical wisdom. Consequently, Socrates was wrong in saying that all virtues are forms of knowledge, but was right in thinking that there is no virtue without knowledge. Virtue has been defined as an attitude of mind directed toward choice, which is guided by right reason, or practical wisdom. Right reason is thus a part of virtue, but is not the same as virtue. In one sense, practical wisdom can be said to imply all the moral virtues. The man who lives by reason and does not follow his instincts, must necessarily develop his moral character.

SUMMARY OF PRACTICAL WISDOM: In summary, Aristotle says that practical wisdom is necessary if a man wants to be truly virtuous. 1) It is the excellence of an essential part of our soul, namely the deliberative faculty. 2) There can be no right choice without it, in view of the fact that virtue "makes us aim at the right end, and practical wisdom makes us use the right means." 3) Practical wisdom is not the same as virtue, as Socrates thought, but all the virtues are united to practical wisdom as to a rational principle.

PRACTICAL WISDOM AND THEORETICAL WISDOM: Aristotle ends his discussion of the intellectual virtues by summarizing the relation between practical and theoretical wisdom. He thinks that practical wisdom is subordinate to theoretical wisdom. "Practical wisdom has no authority over theoretical wisdom or the better part of the soul, any more than the art of medicine has authority over health." Theoretical wisdom determines eternal principles. Practical wisdom, as the executor of theoretical wisdom, issues commands on the basis of these principles, not to theoretical wisdom, however, but in its own interests. To say that practical wisdom is not related to theoretical wisdom in this way, says Aristotle, is to say that "politics governs the gods."

BOOK VII
MORAL STRENGTH
AND MORAL WEAKNESS

SELF-CONTROL AND LACK OF CONTROL: In the first part of Book VII, Aristotle investigates another method of finding out the relation of the rational soul to desire. First he looks at those vices which are generally thought to be a sign of moral weakness: vice, lack of self-control, and bestiality. Then, he looks at their corresponding virtues: moral virtue, self-control, and the opposite of bestiality, which Aristotle thinks is some kind of superhuman virtue. The purpose of this inquiry is to determine the cause of moral weakness. Is moral weakness the result of knowledge or of ignorance? At the outset of his inquiry he defines moral weakness as the absence of proportion in personal conduct. He then goes through an intricate and involved analysis of the problem, which leads him to the conclusion that a man who is morally weak really acts in ignorance. 1) At the moment when he acts, he does not know that he is doing the wrong thing. His action seems good to him because it gives him pleasure. 2) It is incorrect to believe that the morally weak man merely *thinks* that what he is doing is right. If his action was simply the result of a little rationalization, you could convince him by reasoning with him that he is wrong. The reason you cannot persuade him to change his behavior is that the opinions he holds about his conduct have become an indelible part of his character. As practical wisdom becomes an essential part of the virtuous character, so opinion becomes rooted in the life of a morally weak character.

THE CAUSE OF IMMORALITY IS NOT THE IMMORAL: Aristotle's analysis of moral weakness is full of sound observations. In his view, the cause of immorality is almost never the immoral, insofar as it is immoral and therefore wrong. The cause of immorality in most cases is the desire for something which seems good, both because it is immediately pleasing and because the morally weak man has accustomed himself over a period of time to think it *is* good. Moral weakness is thus ingrained insensitivity to moral principles. In his account of moral weakness, however, Aristotle makes no mention of those situations where you know the right thing to do but your desires pull you the other way. He makes no room for the existence of a real moral struggle. A true Greek, Aristotle believed that the truth was so attractive that no lesser object could divert the attention of a moral man from it. Nevertheless, he did suggest in Book I of the *Ethics* the possibility of there being a moral victory, such as attends the man who has struggled over his baser desires and conquered them.

BOOK VII
PLEASURE

WHAT IS PLEASURE?   In the last part of Book VII and in the first part of Book X, Aristotle turns to a discussion of pleasure. He starts by saying that pleasure is the cause of both good and bad actions, and gives three popular views on the subject. 1) Some say that pleasure is not a good at all. 2) Others say that some pleasures are good, while some are not. 3) A third group thinks that pleasure may be some kind of good, but is not the highest good.

ARGUMENTS IN SUPPORT OF THE THREE VIEWS: Those who say that all pleasures are bad, says Aristotle, give the following arguments to support this thesis. 1) Pleasure is a process, a coming-to-be, leading to the natural state of the subject. But the process of change is not of the same worth as its end. For example, a house is the end of the process of building. As such, the house is the real good of the building process. 2) Self-controlled men avoid pleasure. 3) A man of practical wisdom does not pursue the pleasant, but what is free from pain. 4) Pleasures are an obstacle to good sense; they prevent a man from sound reasoning. 5) There is no art of pleasure, but every good is the result of some art. 6) Finally, pleasure cannot be a good, because children and animals, who do not know what the good is, still run after pleasure.

Those who hold that some pleasures are good and some are not, give two reasons for their view. 1) Some pleasures are disgraceful and a source of shame. 2) Some pleasures are harmful, such as those which cause disease.

Those who argue that pleasure is a good, but not the highest good, say that pleasure is a coming-to-be, not an end or objective of human activity.

ARISTOTLE'S VIEW OF PLEASURE: Aristotle answers all these arguments in turn. He refuses to believe that all pleasures are wrong, but says that those pleasures we consider disgraceful are not really pleasures at all, and concludes that even though pleasure may not be the highest good, nevertheless, it is part of the highest good. The basis of his view of pleasure is his observation that pleasure is not a process, or coming-to-be; it is an activity.

ARISTOTLE'S ANSWER TO THE THEORY THAT ALL PLEASURES ARE BAD: Aristotle gives three reasons why all pleasures cannot be bad. 1) "Good" can be used in two ways. A thing may be absolutely good, such as a good man or a good horse, and it may be *good for* a particular person. Thus, even though you argue that all pleasures may not be absolutely good, you have to admit that there are some which are relatively good, in the sense that they are good for some person. 2) The good has two aspects: it is both an activity and a characteristic state of being. Now, it is obvious that the processes which restore us to our natural characteristic state of being are not pleasant in themselves, but only incidentally pleasant. For example, when we are sick, we enjoy drinking bitter medicine because we know it will make us well. But when we are well again, that is, restored to our natural state, nothing can make us drink bitter medicine. Pleasure, therefore, is not a process of restoration or "replenishment." It is no kind of a process at all. We say we take pleasure in desiring. But the activity of desiring is the proper functioning of that part of us which is in its natural characteristic state. Furthermore, some pleasures, like that of learning, do not involve the appetites, but only the rational part of the soul. In both cases, our soul undergoes no change, but continues to function in its natural state. Pleasure, therefore, must be some kind of good, since it is both an activity and a characteristic state of being. 3) The third and final argument against the view that all pleasures are bad stems from the second argument. Pleasure is a good because it is not a process, but an activity, and therefore, an end. For example, both the activity of desire and the activity of knowing are the actual characteristic functioning of the faculties of desire and knowing. Knowing, moreover, is an *entelechy*, which Aristotle defined in the *Metaphysics* as activity which has no other end than its own activity. Now, the pleasures of desiring and knowing result not from the process of developing these faculties, but from their proper unhindered functioning. Learning, for example, may be a torture to the schoolboy. But once he has grasped an idea, he takes pleasure in showing off the knowledge he has acquired.

DEFINITION OF PLEASURE: On the basis of these arguments, Aristotle defines pleasure as the "unobstructed . . . activity of our characteristic condition as determined by our natural state." 1) Aristotle insists that pleasure must be unobstructed. For example, as long as I can read a book without getting tired, I am taking pleasure in the activity of reading. When, however, sore eyes and a weary body begin to fill my thoughts more than the words in the book, my pleasure in reading is obstructed and soon ceases altogether. 2) It is important to note that Aristotle does not say that pleasure is an emotion. Feeling happy or gay can accompany pleasure, but it is not pleasure itself. Pleasure is not a *response* to a situation, as joy or sadness is; it is the *proper functioning* of the soul *in* a particular situation.

IS PLEASURE THE HIGHEST GOOD?   In answer to the third theory that pleasure is a good of some kind but not the highest good, Aristotle relates his definition of pleasure to his definition of happiness. Happiness, he reminds us, is the functioning of all our powers in conformity with their proper virtue. Since pleasure has been seen to be some sort of activity, it follows that the highest good must be some sort of pleasure. Furthermore, happiness is perfect and complete activity. No activity is perfect when it is interrupted. But pleasure is unimpeded activity. Therefore, pleasure must be part of the highest good. Finally, no matter what their particular object of desire, all people pursue the same thing, namely, pleasure. Therefore, pleasure must be the highest good.

ARE MOST PLEASURES BAD?   Aristotle briefly dismisses the second view that some pleasures are bad with the argument that pleasure cannot be an absolute evil. No pleasure is absolutely bad, he says, but is bad in relation to some thing. Studying, for example, can be harmful to health. The fact that pleasure is a relative thing, however, does not explain why self-controlled men avoid what the general run of people call pleasure. If these pleasures were not bad in themselves, why should the wise man avoid them? To answer this question, Aristotle devotes the end of Book VII to an analysis of the psychology of pleasure.

THE PLEASURES OF THE BODY ARE NOT NATURALLY BAD: Aristotle begins his discussion with the observation that when most people talk of pleasure, they really mean the pleasures of the body. Aristotle is too much of a naturalist and a biologist to believe that such pleasures can be bad. How can they be bad, he asks, when we consider pains of the body, which are the opposite of these pleasures, an evil? Nevertheless, it would be inconsistent with his ethical theory if he did not think that bodily pleasures can become bad if they are not used in moderation. When we say that bodily pleasures are "good," however, do we mean by this that they are good, in the relative sense of "not bad," or do we mean they are good up to a certain point? Most men think that the pleasures of the body are the most desirable. Why should they do so, if bodily pleasures are considered good only to a certain point?

BODILY PLEASURES MOST DESIRABLE?   Aristotle's answer to this question shows his deep psychological insight into human nature. He gives two reasons why most people think bodily pleasures are the most desirable. 1) Pleasure is desirable in itself because it drives out pain. The more intense a pleasure is, the more thoroughly it acts as a panacea to pain. Bodily pleasures are more in--

tense than mental ones; therefore, they seem more desirable. 2) Because of their intensity, bodily pleasures are pursued by those people incapable of enjoying more delicate forms of pleasure. Overindulgence in the pleasures of the body implies insensitivity to mental ones. Many people, he shrewdly remarks, have nothing in the world to give them joy. It is painful for them to be in a dull gray world where neither pleasure nor pain is intense. For this reason, they rush after every bodily pleasure to drown out their pain. As their boredom increases, their pleasures take more and more abnormal forms in the attempt to heighten the intensity of the pleasant feeling. On the other hand young people pursue bodily pleasure for the opposite reason. Since they are in a constant state of restlessness and excitability, bodily pleasures bring them relief from such "pain."

BODILY PLEASURES AS A PANACEA FOR PAIN ARE NOT REALLY PLEASURES: Aristotle rejects the opinion of "the many" that bodily pleasures are more desirable. If we look at the problem honestly, he says, we will admit that bodily pleasures which are pursued as a remedy for pain are not really pleasant in themselves. They are only pleasant incidentally. Drinking to drown out sorrow only temporarily cures the pain of sadness. It does not get at the root of the sorrow.

THE TRUE PLEASURES: It follows from the foregoing that Aristotle thinks that no pleasure which is capable of excess (i.e., of which you can have either too much or too little) is really a pleasure. This means that he does not consider sex, drink, or gluttony true pleasures. The habitual smoker, for instance, is constantly obsessed by the gnawing desire to have "another smoke." But the lover of knowledge is haunted by no such obsession, because it is impossible to have "too much" knowledge. Thus, those pleasures are truly pleasant by nature which stimulate the activity of our faculties in their *natural* state, such as the pleasure which accompanies knowing or healthy exercise. To eat too much or to drink too much are unnatural states, because they are excesses. For this reason, we do not really get any pleasure out of them. Aristotle thinks that most of the world is in the unfortunate unnatural condition of the man who drinks too much. If we functioned as it is our nature to function—moderately and virtuously—we would realize that the real pleasure in life is the pleasure of knowing. For "all men by nature desire to know," and knowing is the specific, particular function of man in his natural state.

REAL PLEASURE—*MENS SANA IN CORPORE SANO*:   This view of pleasure leads Aristotle to the conclusion that real pleasure is a "healthy mind in a healthy body": it is a state of mental and physical balance. Unfortunately, however, it is impossible for men to enjoy the state of real pleasure for a continued period of time. Aristotle says the continuous experience of pleasure is not "natural" to human nature. Man is not a simple body, but one composed of body and soul. This means that there is something in our very nature which tends to decay. For this reason the objects of pleasure never remain the same for us. Sometimes we run after money, and sometimes we run after women; we have a constant desire for change. Frequently, our inborn tendency to decay drives us to want a change, simply to have a change. "Change in all things is pleasant, because of some evil in us." These words of the great Greek tragedian, Euripides, go to the heart of Aristotle's concept of natural human imperfection. "Just as a man who changes easily is bad," he says, "so also is a nature [namely, human nature] that needs to change. The reason is that such a nature . . . . is not entirely good." As we saw in the *Metaphysics,* God does not change; His activity is one single and simple pleasure. Consequently, true pleasure, or the pleasure of the gods, consists in the activity of rest, rather than in the activity of motion. If we could preserve our state of balance and overcome our tendency to decay, we would also experience continuous, simple, and real pleasure.

REVISED THEORY OF PLEASURE: In Book X, Aristotle revises his theory of pleasure. In Book VII, he identified pleasure with happiness or the highest good. In Book X he says it is not the same as, but is the perfection of, the good. In developing a more complete definition, he re-examines the two most well-known views of pleasure of his day. 1) The great astronomer, Eudoxus (who was so impressed with Plato's scientific work at the Academy that he moved his own school from Cyzicus in Sicily to Athens in 368 B.C.) argued that pleasure was the Absolute Good. 2) The head of the Academy after Plato's death, Speusippus, took the opposite view. He said that pleasure was an evil. In answer to these theories, Aristotle reiterates his view that pleasure is not a process (a kind of motion), but an activity. His method of proof in Book X differs from that in Book VII and leads to a reformulation of the definition of pleasure. Process, he says, involves motion. But pleasure, like seeing or knowing, is not a motion. 1) It does not have a beginning or an end by which we can say that its motion is complete. For example, when we see a tree, our seeing is immediate and complete the moment we see the tree. We do not *start* to see and finish *seeing*. As long as we see, our act of seeing is complete and perfect. 2) Pleasure does not take place in time and space. It is not like walking, for instance. We can walk slowly or fast. We can walk in different directions in different ways. There are different parts to our walking. Pleasure has none of these qualities. It is complete and perfect at any given moment.

PLEASURE PERFECTS ACTIVITY: On the basis of these observations Aristotle comes to a more complete definition of pleasure than in Book VII. In Book VII he said that pleasure was an activity. In Book X he points out that each activity has its proper pleasure. There is one pleasure of knowing and another of smelling flowers. In this sense, the pleasure which accompanies an activity can be said to complete or perfect that activity. It is like the "bloom of youth," or the "icing on the cake." If pleasure is such a wonderful thing, why can't we feel pleasure all the time? Aristotle says we cannot because no man is capable of continuous activity. The eyes need to relax, the body needs to rest. As the eyes tire, the pleasure of seeing loses its appeal.

DO ALL MEN DESIRE PLEASURE TO LIVE, OR LIVE FOR PLEASURE?   Since pleasure perfects activity, and life is the most complete activity known to man, the question may well be asked whether all men desire pleasure, because all men desire to live, or whether all men desire life, because they love pleasure. Aristotle suggests that pleasure and life are interdependent. Each man finds that pleasure which perfects his life. This, in turn, makes life more desirable to him.

THE VALUE OF PLEASURE DEPENDS ON THE TYPE OF ACTIVITY: In reformulating his definition of pleasure, Aristotle makes the valuable observation that every activity has its own type of pleasure. This enables him to refute Speussipus' view that all pleasures are bad. Whether a pleasure is good or bad depends upon the type of activity it perfects. Not all activities are generally considered good. Thus, we cannot call pleasures those which accompany activities which are agreed to be bad. Some pleasures, for example, are only pleasures to those whose natures have been corrupted. Such pleasures cannot be called pleasures in the strict sense of the word. We should rather call them secondary pleasures. Only those pleasures "which complete the activities of a perfectly happy man, can be called pleasures in the true sense." This means that the good man is to be our standard in matters of pleasure as he was in matters of virtue.

PLEASURE COMPLETES HAPPINESS: In answer to Eudoxus, Aristotle says that pleasure is not the highest good, or happiness, because it is something which perfects an activity. It follows therefore that when pleasure accompanies the activity of happiness, it must transform the happy life into something blessed by the gods. Happiness perfected by pleasure is beatitude.

SIGNIFICANCE OF ARISTOTLE'S VIEW OF PLEASURE: We may object to Aristotle's insistence that pleasure is primarily of an intellectual nature. But his whole view of the nature of man emphasizes the fact that man is a rational animal. It is man's function to know. Consequently, real pleasure can only be the pleasure that accompanies the activity of knowing. In the *Metaphysics* Aristotle described the nature of God as pure knowing, whose very activity was pleasure. There is little doubt that he believes man's chief end is to realize this activity insofar as it is humanly possible. If we accept Aristotle's view of human nature, we must admit that his treatment of pleasure carefully avoids two very modern pitfalls. The first is the tendency to consider pleasure an end in itself. The second is the puritan approach that all pleasure is evil.

BOOKS VIII AND IX
FRIENDSHIP

INTRODUCTION: In the previous books, Aristotle has looked at morality from the standpoint of the individual alone. In Books VIII and IX he considers the problem of virtue as it is involved in personal relationships or in what he calls *friendship*. The Greek word *philia* has a much wider usage than our word, friendship. 1) It refers to the relationship toward a person to whom one is attached, just as our word friendship does. 2) It is used to describe the relationship one has toward one's wife and children or toward anything that is "dear" to one's heart and mind. 3) Finally, *philia* can mean the bond which holds members of an association or a community together, such as the relation between a buyer and seller or the relation between rulers and ruled. *Philia* in this sense refers to the kind of bond that gives otherwise unrelated individuals "something in common." Because friendship has personal, social, and political significance, Aristotle devotes more space to it than to any other subject in the *Ethics*. "Friendship seems to hold states together," he says. Man can only fulfill his function of acting intelligently by living in a community. His relation to others is thus an important factor in the development of his character. Much of what Aristotle has to say on the nature of friendship, however, seems rather remote to us. Therefore, since it does not contribute anything to his fundamental principles of ethics, but is the logical outcome of them, we shall but briefly review his discussion of friendship here.

DEFINITION OF FRIENDSHIP: "To be friends," Aristotle says, as always starting with a definition, "men must have good will for one another, must each wish for the good of the other, and must each be aware of one another's good will." There is no friendship unless all three of these conditions are present.

THREE KINDS OF FRIENDSHIP: Aristotle's broad interpretation of friendship is evident in this definition. Friends must each wish for the good of the other. What distinguishes the various kinds of friendship is the kind of good which is the object of our affection. Aristotle shrewdly observes that it is what we love which determines the kind of friendships we make. Broadly speaking, we love three things: the good, the pleasant, and the useful. Thus, 1) we can be friends with someone because we think he is going to be useful to us, either socially, politically, or in business. This type of friendship is best understood through our expression "to use our friends." 2) We can be friends with someone because we take pleasure in his company. Friendships based on the natural delight in another person's company are particularly common among young people, although most social friendships fall into this category. 3) Finally, we can be friends with someone from a pure and good motive. We wish our friend good for his sake, not for what we can "get out" of the relationship. Needless to say, this is the best kind of friendship there is, and indeed, the only perfect friendship in the strict sense of the word. For friendships based on pleasure are unstable. When the reason for the friendship is gone, the friendship is destroyed. But friendship based on virtue will last as long as the friends keep the same character.

FRIENDSHIP BETWEEN EQUALS AND UNEQUALS: Friendships are based on two types of relationships. There can be friendship between equals and friendship between unequals. Friendships between unequals are those which exist between a man and his wife or a man and his son. In social significance, both equal and unequal friendships are present in the state and form the bond which distinguishes the kind of a state it is. A democracy is friendship between equals. Monarchy is parental, or unequal, friendship. And a tyranny is no friendship at all. As Aristotle suggested in his discussion of justice, the bond of friendship is dependent on the idea of "the just" which governs a given society.

IT IS BETTER TO GIVE THAN TO RECEIVE: Much that Aristotle has to say about friendship seems mechanical and lacking in human kindness. As one would expect from his concept of the mean in regard to the other virtues, friendship is also a kind of mean. It is giving your equals what they deserve and not wanting more than your due from them. And it is giving your unequals what you think they deserve and accepting the honor due you from them. Nevertheless, Aristotle is too shrewd an observer of human nature not to be intrigued by the question: is it better to give or to receive affection? Most people, he comments dryly, prefer to receive affection. To have a lot of friends gives one status. It seems as if other people are paying you honor. Aristotle is sure, however, that the essence of friendship is the giving of affection. In one of his favorite examples, he notes that giving more than she receives is the mother's typical way of showing affection to her children. Still, this type of relationship is a very special one. Aristotle feels that giving as much affection as the other partner is worth is the best rule for a long friendship.

OBLIGATIONS OF EQUAL FRIENDS: To give your friend as much friendship as he deserves raises the question of the obligation of equal friends to one another. Aristotle says that relations based on usefulness or pleasure demand a "tit-for-tat" arrangement. The giver expects a favor in return. In a relation based on virtue, however, the man who gives expects to receive an even greater gift in return—in the sense that both friends are looking for the good and expect to receive the good in return for giving virtue. Book IX goes farther into defining the obligations of business partners to one another in an effort to determine what friends owe to each other.

WHY FRIENDSHIPS BREAK DOWN: Aristotle is perceptive in his analysis of why friendships fall apart. Friendships break down, he says, when the two friends discover that the basis of the friendship was not what they thought it was. A social friendship, for example, breaks down, when one partner says, "I thought he liked me for myself, but I see he just wanted to use me." Friendships also break down when one of the partners becomes more mature than the other, or in some way becomes superior to the other. Marriages, for instance, frequently "go on the rocks" when the husband realizes that his wife has not kept up with his mental development.

SELF-LOVE—THE FIRST PRINCIPLE OF FRIENDSHIP: The most significant part of Aristotle's discussion of friendship is his theory that self-love is the basis of all friendship. The true friend is an egoist (a self-centered person) in the fine sense of the word. For the true friend is he who wishes all the goods he would wish for himself for his friend, for his friend's sake. In order to do this, he must first learn to love what is lovable and desirable in himself, namely, the rule of right reason in his soul, and then he can wish this good for his friend. A true friend considers his partner another self. To prove his point, Aristotle analyzes the difference between a good man and a criminal. A good man, he says, wishes and does what is good for himself. He wants what is good with every faculty of his soul, because he is at peace with his soul and not torn by conflicting desires. This is not selfish self-centeredness. It is the product of the hard discipline of learning to know one's self for what one is and making the best of one's abilities. For Aristotle, self-knowledge is really self-love. The criminal, on the other hand, possesses none of these qualities. He is not at peace with himself. This is evident from the fact that men who have committed crimes frequently take their own lives. Moreover, most criminals hate to be alone with themselves and always have to be with other people. Aristotle concludes that a bad man really hates himself because he finds nothing lovable in himself.

SIGNIFICANCE OF ARISTOTLE'S VIEW OF THE FIRST PRIN- CIPLE OF FRIENDSHIP: In his view of self-love as the basis of friendship, Aristotle is expressing a concept familiar to present-day analytic psychiatry. In simple words, he is saying, "if you don't love yourself, you cannot love anyone else." For you judge or evaluate other people by what you are yourself. Your own character is your standard for measuring other people's character. The average man realizes the many defects he has, how full of suspicion he is, and how lacking in capability he is. He tends to attribute his own weaknesses of character to those around him. Distrust breeds mistrust. Since few people can directly experience any type of character other than their own, it is almost impossible for them to conceive of anyone being *really* different from them. Aristotle says that the good man is one who knows what is good in himself. Thus he can see the good in another man, for all goods are lovable, by defini- tion. As he loves the good in himself, so he loves the good in his friends.

CRITICISM OF ARISTOTLE'S VIEW OF FRIENDSHIP: Al- though Aristotle shows psychological insight in saying that self-love is the basis of friendship, his application of this principle is not very satisfactory. It tends to make friendship a very self-centered activity. Aristotle tries to make his position more clear by distin- guishing between different types of self-love. Some men, he says, try to get all they can out of a relationship by way of money, honor, or pleasure. Obviously, there is nothing praiseworthy in their kind of self-love. Good men, however, are anxious to stand out from the general run of men by their reputation for virtuous and noble actions. It is this kind of self-love which motivates the virtuous man to give away all the money he has to his friends. In so doing, the virtuous man believes he is "getting more" from the friendship, for the friend merely "gets" money. But the good man "gets" the noble deed. Similarly, the good man will even give up his public office so that he may get the credit for a virtuous action. It is evident that this view of friendship as an extension of the self is not very successful in explaining the real motives for altruism or generosity. Aristotle has been justly criticized for it.

THE IMPORTANCE OF FRIENDSHIP: Aristotle insists that friendship is one of the most important things in our life and one of the hardest things to acquire. 1) Friendship is necessary for our character development. For this reason, we need different kinds of friends at different periods in our lives. Friends are particularly needed during periods of misfortune. Moreover, a man is known by the company he keeps. A man can only become good in the company of good friends. Consequently, Aristotle feels that it is not important to have many friends, but to form those few valuable friendships which are based on character and virtue. 2) Friendship is necessary for the attainment of happiness. Aristotle's view of happiness is much influenced by Plato's theory of *koinonia,* or fellowship. Plato taught that knowledge could be achieved through the dialectic. He viewed the dialectic as a continuous conversation between like-minded individuals who were joined together in the common desire to find the truth. In many ways, Plato's *koinonia* was similar to a religious fellowship. Aristotle agrees that the good life can only be achieved through the intellectual companionship of one good man with another. His final definition of friendship is that it is "a partnership for life in search of the truth." He believes friends should live together, because "from the mold of the other, each takes the imprint of the traits he likes, whence the saying, 'Noble things from noble people.' "

BOOK X
HAPPINESS

INTRODUCTION: Aristotle has completed his discussion of the moral and intellectual virtues. He has determined the role that friendship and pleasure play in acquiring these virtues. Now he is ready to return to his original interest in Book I, the nature of happiness. Aristotle considers the subject of happiness a fitting conclusion to the *Ethics* because every part of the moral life has been shown to have happiness as its goal.

DEFINITION OF HAPPINESS: From Book I, we know that happiness is essentially an activity. It cannot be an amusement because amusement is not desired for itself, but for the sake of something else. For these same reasons, happiness is not study, leisure, or a practical pursuit, although it depends on all of these. Happiness is activity in conformity with virtue, especially in conformity with the highest virtue. Thus, happiness is activity in conformity with the intellectual virtues of intelligence and theoretical wisdom. True happiness is *theoria*, or the contemplation of eternal truths for an entire lifetime.

> **COMMENT:**   The Greek word *theoria* is usually translated as "contemplation." It is derived from the word "to see," or "observe," as is our word "theater." *Theoria* is really a "seeing" or "observing" of the truth, in the same way that theater-goers see a play. Consequently, we must not think that Aristotle understands happiness as "a thinking about" the truth. Happiness, for him, is the mind's direct seeing of the true and the good. Thus, *theoria* is an experience, or a kind of life, as seeing is a kind of life. This means that our knowledge of the truth is certain knowledge based on experience. As you know the tree is, by seeing, so you know the truth is, by *theoria*.

WHY THE HIGHEST HUMAN HAPPINESS IS THE CONTEMPLATION OF THE TRUTH: Aristotle gives many reasons in support of his view that *theoria* is the highest happiness of man. 1) Reason is the highest faculty in man, and *theoria* is the activity of reason. 2) *Theoria* is the most unimpeded kind of human activity. We can keep it up longer than any other kind of activity, such as exercise or artistic creation. 3) Pleasure has been shown to be a part of happiness, and Aristotle has proved that intellectual activity gives the most pleasure. Furthermore, "the life of he who knows is pleasanter than that of he who is learning." 4) The philosopher is the most self-sufficient of all men. Although he too needs the basic necessities of life, such as external goods and friends, nevertheless, he can live on only moderate means because he is happy and virtuous. Moreover, he is not dependent upon his friends. Although he enjoys their company, he can get along better than others without them, for he is able to stay alone with himself and "to think his thoughts in solitude." 5) Philosophy is loved for its own sake and not for the sake of something else. 6) The life of contemplation is the only kind of life we attribute to the gods. If *theoria* is divine, it necessarily must be the highest human happiness.

A LIFE OF CONTEMPLATION IS NOT HUMANLY POSSIBLE: Aristotle is realistic enough to realize that a life spent in contemplation is more than a human life. Man is made of both a rational and non-rational soul. Consequently, to live only the life of the rational part is not within human power. A life guided by intuitive intelligence (*nous*) is as far above human life as the virtue of intuitive reason is above the virtue of practical wisdom. A life guided purely by intelligence is divine. Nevertheless, Aristotle says we should not listen to those people who say that we should forget the divine and only have human thoughts. "On the contrary, we should try to become immortal as far as that is possible and do our utmost to live in accordance with what is highest in us. For this small portion of our nature far surpasses everything else in power and value. One might even regard it as each man's true self."

THE LIFE OF PRACTICAL WISDOM ALSO IS HAPPINESS: Although Aristotle feels that a life of *theoria* is the highest form of human happiness, he is ready to admit that a life guided by practical wisdom and moral virtue should also be considered happiness. 1) The life of practical wisdom is concerned with the whole man. It involves our emotions and actions, as well as our rational soul. Since it involves the composite being of man, Aristotle says that a life guided by practical wisdom is "particularly human." The life of the intellect, he says somewhat strangely, is "separate," presumably from the particularly human. 2) A life lived according to practical wisdom and moral virtue prepares us for the life of contemplation. Without practical wisdom and virtue, we would be unable to live the higher life. We cannot attain the highest human happiness until we have disciplined our passions. Just how a life of practical wisdom prepares us for the life of *theoria*, Aristotle never makes clear.

THE OBJECTS OF CONTEMPLATION: In this last book of the *Ethics*, Aristotle does not tell us what the objects of *theoria* are. What do we see, when we see the truth? In his discussion of theoretical wisdom, he said that the subject matter of mathematics, natural science, and metaphysics are the objects of *sophia*, or wisdom. It is therefore probable that the life of contemplation is also directed at these objects. We should not think, however, that Aristotle assigns any religious meaning to *theoria*. As we saw in the *Metaphysics*, the Greek mind did not fuse together the highest object of metaphysics, namely, the First Cause, and the objects of religious adoration, the gods. Thus, we should think of *theoria* not in terms of religious contemplation, but of direct contact with the truth, whatever that may be.

IS THE REALLY HUMAN REALLY DIVINE?   Aristotle's two statements that a life of *theoria* is divine and that the life of the intellect is "separate" bring out the essential dilemma of Aristotle's ethical theory. Its moral relativism conflicts with his view of human nature. Aristotle has devoted a whole book to a discussion of human virtue as it relates to human action. In most of this discussion he has said that we can find out what is the good, wise, and pleasing from the good man. This good man is not an Ideal Man, however; he is merely good, relative to us. Indeed, Aristotle's whole approach to morality is rooted in the conviction that human goodness as an absolute, objective value does not exist. Yet, despite his relativity, at the end of the *Ethics* he cannot rid himself of the feeling that there must be something *more* than human in us, which alone enables us to become perfectly human (i.e., good). In *On the Soul*, Aristotle mentions the possibility of what he calls an "agent intellect" existing as something eternal and divine within us. In the *Ethics*, we find him still indefinite as to whether *nous*, or the intellect, is divine or not. Socrates had a direct experience of ultimate value, if we are to believe Plato's account. Plato shared in this experience as his pupil. So profound was the effect of Socrates' experience upon Plato that Aristotle cannot lightly dismiss the mystical aspect of Plato's philosophy. Consequently, he is unable to resolve the paradox that in living up to his "true self," man is living beyond the purely human, and participating in something divine. This means that by virtue of his "natural" ability to participate in the divine, man is subject to an absolute value. The moral virtues prepare us for this life, while the intellectual virtues enable us to lay hold on it. The problem of the *Ethics* is the major problem of Aristotle's philosophy. In none of his writings is he able to explain why man, to be truly human, must live his life according to more than human standards.

ETHICS—A PREPARATION FOR POLITICS: At the end of the *Ethics*, Aristotle returns to the world of human action. The study of individual and social morality has been shown to be necessary if we want to become good statesmen and lawgivers. Aristotle has proved that we can only become good 1) through knowing what the good is, and 2) through habit and training. He has also defined the nature of man's true happiness and demonstrated what the various virtues are. He is now ready to take up the larger investigation, the nature of politics.

THE *POLITICS*

POLITICS—THE STUDY OF THE STATE: We have seen in the *Ethics* how a man's character depends on the society in which he is brought up. To learn how to act intelligently, one must live in a community which believes that it is important to act intelligently. In order to perform his function of living according to reason, a man must have a field of action in which to operate. This field is the state. In the *Politics,* Aristotle investigates "that larger science" of which ethics is a part. The *Politics* is thus Aristotle's book on government. It tells us what Aristotle thinks government is and what good government *should be.*

ORDER OF THE BOOKS: Like all the rest of Aristotle's books, the *Politics* is a collection of teaching notes, which Aristotle used while he was at the Lyceum. For this reason, it has come down to us in a confusing form, and there has been much speculation about the "early" or the "late" politics. None of the books seems to relate directly to the one which follows. But we shall put aside the interesting question of the development of Aristotle's political theory. If we take the books in order, we shall find Aristotle at work with his usual method. The work falls into four sections, corresponding to Aristotle's four causes. In Book I, he states the first principles and definition of the state. He then proceeds to examine the "out of what" the state comes, namely, the *material cause* of the state. In Books II-IV, he deals with the structure of government, the *formal cause,* or the constitution of the state. In Books V and VI, Aristotle looks at the sources of change and stability in a given society, or the *efficient cause* of change in the state. Finally, in Books VII and VIII, Aristotle investigates the *final cause* of government. What is the purpose of government? What should be the aim of good government?

BOOK I
THE RAW MATERIAL OF THE STATE

DEFINITION OF THE STATE: In his discussion of friendship in the *Ethics,* Aristotle had said that the state was some kind of

193

association. In the opening chapter of the *Politics*, he explains what kind of association the state is. It is that association which is "most sovereign"; it includes and controls all other associations for the purpose of attaining the highest good, namely, happiness.

THE NATURAL ORIGIN OF THE STATE: "Man by nature is a political animal." This is perhaps the most important sentence of the *Politics*. In saying that man is a *political* animal, Aristotle means that man is meant to live in a civil community. He has what is known as a social instinct, which tells him that he should live with others like himself. This instinct may be likened to the instinct that tells birds that they should fly in flocks; Aristotle calls it a *natural* instinct. Man does not have to go to school to learn that he must live in groups. He is simply born with the desire, or inclination, to do so.

THE STATE: The organization which makes man's group-life possible we call the state. Aristotle and the Greeks called it a *polis*. Aristotle wants to make it quite clear that the state, or *polis,* is not just another association. The principle of *rule* or subordination is present in every type of association and, indeed, in nature at large, he argues. But political authority is different from all other types of authority. To prove his point, Aristotle turns to consider the nature of the *polis* in relation to what he holds are lesser forms of human association. The rest of Book I is taken up with this problem. First, Aristotle examines the state as the formal cause of man's development. Then, he discusses the state as the final cause, the end product of man's historical search for self-sufficiency. He gives special attention to the association of the household in order that there be no confusion later as to the difference between household management and political rule.

COMMENT: The ancient Greeks did not think of themselves as citizens of a particular country, as we think of ourselves as citizens of the United States. The form of state they knew was the city. Actually, the city of Athens was much smaller than any modern city, but these small cities were the kind of state Aristotle and the men of his time were used to. From the Greek word for city, *polis,* come our English words, "political" and "politics." Originally, these words had to do with the running of city affairs. Now they refer to the running of national affairs. Aristotle uses the word *polis* throughout the *Politics* in two senses: 1) in the particularly Greek sense of city-state, and 2) in the more general sense of "state" or "society."

STATE—THE ONLY ENVIRONMENT WHERE MAN CAN BE MAN: Aristotle tells us that the *state* answers man's social instinct to live in groups, to form a community. Thus, like the instinct, the state is also natural to man. A strictly human life is difficult to live all by one's self. In this sense, the state is the only place where one can say that man exists as man because he is endowed with the gift of language. For example, if a man lived all his life in the jungle, he would be more like the wild animals than a man. Probably, he would not be able to talk, and he would have no idea of culture, science, and all those things we think are part of our daily life. Because man *is* a social animal, Aristotle says that the state is *prior* to the individual. "Prior" comes from the Latin word meaning "before." The idea, "state," comes from the idea, "man." You cannot understand what man is without first knowing what the state is, in the same way that you cannot understand what a seed is without first seeing the tree.

HISTORICAL DEVELOPMENT OF THE STATE: Historically, of course, man came before the state, as Aristotle makes clear. 1) First there was the union of man and his wife. This was the smallest kind of what we call a *family*. 2) The family changed into a *household* after children were born, and slaves or servants were employed.

> **COMMENT:** Ancient Greek society was a slave society. A family did not hire a maid or butler who would work for pay. The master of the house went down to the market, and bought the number of slaves he needed. Aristotle talks about the rule of a master over his slave, not about relations between an employee and his employer. For the slave is the property of his master, and is owned by him. We shall learn more about the master-slave relationship later.

3) When a group of families got together, they formed what Aristotle calls the *village*. Finally, the last step was taken. A group of villages agreed to unite and formed the first state.

> **COMMENT:** It has been pointed out that Aristotle's state was a small city. In his view, a group of villages united to form a city. Today, we could go further. From history we know that a group of cities can unite to form a province or a state, for example, New York State. Finally, our own history tells us that groups of states can unite to form one nation. It is even possible for several nations to unite and form a federation, such as the Soviet Union or the Federation of the Congo.

REASON FOR SOCIAL EVOLUTION—A BETTER LIFE: Aristotle tells us that the reason for this development from the family to the state is that with each stage man sees that he can live a fuller and happier life. 1) Only the state provides man with self-sufficiency. Not being self-sufficient, "all individuals," Aristotle tells us, "are so many parts all equally depending on the whole, which alone can bring self-sufficiency." 2) The state is the only association where man's subordination to other men is ordered on principles of justice, fairness, and equality. The structure or ordering of the political association, Aristotle asserts, is based on "the determination of what is just." The *polis* makes men of unequal economic, social, and intellectual backgrounds equal by virtue of their sharing fairly in the benefits the political association has to offer. The members of the household are not equals. The father is the head of the house, while his wife is his near equal. The children are under their father's control until they are old enough to take care of themselves. The slaves are the property of their master, living an almost subhuman kind of life. For this reason, they can never become citizens in Aristotle's view.

"STATE" AND "NATION":   How big should the state be? How much land should it cover, and how many people should live in it? A state is bigger than a village, since it is made from a group of villages. On the other hand, Aristotle thinks that a community can be too big to be a state in the proper sense of the word. "There is a limit to the size of the state as to other things, plants, animals, tools; for none of these keeps its function when it is too big or too small. Either it wholly loses its identity or is spoiled." The largest population which Aristotle would like a state to have is "the largest number which suffices for the purposes of life, and can be taken in at a single glance."

     COMMENT: Aristotle's idea of the proper size of the state fits in with his view of the Greek city which we mentioned above. The Greek city-states were small, close-knit societies. Since they were small, it is likely that everyone knew everyone else and identified himself with his city. In Greek cities, the community played a more important part in the lives of the citizens than it does for most of us now. Obviously, the deep loyalty we would feel toward a city which has become the center of our lives cannot be shown so easily towards a large country or a nation. Even Brooklyn or Queens is probably too large to call forth the feelings which Aristotle thinks are necessary for his city-state.

THE FUNCTION OF THE STATE: From what has been said above, it can be seen that what Aristotle calls a state means a pattern of living, *a way of life.* He does not believe that a state has done its duty when it sees that there is a police force or a sanitation system. Aristotle thinks that the state is not just a "society," established for the prevention of crime where men can buy and sell. These are conditions without which a state cannot exist, but all of them together do not make up a state. A state is more than an economic unit. It is "a community of well-being in families and groups of families for the sake of a perfect and self-sufficient life."

THE COMMUNITY OF WELL-BEING: The key to what Aristotle thinks the state is, is found in the words, "a community of well-being." For example, Aristotle would not agree that a policeman is a guarantee of a good life to a group of citizens. Policemen are necessary because there are thieves and murderers in every state. But a policeman does not make a healthy society. He just lays the foundations for one. "A community of well-being" suggests a kind of life in which men *live well.* For instance, when we talk of the American way of life, we are not talking only of our government or our supermarkets. We are referring to everything that makes up America: the countryside, the government, the high standard of living, free enterprise, democracy—in a word—all of what are called our values and social relationships.

STATE'S WELL-BEING—ITS CONSTITUTION: Should a Frenchman or a Japanese ask us where he could find the best picture of what we mean when we say, "the American Way of Life," we would tell him to read our Constitution. In the same way, Aristotle tells us that what a state's "well-being" is can be found in its constitution. For a constitution best explains the many strands of the web of social relationships. Change the constitution and you change these relationships. In other words, if the form of the constitution is changed, the pattern of the state's way of life is changed, and thus the state itself changes its form. To put it in Aristotle's words, "the sameness of the state consists chiefly in the sameness of the constitution, and may be called or not called by the same name."

LIMITS ON THE STATE'S UNITY: Aristotle does not think that the state is so important that the individual is nothing in comparison to it, or lives only to serve it. This is the view of totalitarian governments. Aristotle attacks his great teacher, Plato, precisely because the latter taught that the "state is the individual written large." As the hands move at the command of the man, so the individual must carry out the wishes of the state, in Plato's view.

Aristotle argues that the state should not be so uniform that the individual has no other wish than to obey his rulers. "Is it not obvious that a state may at length reach such a degree of unity as to be no longer a state—since the state is to be a plurality?" Plurality means made of many; unity means made of one. Aristotle thinks that a state is made of many kinds of men. To turn the individual into a cog in the wheels of the state destroys the purpose of the state, which is the "cooperation in living of different kinds of men."

THE FAMILY AND FORMS OF THE CONSTITUTION: As we said earlier, the family historically comes before the state. Thus, the kinds of relationships that are found within the family, husband-wife, father-son, serve as models for the kinds of organization of society that are found in the state. Aristotle sees in the family models for what he calls the three "natural" forms of government: monarchy (the rule of one man, or king), aristocracy (the rule of the best man or nobility), and a constitutional state.

CONSTITUTIONAL MODEL: The models for two of these types of government are found in the way the head of the household rules his family. Aristotle thinks the way a husband rules his wife is constitutional, as husband and wife manage the affairs of the household together as near equals. The relation between husband and wife differs in one way from a constitutional state. In the state, different citizens hold the highest office at different times. In the United States, for example, we elect a different President on the average of every eight years. In the family, the husband remains the head of the household and makes the final decisions.

MONARCHICAL MODEL: The rule of a father over his children is that of a king over his subjects. The children are not slaves; they are free persons. But they must do what their father tells them to do, as a king's subjects must obey their lord or be punished. The father has a right to be "king" over his children, Aristotle tells us, because he takes care of them until they are grown men and women. He is thus their "natural" superior.

DESPOTIC MODEL: The master–slave relationship is the model for another form of government, which Aristotle does not call truly good, however. He calls the relation between a man and his slave despotical. The word comes from the Greek word *despotes* or tyrant. The Greeks used it to refer to the rulers of Asia, for they believed that there were no really free men in the

East. Everyone was owned body and soul by the all-powerful ruler. Aristotle likens this master–slave relationship to the rule of the mind over the body. If my mind orders my hand to move, my hand will move unless it is hurt in some way. It has no mind of its own. To be a slave means to be a human being who cannot think or act by himself, but must be told what to do. Aristotle believes that some men are born slaves, because their lack of intelligence makes them easily "owned" by others. A "natural" slave is one who was born or has fallen into slavery and lacks enough reason to govern himself. As the master–slave relationship is "natural," because some men are born slaves, so Aristotle thinks that despotism is a natural form of government, because there are races of men who have the minds of slaves.

COMMENT: The reason that Aristotle holds what seems to be an intolerant view of men in general is that slavery in Greek society was commonplace. Slaves were treated somewhat like domestic animals, as the property of their masters. Poorer people, of course, could not afford slaves, as is evident from the old Greek proverb, "an ox is the poor man's slave." A despotism is made of many slaves and one master. The other three forms of government—monarchy, aristocracy, and a constitutional government—are made up of freemen, men who own property, earn their own living, and are able to make decisions for themselves.

SLAVERY: Slavery was an accepted institution in Aristotle's time. Almost no one thought that owning slaves was a bad thing. As we said above, the slave was a member of the household, and if the family were rich, he lived well. In Greek times the cruelty that was shown slaves in later Roman times, or in our Southern states, seems not to have been very widespread. Nevertheless, Aristotle feels he should not call all slaves, slaves. Some are worthy of better things. There is thus "slavery by law" and "slavery by nature." "Slavery by law" covers those poor souls who were bought in the marketplace, were captured in war, or were born the sons of slaves. "Slavery by nature" has already been talked about above. Aristotle thinks no Greek is a slave by nature, since Greeks in general are the most intelligent of all men. The best "natural" slaves are the Southern peoples, who have some intelligence but little spirit. When Aristotle discusses the fate of prisoners of war who have unjustly been made slaves, he raises the whole problem of what is an unjust war, and whether it is unjust that the losers be made slaves. This problem will be brought up later in the *Politics.*

PROPERTY AND HOUSEHOLD MANAGEMENT: Since slaves were considered forms of property in Greek times, it is fitting that Aristotle should take the last chapters of Book I to discuss the relation of property to *oekumenia* or household management.

> **COMMENT:**   From the Greek word, *oekumenia,* is derived our modern word "economics." At first economics referred only to the household. Property was a private affair to the Greeks. The state regulated relations between owners of differing amounts of property, but it was not the business of the state to say how much property each man could acquire. Aristotle would agree with John Locke, the famous English philosopher of the seventeenth century, that property was prior to the state, and the foundation of the state. But he did not believe that the state existed chiefly either to protect individual property rights or to say who should have how much. The rest of the *Politics* will show how aware Aristotle was of the relation of economics to political action.

HOUSEHOLD MANAGEMENT AND NATURAL PROPERTY: Aristotle first distinguishes between the art or *techne* of household management and the *techne* of acquisition of property. The first, he says, makes use of the property acquired. The second provides the means of substance for the household. A family has to live on something. It has to eat, have shelter, and be clothed. Aristotle says that the goods which form these basic provisions of life— food, shelter and clothing—are provided by nature. Thus, the acquisition of the means of substance is "natural" and proper to man. The way in which he acquires these basic goods determines his way of life, whether it be farming, hunting, or stockraising. That property which is the means whereby a man maintains his livelihood, Aristotle calls *natural property*. Because it is natural, it is *limited* to the amount required for the needs of the household. True wealth, then, is defined as "the number of instruments used in a household or state and needed for their respective arts."

UNNATURAL ACQUISITION OF PROPERTY: There is a second way of acquiring property, the unnatural way. It is this second way which has made men believe that there is no "natural" limit to wealth and property. The second way of acquiring property takes place in the exchange of goods. A shoe, Aristotle says, can have two functions: It can be used for wearing and used as a means of exchange. But to sell a shoe for money is not the "proper" use of that shoe. Nevertheless, shoes are sold for money, because some men naturally are able to produce more than they

need and others less. The law of supply and demand regulates a
barter economy. He who produces more shoes naturally sells to
the man who has produced no shoes. The unnatural form of
acquisition comes into being when the shoes are sold for a profit.
This form Aristotle calls the retail trade, where one man buys
from one source and sells to another for a profit. It is unnatural
because in the true sense of the word, the retailer "makes money."

TWO THEORIES OF MONEY: 1) Because a man makes
money through exchange, most people think that the art of acquisition is directed toward accumulating a pile of money. They
believe that money has a *value of its own*. Aristotle thinks this is
not true. Money or currency first came into being when men
became dependent on outside sources for articles they needed. In
exchange for these articles, they sold their own products. As he
explained in the *Ethics*, the great equalizer in the exchange process is money, because it reduces every commodity to a common
measurable denominator. At first, Aristotle says, no one thought
of making a profit. Only a barter system existed. But gradually,
men came to the realization that you could exchange your goods
for a profit, and the retail trade was born. Money thus became
the starting point and goal of all exchange. 2) Other people
believe that money grew up as a *convention*, as a standard measure
by which to measure the value of concrete goods.

DIFFERENCE BETWEEN NATURAL AND UNNATURAL GAIN:
Aristotle agrees with the second view that there is a difference
between natural and unnatural (i.e., profit-making) acquisition
of property. The natural form of acquisition aims at accumulating
true wealth, in the form of tools and supplies needed to run the
household; this form of acquisition, Aristotle repeats, is limited
by the needs of the household. Unnatural acquisition aims only
at acquiring money. Some people believe that happiness means
having a super-amount of everything. This leads them to try to
accumulate money. The point Aristotle makes is that excess capital
has no real or natural use and is therefore unnecessary. As with
every activity, money-making has its proper mean, which is determined by the use to which it is to be put. The urge to make a lot
of money shows, says Aristotle, that a man is more concerned
about his livelihood than about his well-being or true happiness.
The virtuous man does not make money for the sake of making
money.

    COMMENT: Nowhere does Aristotle show himself more
a product of his aristocratic upbringing than in this section

of the *Politics*. He condemns the Greek commercialism of his day because it is inconsistent with his aristocratic outlook. As a landowner and a nobleman, Aristotle doubtless 'had all of his basic wants taken care of. It thus is difficult for him to understand the problems of, and to sympathize with, the man who has to work for a living. Most probably he takes such a firm stand against profit-making because he saw how aristocrats of his day were accumulating capital for private pleasures when they really had no need to do so. Aristotle believes that it is unaesthetic for the man who is well off, and who is of good social standing, to run after money. He feels that such a person should devote his life to philosophy and to public service. It must be admitted that his view is not very far from the nineteenth-century British ideal.

HOUSEHOLD MANAGEMENT—THE USE OF MONEY: Returning to the relation of household management to the acquisition of property, Aristotle says that household management is concerned with the *use* of property, not its *acquisition*. In general, the good housekeeper can count on nature's supplying him with what he needs. Aristotle says the only truly natural form of acquisition is taking from fruits, vegetables, and animals. The other form of acquisition, namely, money-making or retail trade, is to be censured because the money resulting from trade is made at the expense of other men.

THE WORST FORM OF UNNATURAL ACQUISITION—LENDING ON INTEREST: For interest is earned on the money itself, rather than on the exchange process which money was made to serve. Interest, therefore, is three steps removed from the results of natural acquisition.

DIVISION OF LABOR: Aristotle sets up his economic divisions of labor on the basis of the different methods of acquiring property. The natural forms are stockbreeding and agriculture. The unnatural forms are commerce, investment at interest, and selling service for hire. Examples of this last are craftsmen hired to do a particular job, or an unskilled workman selling his bodily labor for pay. Aristotle also sees a middle form between the natural and unnatural forms based on the extraction of natural resources, for example, mining metals, or gold, and silver.

MONOPOLIES: Aristotle admits that monopolies are possible and do exist in every society. Monopolies can be private or state monopolies. Their purpose is to give the man or state who owns the monopoly a sure source of money.

HOUSEHOLD MANAGEMENT AS A MORAL ART: In the last two chapters of Book I, Aristotle reviews the nature of authority in the household, which we have already mentioned. He insists that household management is concerned more with the moral goodness of its members than with economic problems, since it only deals with the use made of property after it has been acquired. He does not go into detail about what the moral goodness of the household is. Nevertheless, he does say that the goodness of each member depends on the task or function he performs in the house. It is the master's duty to guide the slaves and the slaves' goodness or duty to obey. The subject of marriage and relations between a father and his children are put off for further discussion.

BOOK II
IDEAL CONSTITUTIONS AND IDEAL STATES

INTRODUCTION: In Book II, Aristotle considers the various best forms of the state. He remarks that not only have Plato and other famous philosophers proposed models of what they thought the Ideal State should be, but many people have thought very highly of constitutions which have actually existed in history. True to his conviction that all knowledge is based on experience, Aristotle turns to find out what the "many and the wise" have thought and done in the field of constitution-making.

A CRITICISM OF PLATO'S REPUBLIC: It is to be expected that Aristotle should first look at the suggestions his master and teacher, Plato, made. Aristotle discusses in detail two ideas presented in Plato's famous work on government, The *Republic:* 1) the community of wives and children, and 2) the community of property. He starts out by saying that a political association means that the citizens have something in common. The question is what and how much should they have in common. "To be fellow citizens is to be sharers in one state," but what should the citizens share?

1. COMMUNITY OF WIVES AND CHILDREN: Plato suggests that wives and children be shared in common. Aristotle objects to this idea for two reasons: one based on the nature of the state, and the other based on the nature of man. First, he questions the purpose of this type of sharing, namely, unity. Socrates, Aristotle says, was wrong when he said that the supreme good of the state was the greatest possible unity. He gives the following reasons why a state must be composed of many different interests. 1) When a state becomes too much of a unit, it will first turn into a household, and ultimately it will evolve into a one-man state. By definition, when the state becomes only one man, it ceases to be a state. 2) A state, by definition, is a grouping of different kinds of people, all of whom perform different functions. For example, some are farmers, some are lawmakers, some are soldiers. 3) Not only is the state composed of groups of people performing different economic and social functions, but also of people who have different political positions. Even in a state where the citizens are free and equal, the fundamental political distinction between those who rule and those who are ruled always prevails. 4) Finally, a state must be self-sufficient. No state can be self-sufficient when there is too much unity. It must possess a sufficient number of different kinds of people performing those functions which will provide the necessites of life essential to its survival. Each individual makes his own contribution, and that contribution is vital for the survival of the state.

A STATE MUST BE FOUNDED ON HUMAN NATURE: The second part of Aristotle's criticism of Plato's community of wives and children is based on psychological factors, and springs from his belief that the family is a "natural" social group. 1) To do away with the family, as Plato desires, he says, is contrary to human nature. Both children and property are natural extensions of the individual. Plato says that unity will be achieved when all the citizens of a community say, "This is mine," and "This is not mine" together. Aristotle points out that this sort of collective "mine" is unhealthy. "Men pay most attention to what is their own; they care less for what is common," he wisely points out. The result of a community of wives and children will be that all children are equally neglected by every father. He imagines a sort of "watery fraternity" between relatives where 1000 are father to the same child, and each father is only 1/1000 part of a father. "It is better to be a cousin to a man, than to be his son, in Plato's fashion," he concludes. 2) Aristotle not only objects to a community of wives and children on the grounds that what is every man's business is no man's business, but gives a more basic reason. "Just as a little sweet wine, mixed with a great deal of water, produces a tasteless mixture, so family feeling is diluted and tasteless when family names have so little meaning," he says. In the *Ethics*, Aristotle indicated that the state rested on *philia*, or friendship. In the *Politics*, he argues that destroying the natural forms of affection such as the father-son relationship, will not create more love for the state, but will destroy the basis of all patriotism, namely, loving that which is your own. Second, it will eat away at the foundations of the state because it promotes an unnatural system of social mobility which will foster unrest and immorality.

COMMENT: It is interesting to remember that one of the means the Soviet government used in the 1920's to destroy the roots of the old Tzarist regime was the abolition of the family. Later, when Stalin was interested in consolidating his new state, he reversed the laws on easy marriage and divorce and introduced legislation to strengthen family ties. At the present time, there is increasing emphasis in Soviet ideology on the institutions of marriage and the family. The Soviet experience proves Aristotle's argument that the family unit is essential to a well-ordered state.

2. COMMUNITY OF PROPERTY: According to Aristotle there are three possible systems of property: 1) common ownership and common use; 2) private ownership and common use; 3) common ownership and private use. He does not consider the possibility of private ownership and private use.

PRIVATE PROPERTY—THE BEST: Plato argued for common ownership and common use. Aristotle says that the best form is private ownership and common use, for four reasons. 1) A system of common ownership of property will limit the field of action where moral goodness can develop. Your character develops when you consciously put your property at the disposal of your friends, or at the disposal of your country. When you have no property to give away, because all property is in common, you cannot learn the virtue of generosity. Plato's system would thus deprive a man of one of the chief means of acquiring virtue. 2) Plato would cut off men from a natural and rightful pleasure, such as men have when they have done someone a favor. There are pleasures, he says, which arise from the satisfaction of a natural feeling of self-love and from the satisfaction of the natural impulse to help others. 3) Finally, Plato is mistaken when he says that common ownership of property will increase the harmony and unity of the state. Lawsuits about contracts, convictions from perjury, and flattery of the rich are not a result of private property. Communism will not solve the evils that arise from human nature. Aristotle observes that those who own property in common quarrel much more with one another than those who own property separately. Aristotle insists that it is not

the economic system which produces unity and harmony in a
state. Education is the sole means of making an association of
individuals a community. By education, Aristotle means social
customs, mental culture, or what we call formal education and
legislation. These three things, and these alone, will cultivate the
right spirit toward the use of property, he says. 4) Plato's system
of communism has left out the farmers and ordinary citizens.
There is thus a danger of there being two states, not one. Consequently, the ruling class will more resemble a miltiary occupation
force in a city dependent on its wishes. If communism is the
supreme happiness, why do not the farmers benefit from it?
Moreover, Plato condemns the ruling class to rule always, de-
priving them of happiness in the interests of the happiness of the
whole state. But if the ruling class is not happy under communism because they have to rule, and the farmers are not happy
because they do not have communism, who is happy in Plato's
state? It is impossible for a state to be happy unless its individual
members are happy.

> **COMMENT:**   Many scholars have said that Aristotle was
> too harsh towards Plato in this passage. They criticize Aris-
> totle for not having read Plato carefully enough. For instance,
> Plato *did* make class divisions, according to the function of
> the various members of his state, in the *Republic*. The com-
> munity of wives and children was restricted to the two top
> classes: the warrior and guardian class. And, Plato makes it
> clear that the farmers owned private property. It can be
> argued that Aristotle was too literal in his use of the word
> *unity* in his defense of farmers and in his whole attitude
> toward the question of happiness in the state.

THE EQUALIZATION OF PROPERTY IN THE STATE: In the
next chapters of Book II, Aristotle considers three proposals to
regulate property—either by making all property equal, or by
balancing property interests one against the other.

PLATO: Aristotle first looks at the view expressed by Plato
in a later work, the *Laws,* where Plato argues for some type
of private ownership of property. Aristotle says he fails to say
how much property each citizen should have, nor does he specify
how many citizens should live in a state of a given territory. More
important, Plato does not show how one combines the elements
of democracy (common property) with monarchy to form what
he considers the best .practicable constitution. Aristotle says that
Plato's neglect of these vital problems is evident when we look

at the system of elections and the ownership of property and voting qualifications proposed by Plato in the *Laws*.

PHALEAS OF CHALCEDON: Aristotle next turns to the proposals of a contemporary of Plato, Phaleas of Chalcedon. He suggested that every citizen should have the same amount of property as everyone else. Aristotle gives several objections to this view. 1) The main one is that Phaleas stresses material factors too much and overlooks moral factors, such as education. 2) What happens to the principle of equality of property when the population has grown considerably larger? Some will be the original property owners, while others will own no property at all. 3) Equality of property does not necessarily mean equality of office. What is to be the standard for holding office? 4) Crime and vice are not due to economic causes. You can't cure crime by giving everyone the same amount of property. But you can cure it by giving everyone the same quality of education. 5) The question of how much property you distribute depends on your foreign policy, and defense needs. Aristotle feels that Phaleas has not set up a standard "best" amount of property which effectively deals with all these problems.

HIPPODAMUS OF MILETUS (480 B.C.): He suggested a threefold division in a community. There were to be three types of classes, three amounts of property, and three kinds of law. Aristotle criticizes his proposal for much the same reasons. A law-abiding habit is better than all the reforms you can propose.

CONSTITUTIONS WHICH HAVE BEEN VALUED IN HISTORY AS ALMOST PERFECT: In the last chapters of Book II, Aristotle looks at the constitutions of three of the foremost states of his day: Sparta, a city on the Greek mainland; the island of Crete; and Carthage, a Greek colony in North Africa which was a famous Mediterranean seaport. His purpose is to identify both the good and bad features of these constitutions in preparation for his analysis in Book III of what a constitution should be. As the discussion of these constitutions does not form an essential part of Aristotle's political theory and is of little general interest to the modern reader, we shall not go into it here. The important thing to notice throughout Aristotle's discussion is his emphasis on the "mixed nature" of the three constitutions. He says that all three are a mixture of democratic, monarchical, and aristocratic elements, but each of them tends to emphasize one of these elements more than the other two. Aristotle favors the Spartan constitution because he thinks it is more rooted in popular consent. He criticizes both the Cretan and Carthaginian constitutions, for being oligarchies, and observes that, despite pretensions to the contrary, they both are governed by a few powerful members of the nobility or the merchant class. He calls the constitution of Crete an *arbitrary oligarchy*, that is, it is governed by a few feudal nobles who are not subject to any binding laws. He considers the Carthaginian constitution government by the monied aristocracy. The result of Aristotle's inquiry is that he finds he can consider none of these forms of government ideal.

SOLON: The last chapter of Book II is a rough outline of the legislation of the great Athenian lawgiver, Solon, (640–558 B.C.). Since this chapter is so roughly done, many scholars believe that it was not the work of Aristotle at all, but was written by a student or added some time later.

BOOK III
THE CITIZENS AND THE CONSTITUTION

INTRODUCTION: Now that Aristotle has paid lip service to the opinions and actions of the "many and the wise," he is free to develop his own view of the formal structure of the Greek city-state. We must repeat that whenever Aristotle talks about the state, he is always referring to the state he knew, namely, the Greek *polis*, or city-state system. A state is understood in terms of its parts. Aristotle has defined the state as an association of citizens. Thus, his first important task is to define who the citizen is. As everything for Aristotle can only be understood in terms of its function, he starts by asking what a citizen does.

WHAT A CITIZEN IS NOT: In order to know what anything is, you must first determine what it is not. A citizen is not a citizen because he happens to live in a particular state. Foreigners and slaves, for example, are not citizens. A citizen is not anyone who shares in either the private or the constitutional right to sue and be sued. Foreigners also may have this right by virtue of a treaty between two states. The very young and the very old have this right, but they are not citizens, as they are considered unfit to assume the duties of citizenship. Aristotle then gives a trial definition of citizen as "one who shares in the administration of justice and in the holding of office."

DEFINITION OF CITIZEN: The problem is that citizenship means a different thing in different kinds of states. The basis of citizenship is the constitution, but constitutions differ. One could argue that citizens of a conservative oligarchy and citizens of a radical democracy have little in common. Aristotle thinks that the definition he has just given best suits the citizen of a democracy. He, consequently, amends his definition to include all types of citizenship. "He who enjoys the right of sharing in deliberative or judicial office for any period, fixed or unfixed, attains the status of citizen." A citizen is anyone anywhere who has 1) the right to have a say in the administration of justice, and 2) the right to be a member of the policy-making body of his state. For Aristotle, a citizen is essentially a person who has the right to *initiate action* by formulating policy, (i.e., making laws), and to *control* action by administering justice. In other words, a citizen is anyone who has the right to participate in the rational life of the state. It is obvious from his definition that Aristotle thought of government primarily in terms of who makes the decisions, not in terms of who carries them out. The difference between the ruler and the ruled is the difference between he who makes and he who executes the decisions. A state, therefore, is "a body of citizens sufficient to make the state self-sufficient."

> **COMMENT:** The word for rule in Greek is *arche*. It was shown in our discussion of Aristotle's method that *arche* means many things, all of them having to do with the starting of action. It may be translated as a rule, control, principle, starting point, or regulation. A ruler is primarily one who initiates action. He is the controlling or first principle in the state. It follows that he who executes action is in an inferior position. He is simply a doer. As the intellectual life rules and controls the practical life, so the ruler of a state controls those who are engaged in the practical life of the state.

CITIZENSHIP—THE RIGHT TO RULE AND TO BE RULED: There is no doubt that Aristotle excludes the majority of those who live in any state from the privilege of citizenship. It follows from his aristocratic view of human nature that not everyone is capable of participating in the rational life of the state. If we look at the relation between the ruler and the ruled, as the relation between actuality and potentiality, we will see that Aristotle thought of citizenship primarily in terms of the *right to rule*. To be ruled is potential to the act of ruling. He would argue that an unskilled workman should not be a citizen, although he might be able to say who should make the laws, because it does not necessarily follow that he is capable of making laws himself. Despite Aristotle's insistence on the value of education and tradition, he quite obviously does not believe that participation in self-government has an educative value in training men to rule.

> **COMMENT:**   In making our evaluation of Aristotle's definition of citizenship, we should recall once more that his was a slave society. Those who were free were essentially the nobility. Given his aristocratic views of human nature, Aristotle could not but believe that slaves and hardworking freemen were unfit to rule. In the *Ethics*, he stressed the point that to be truly happy, a man needed not only the goods of the soul, but external and bodily goods as well. A typical member of his society, Aristotle was convinced that a man had to have a certain number of internal and external advantages to start with in order to be a good citizen. Such an attitude, however, is not only representative of Greek society of the third century, B.C. Our Founding Fathers talked righteously of "men of property and of principle," as somehow being better and more responsible than the common mass of men. One of the great controversies of the Philadelphia Convention was over the basis of citizenship, or, as we would call it now, voting qualifications. Many of the men who wrote the Constitution firmly believed in an aristocratic view of human nature. It took till the twentieth century before men generally realized that virtue and property do not necessarily go together.

WHO IS A CITIZEN?   Some people, Aristotle says, think that being descended from citizens qualifies a man to be a citizen. But such a distinction can only apply to "old families" in the community, and is useless in saying how we are to treat newcomers. An even more difficult problem arises when there is a revolution, and when foreigners or slaves are allowed to enter the citizen body. Are these to be considered citizens on the same basis as the other citizens or not?

THE IDENTITY OF THE STATE: In asking these questions, Aristotle is trying to determine what makes a state a state. In what does its identity, or individuality, consist? During his lifetime, Aristotle was witness to countless revolutions and changes of constitution among the Greek city-states. In some cases, the government coming to power after the revolution refused to honor the contracts and obligations of the old government. The problem such situations presented was the following: in the course of a revolution, does a state forfeit its identity? In other words, does the new constitution which comes into being after a revolution represent an entirely different state, or is the new government merely a continuation of the old? Does the state as state remain the same throughout the period of upheaval? The Soviet Union posed a similar problem to the nations of the world in 1917. It refused to honor the obligations of the Tsarist Government and cancelled all its foreign debts. In evaluating the rightness or wrongness of such an action, we have to ask, "was the Soviet state the same state as the Tsarist state, or a different state?" The Soviets said they had formed a different state, but was this really the case? What makes the state what it is? Aristotle says the identity of the states does not consist in its population or territory, nor in the walls or boundaries which surround it. It is not based on sameness of ethnic stock or sameness of race; the state can change, even if its racial composition does not change, and vice versa. Aristotle believes the identity of the state is based on the constitution. When the constitution changes, the state will become a different state. The state remains the same as long as the constitution remains the same. According to his view, the Soviets would be right in saying they had formed a new state.

THE VIRTUE OF THE CITIZEN: The fact that the nature of the state is understood by its constitution helps answer the question, "what is the relation of the virtue of the good man to the virtue of the good citizen?" Aristotle considers this question from two points of view. There are many types of constitutions. It follows, then, that there must be many different standards of good citizenship. Consequently, there cannot be one single virtue of the good citizen, as there is of the good man. Aristotle discusses the question from the viewpoint of a particular constitution. Observation shows him that there must be different types of good citizens within one state, depending on the function each performs in the state. Nevertheless, in performing their functions, all citizens may be said to have a common objective: namely, the safety of the state. Thus, to ensure the safety of the state, the good man must have the virtue both of the good ruler and the good subject. To be a good citizen, one has to know how to rule and how to be ruled. Aristotle says that the difference between the two types of virtue is not so big as he first imagined.

THE CIVIC VIRTUES: The difference between the virtue of the master and that of the slave or the laborer is enormous, but citizenship, by definition, implies the rule of freemen over freemen, that is, the rule of equals over equals. One starts learning how to rule by first learning how to obey. Consequently, a good citizen will "need knowledge of government from both points of view."

CIVIC VIRTUE AS DISTINCT FROM MORAL VIRTUE: Aristotle says that the ruler and the ruled each have their own particular virtue which is the excellence of their function. The virtue of the good man, which belongs to the ruler, is prudence or practical wisdom. To the ruled belongs the virtue of "right opinion," or right feeling (i.e., the proper disposition to obey). The other moral virtues are common to both the ruler and the ruled. Aristotle concludes that the virtue of the good man, and the virtue of the good citizen can only be the same in the Ideal State, where the good citizen has acquired the virtue of practical wisdom (the essential intellectual virtue for the good man), which enables him to rule well, and the qualities necessary to make him a good subject.

SIGNIFICANCE OF ARISTOTLE'S SEPARATION OF CIVIC FROM MORAL VIRTUE: The reader may consider Aristotle's concern over the relation between the good man and the good citizen unnecessary. But we should not forget that Aristotle believes that true virtue can only be acquired in a state which provides the right conditions. The right conditions in turn depend on the type of constitution a state has. As we have seen, a state's constitution determines the identity of the state, and therefore, the relation of the virtue of the good man to the virtue of the good citizen. It follows that only in the Ideal Constitution are the good man and the good citizen identical. Aristotle's conclusion raises the whole question of whether it is possible to be a good man and not a good citizen. It raises the problem of the relation of morality to politics. Like Plato before him, Aristotle in this chapter of the *Politics* holds that politics is the master science governing human action. Yet, he distinctly separates individual virtue from the virtue of the good citizen. In proving that the virtue of the good man cannot be the same as that of the good citizen, except in an ideal situation, Aristotle suggests that the virtue of character is in some way more important than the virtue of the good citizen, because it is the test of a good man everywhere. In taking this position, Aristotle shows himself a child of his time. The Greek city-state in which he had been brought up was experiencing a slow decay. Everywhere, its values were being questioned. Aristotle is the first Greek philosopher consciously to reject the traditional identification of public and private values, not because he was skeptical of "convention," as were the Sophists, but because such an attitude did not fit the facts of the world around him. He finds a more suitable explanation of human excellence in a theory of individual values. For this reason, Aristotle becomes the first Western thinker to give expression to the view that the individual conscience is independent of any man-instituted moral authority, including that of the state.

THE QUALIFICATIONS FOR CITIZENSHIP: Aristotle asks one final question about the nature of the citizen. Who has the right to be a citizen? Can mechanics and laborers be citizens, for instance? Aristotle says they cannot or at least should not be citizens in the best state, because they are incapable of acquiring the virtue of a good citizen. Those who have to work all the time at some menial task, he says, will never have the leisure to learn the art of citizenship. As it takes leisure to become a good man, so one must have free time to become a good citizen. Aristotle says workmen and mechanics should be described as "necessary conditions" of the state. He admits, however, that in actual constitutions, mechanics are frequently, although not always, citizens. In an oligarchy, for example, he says, a rich mechanic can be a citizen. There is no doubt that Aristotle believes that labor is the means of existence, the basis of the state, not part of the state itself. He was not alone in this belief. Plato believed it before him; and, in general, the Greeks looked on the working world as supplying them with the necessities of life. We must not forget that Greek democracy was a democracy of aristocrats to a large extent. The Greek attitude toward labor was the expression of an aristocratic slave-owning class.

Aristotle has said that the qualifications for citizenship of a given society depend on its constitution. This conclusion leads him to a discussion of the various possible types of constitutions. He thus devotes the larger part of Book III to the classification of constitutions.

DEFINITION OF CONSTITUTION: Aristotle views citizenship as the right to hold the highest offices of the state. He defines a constitution as "the organization of a state in respect to its offices generally, but especially in respect of that particular office which is sovereign in all issues." In his opinion, a constitution establishes and defines the structure of political authority. This means that Aristotle classifies constitutions according to where the supreme authority is located, whether in the people, the nobility, or the king.

THE CLASSIFICATION OF CONSTITUTIONS: Aristotle says that two factors must be considered in making the classification of constitutions.

1. THE COMMON INTEREST: The first factor is the *end* or *purpose* for which a state exists. Aristotle says that human behavior in society is motivated by three basic interests. One of these interests is the interest in life itself, as being a thing of value. The second interest is the natural human impulse toward self-preservation which, Aristotle says, provides motivation for the social and economic activity of the state. The third interest is the interest in the good life, in "living well." In Aristotle's view, only this last can be considered the proper concern of society as a whole. He has defined the state as an association of people with a common interest in the good life (i.e., in the life of happiness and well-being which is proper to man). This means that the primary purpose of any society is the welfare of its citizens as expressed in the common interest. Thus, the only interest that can be considered the specific province of politics is the common interest. Aristotle does not underestimate the importance of other interests. He realizes that the state plays a part in satisfying these as well. It enables man to live; and it satisfies man's impulse for a social and economic life. Nevertheless, he insists that the common interest alone is the proper concern of the state, for the state exists to give man the opportunity to share in the good life.

2. RIGHT AND WRONG: The second factor which Aristotle considers important in the classification of constitutions is the *nature of the political authority* exercised by a government in a given society. Aristotle says that there is a right kind and a wrong kind of political rule. The right kind is that authority which is exercised in the common interest. The distinction between the right and the wrong kind of political authority as understood in terms of the purpose for which it exists, leads Aristotle to the major division in his classification of constitutions: right forms of government and their perversions. When a government is directed toward the common interest, which is the well-being of the state, you have a good constitution. When government is in the interests of a part of society, the rulers only, for example, you have a wrong constitution.

DIVISION ACCORDING TO NUMBER OF RULERS: Aristotle makes the second division of constitutions upon the basis of the possible variations of ruling authority. He says there are only three types, based on the possible number of rulers a society can have. You can have government by the one, the few, or the many. When you combine the right *kind* of authority with the different *types* of authority, you get what Aristotle considers the three right types of constitutions: monarchy (government by the virtuous one); aristocracy (government by the few best); and constitutional government, or what Aristotle calls *politeia* (government by the many, under the rule of law). The perversions of these constitutions are, in the same order: tyranny (government by one despot); oligarchy (government by the wealthy few); and democracy (government by mob rule).

COMMENT: In making these divisions, Aristotle does not base his distinctions upon whether or not a constitution upholds the rule of law. He takes up the subject of the supremacy of law later on. Aristotle's classification of constitutions is not original. Plato made a similar classification in the *Republic*. His system was more simple and was based on the degree of justice present in society. In descending order, he classified constitutions as follows: monarchy (the rule of the philosopher king), aristocracy, oligarchy, democracy, ochlocracy (mob rule). In keeping with his doctrine of Ideas, he held that every constitution was good insofar as it participated in the Ideal Government, which he described in his *Republic* as the rule of the philosopher king. Consequently, all other forms of government were inferior to his Ideal Monarchy. Aristotle's contribution to political science was his division of constitutions according to their avowed purpose. The distinction between right and wrong forms of government gives him greater flexibility in analyzing all forms of government, and provides a useful framework for interpreting political problems. His distinction has had great influence on the development of political theory. Although the principle upon which the distinction was made has changed over the centuries, political scientists and politicians, as well, still distinguish between right and wrong forms of government. Our opposition to Communism, for instance, is because we do not consider it a right form of government.

DIVISION ON THE BASIS OF CLASS: To classify constitutions strictly according to the number of people in the governing group does not seem adequate to Aristotle. He thinks that there is another distinction which is particularly applicable to oligarchy and democracy. All societies, he observes, have an economic and social basis, namely, class. Oligarchy, for instance, is not only the rule of the few, but the rule of the wealthy class. Likewise, the chief characteristic of democracy is that it is ruled by the poor (who happen to be the many), while a constitutional government is government by the middle class.

COMMENT: Aristotle was firmly convinced that economics was the basis of all social organization. He did not believe, however, that economic factors were of primary importance in determining the rightness or wrongness of a constitution. The value of a given constitution could only be judged on the basis of its purpose for being.

DIVISION ACCORDING TO JUSTICE: Aristotle says that constitutions may also be classified according to the concept of justice which is operative in the way public offices are distributed in society. For example, in an oligarchy, offices are distributed on the basis of excellence; in a democracy, on the basis of equality. This division introduces a new dimension into our evaluation of right and wrong constitutional forms. Aristotle questions whether the concept of justice which operates in either a democracy or an oligarchy is really justice at all. In a democracy, he observes, equality is supposed to be the principle of justice, but democrats do not really believe in equality at all. They simply want to justify their own position. When they say equality, they mean equality of free birth, not absolute equality. Similarly, when the oligarchs base their constitution on excellence, they mean excellence in wealth, not in anything else. Aristotle believes that in a democracy and an oligarchy true justice cannot exist. True justice means that those who have contributed to the constituted end of the state are assigned offices in proportion to their contribution on the basis of personal merit.

THE STATE EXISTS FOR THE GOOD LIFE: Aristotle concludes that both the democrats and the oligarchs have disregarded the most important factor in the life of society. The state exists *for the sake of the good life*. Its end is not merely self-preservation nor an alliance for mutual defense. The end of the state is a good quality of life. In this passage, Aristotle gives expression to one of the most noble views of the end of government to be found in Western political literature. The end of government, he says, is not to regulate economic interests, as the oligarchs tend to think. Commerce and production are *necessary conditions* of the state. When, however, economic interests become more important in the life of the state than the common interest of encouraging moral virtue, then, says Aristotle, "a political association sinks into a mere alliance, as when two states sign a commercial agreement." Then, "law becomes a mere covenant, a guarantor of men's rights *against* one another, instead of being, as it should be, a rule of life, such as will make the members of a state good and just." Aristotle develops this idea: if two states border on one another, he says, their common boundary does not make them one state. Neither does intermarriage between heads of states, nor laws which regulate commerce and defense, make a state. Common territory, racial background, and common economic and security regulations are necessary conditions of a state, but neither separately nor together do they constitute a state. A state, Aristotle repeats, is "an association of households and clans in a good life, for the sake of attaining a perfect and self-sufficing existence." All other institutions are but means toward that end.

The state exists not for the sake of economics, but for the sake of noble actions. Those who contribute most to an association with such a lofty purpose should have a greater "share" in the state. This means that they should hold higher public positions than those who may be equal to them in birth, but unequal in civic virtues, or superior to them in wealth, but inferior in good citizenship.

> **COMMENT:** Aristotle's view of the end of government as "noble action" is particularly Greek. As we saw in the *Ethics*, he considered action the most unpredictable and yet most fundamental characteristic of human behavior. Aristotle, and the Greeks in general, thought that man's actions were the key to his nature. A man is how he acts. Aristotle viewed society as the natural stage on which the human drama could be played, because no action can be performed in isolation. In other words, he realized that all action is public and, therefore, political. Because action was the political expression of human nature, he thought the state should exist to promote the best type of action possible.

SIGNIFICANCE OF ARISTOTLE'S VIEW OF THE END OF GOVERNMENT: The chapter of the *Politics* discussed above goes to the heart of Aristotle's view of the state's responsibility in encouraging moral virtue. In his view, the value system which determines the way in which a given society distributes its highest offices plays a vital role in the promotion of virtue among the citizen body. Aristotle does not consider the state the supreme moral authority in human affairs, but he does feel that it provides the only conditions in which morality is possible. The state cannot make its citizens behave morally. But it can and does serve as the frame of reference which makes moral action intelligible.

THE BEST RULER—THE MANY?   In the last part of Book III Aristotle discusses the question of the best form of rule. Should sovereignty reside in the many, the few, the one, or the law? He first considers the advantages and disadvantages of popular sovereignty. 1) His principle argument in favor of the many ruling is that the people collectively are always the best judge. Whenever men act collectively, their judgment is usually better than that of the expert, because they contain within their group a combination of qualities which the single expert cannot have. Moreover, a popular assembly is the best judge of political matters because its immediate knowledge of "how the shoe pinches" enables it to evaluate accurately the behavior of its rulers. 2) The second main reason the people should have a share in the enjoyment of power is that their participation provides some guarantee of political stability. A state which is full of poor people, who are excluded from the vote, is full of enemies, and prey to revolution. 3) What kind of a say should the people have? Aristotle thinks they should have a share in government through participation in the election of magistrates, and through the right to evaluate the achievements of their superiors at the end of their term of office. He does not believe, however, that "persons of poor quality" should actually be permitted to hold office. On the contrary, he recommends that there be some kind of property qualification for holding office. 4) In general, Aristotle thinks that the people assembled as a whole are morally better than the individual expert or magistrate, because they are less likely as a group to be swayed by passion than the individual. This means that their judgment will tend to be sounder. Individually, however, the poor people are more to be distrusted and are of poorer quality than those of the upper classes. This last argument is in sharp contrast to Aristotle's repeated references to the dangers of mob rule or the rule of a demagogue or a popular leader with a huge mass following. 5) Aristotle concludes that good laws should be the final sovereign authority in any popular assembly.

THE BEST RULER—THE FEW?   Aristotle can see no reason why the few should rule. In his view, government by the few involves the delicate problem of the standard of values by which the few can be said to have a right to hold office. Should free birth, culture, or noble descent be your criterion? He seems to think that goodness and culture are the only valid claims to rule by the few.

THE BEST RULER—THE ONE?   There is one other solution, namely, that of one-man rule. Aristotle says a monarch derives his right to rule from the fact that he stands out from his fellowmen in excellence of character and political activity. He feels that kingship involves many risks, however. 1) The chief danger of one-man rule lies in the possibility that the mob may think the monarch is a god among men and turn against him. 2) A second danger lies in the nature of the king's authority. Being an extraordinary man, he is above law, because law by its very nature can only govern those who are equal in birth and talents. In other words, law only applies to ordinary people. It has no control over exceptional people. Consequently, it is to be feared that the monarch will become subject to his passions and cease to act in the common interest. 3) Despite the great risk involved, however, Aristotle believes that if such an extraordinary, uncorruptible individual actually existed, a democratic state would have only two choices in the matter: it would have to exile him or accept his rule. These considerations lead Aristotle to a discussion of the nature of kingship and the value to be derived from placing all authority into the hands of one outstanding man.

MONARCHY:　　Aristotle lists five types of kingship: 1) the Spartan form; 2) kingship among uncivilized people; 3) the elective form of dictatorship, for example, the Roman Empire; 4) the type of monarchy which prevailed during the so-called "heroic age" of Greece; and 5) absolute kingship, where the monarch is above the law.

ABSOLUTE KINGSHIP:　　The last form of kingship interests Aristotle most. He is particularly fascinated by the possibility of there being one man so excellent in character that he is actually above the law. But no matter how he argues the case, he comes out in favor of a limited monarchy where law is supreme. 1) Aristotle gives the practical difficulties which stand in the way of absolute monarchy. a) Although the king may legally be the source of all power, in actual fact he needs advisers and men to carry out his will. Thus one-man rule really means aristocracy. b) There is the problem of succession. There is no way of making sure that the king's children will have any of the superior qualities of their father. c) There is the problem of the king's guards. If he has too many, a monarchy turns into despotism. 2) There is the whole question of the king's position *vis-à-vis* the law. a) The rule of an absolute monarch is unnatural because there can be no justice in the state where he rules. Justice, we have seen, depends on some principle of equal distribution of offices. In other words, an arrangement of public offices necessitates some system of law. If the king holds all the offices, there can be no justice. b) It may be argued that a king is better than law because law cannot deal with particulars, only with general principles. If in the world of the arts, for example, we need a physician to see the relation between the general cause and our particular disease, so in the world of politics, we need a king. Aristotle says the two cases are not the same. The doctor has no reason not to do his best for the patient. But the king can be partial to one cause rather than another. Furthermore, if one man is an expert, two experts will be able to give a better opinion. The king cannot keep an eye on all the problems of his realm. He will have to have advisers. In decision-making, the action of many is better than one, especially if all have been trained in the law. c) If some say written law is too rigid, they will have no reason to find fault with custom or unwritten law which has grown up from the experience of the people. Aristotle concludes that law should rule wherever possible.

> COMMENT: To understand Aristotle's view of law, we must remember that Athenian law was a very old body of rules and custom which was seldom changed. Each citizen had the right to prosecute a magistrate who tried to abuse the law. Thus, the idea of "making a law" in the day-to-day business of government would have sounded strange to Aristotle. *Nomos,* or law, for him, meant the custom, written and unwritten, which had developed with the development of a state. This concept of law is the basis for Aristotle's frequent appeals to tradition in both the *Ethics* and the *Politics.* It also explains his strong sense of historical development. It will be remembered that Aristotle viewed growth as the change of something from its potential to its actual. Change takes place over a certain period of time, as time is "the measure of motion." It was natural, therefore, that Aristotle should consider the passage of time and the slow accumulation of custom of value in the growth of the city state. When the philosopher's idea of law is understood in this way, it is clear that his view that a king should be subject to the law means that a king should defer to the written and unwritten custom of his people, if he is to rule them wisely and well. The idea that legislators could make new laws and change old ones in keeping with changing social, economic, and political conditions did not make its definitive appearance until the seventeenth century.

THE BEST CONSTITUTION A RELATIVE MATTER: Some societies are naturally suited for monarchies, others for aristocracies and others for constitutional governments. That society which is suited for kingship is one which naturally tends to produce some family which is outstanding in its talent for political leadership. The society suited for aristocracy is that in which there are some people who possess the ability to be ruled, and others who are capable of being leaders. The society fitted for constitutional government has a warlike body of citizens who rule and are ruled in turn under a system of law which distributes offices among property owners on the basis of merit.

ONE SITUATION IN WHICH ABSOLUTE MONARCHY IS DE-SIRABLE: Aristotle concludes Book III with his only defense of absolute monarchy. When a man by nature is far superior to anyone else in the state, it is both just and proper to allow him to rule. The god among men should not be exiled, for this type of rule would be the best possible, in Aristotle's opinion.

BOOK IV
CONSTITUTIONS AND
GOVERNMENT INSTITUTIONS

INTRODUCTION: Scholars generally agree that Books IV to VI originally formed a separate work, as they are more detailed in their subject matter, and go into the small points of the divisions and subdivisions of constitutions. Aristotle begins by laying out a five-point program of inquiry: 1) what are the varieties of the main kinds of constitutions given in Book III; 2) what type of constitution is the most practicable; 3) what type of constitution is best for what sort of people; 4) how do constitutions come into being; 5) what are the causes of constitutional decay and how can one keep a constitution in being.

REVIEW OF PREVIOUS MATERIAL: As Aristotle has already discussed aristocracy and monarchy in Book III, he now turns to discuss constitutional government, and oligarchy, democracy and tyranny. In so doing, he reviews much of the material he has already covered. 1) He stresses that the form of constitution depends on the class structure of a given society. This structure may be divided roughly into three parts, the rich, the poor, and the middle class. 2) Each class is subdivided according to occupation. The common people are farmers and laborers, for instance. Not all who belong to the wealthy class possess the same amount of property or money. 3) A constitution is an arrangement of offices, and this arrangement has to be made on some basis. In some states it is made on the basis of power, i.e., the power of the rich or the poor. In others, it is made on the basis of equality between the rich and the poor, such as equality of free birth. The varieties of institutions and laws to be found in constitutions is chiefly due to variety in social composition. 4) A state is made up of parts, i.e., classes and occupations. Aristotle proceeds to analyze both oligarchy and democracy on the basis of different forms of their various parts.

THE VARIETIES OF THE MAIN KINDS OF CONSTITUTIONS: Aristotle begins his inquiry into the nature of democracy and oligarchy by listing how many kinds of each there are. The principle variable in each case is the degree to which the rule of law is upheld in the state.

DEMOCRACY: Aristotle says there are five different types of democracy. He makes his classification according to the measure of equality and respect for law to be found in a democratic state. The first type comes nearest to the principle of absolute equality, for the rich count no more than the poor. The second type is that in which there is a low property qualification for election to office. The third type is one in which everyone of good birth can hold office, and law is supreme. The fourth type is that in which everyone who is a citizen can hold office, but law is still sovereign. The fifth type allows everyone to hold office, but popular decrees have taken the place of law. In such a democracy there is a danger that a demagogue or popular leader will arise, and destroy the constitution. We have experience of the power of demagogues such as Hitler and Castro in our own century.

OLIGARCHIES: There are four types of oligarchies. In the first, the property-qualifications are high enough to keep the poor out of office. In the second, not only is the property qualification high for eligibility to hold office, but only persons with a great deal of property are qualified to vote. In the third, officeholding is hereditary. This means that sons succeed their fathers to the same office. In the fourth, the rule of law has given way to the personal rule of a junta, or small ruling clique.

WHAT TYPE OF CONSTITUTION IS BEST FOR WHAT SORT OF PEOPLE?   It is not enough for Aristotle to classify the political structure of the state according to its respect, or lack of respect, for law. To know what the constitution is, we must see it actually at work. This means that we have to look at the social composition of the state. Of what kinds of people is it composed? In answering this question, Aristotle is dealing with the third area of inquiry of his program: What type of constitution is suited to what type of people?

AGRARIAN DEMOCRACY: Of the varieties of democracy, Aristotle picks out the form which he considers best suited for a farming people: one where there is a low property qualification. This is the second type of democracy. The reason for this choice is that the farmers are usually too busy to attend meetings or hold office, and consequently tend to leave the actual running of the state to those who have the time. Furthermore, even the leisure classes of an agricultural society have relatively little free time. This means that meetings will be held infrequently. The result is that law rules supreme, as there is no danger of a mob forming, and ruling by decree. In this discussion, Aristotle makes it clear that he believes the social conditions, or standard of living of a society, determine how much free time its citizens will have. He feels that free time in a democracy is a dangerous thing, because the great mass of citizens will not know how to use it properly. In a society whose standard of living is sufficiently high to give everyone a certain amount of free time, there is always the danger that the mob which has nothing to do, and is allowed to take part in the political process, will become the sovereign power in the state, instead of law. Aristotle was perhaps thinking of the rise of popular leaders in his own lifetime, or of party strife in Athens, when he was at the Lyceum, when he made these comments.

OTHER SOCIO-ECONOMIC FORMS OF DEMOCRACY: Aristotle thinks the agrarian form of democracy is the best of the four forms he distinguishes. The others are 1) a democracy based on social origin, 2) that based only on free birth, and 3) that based on numerical equality. Aristotle considers this last type the most advanced form of democracy. It appears in those states where there has been a substantial increase in population, accompanied by a corresponding rise in the standard of living.

SOCIO-ECONOMIC FORMS OF OLIGARCHY: Using the same principles, Aristotle distinguishes four forms of oligarchy. The most extreme form of oligarchy, the rule of a small clique, or *junta*, is similar in kind to the extreme form of democracy, the personal rule of the mob. Both are equally arbitrary.

THE BEST CONSTITUTION FOR THE MAJORITY OF PEOPLE— THE *POLITEIA*:   Now that he has discussed the good and bad aspects of the various constitutional forms, Aristotle is ready to discuss what he thinks is the best type of constitution, which can be put into practice. This is constitutional government, or *politeia*: a mixture of democracy and oligarchy and aristocracy. The principles upon which government offices are distributed correspond to the principles of distribution in each constitution: wealth (oligarchy), free birth (democracy) and merit (aristocracy). After going into details as to how these different elements can be mixed, Aristotle concludes that a properly mixed constitutional government should contain both democratic and oligarchical elements. Second, it should be so constructed that no single section of society would be in favor of changing the form of government.

CONSTITUTIONAL GOVERNMENT—A MEAN: Constitutional government is the best type of government for the majority of the people because it is a mean between the two extremes of democracy and oligarchy. In the *Ethics*, Aristotle said that goodness consists in a mean. It follows, therefore, that the well-being of the political community must also be a mean as expressed in its constitution. In every state sovereign power is vested in a particular class. In a constitutional government, power should be vested in the class between the two extremes, i.e., the middle class.

THE MIDDLE CLASS: The class which has neither too much nor too little will be prey neither to the violence nor ambition of the rich, nor to the pettiness and crimes of the poor. The rich will not learn the virtue of obedience, and the poor will not know how to command, and therefore have to be governed like slaves. In a state where there are only these two classes, a permanent class war exists between the "state" of the rich and the "state" of the poor. A large middle class provides a balance between the two factions. For some reason, which he does not make clear, Aristotle thinks the middle class is free from factionalism. Thus both the rich and the poor are more inclined to trust the middle class than their opposite extremes. Without a middle class the state tends toward either a democracy or an oligarchy. And from both of these forms of government a tyranny can readily arise in the person of the demagogue or the despot.

CONSTITUTIONAL GOVERNMENT—THE MOST STABLE: A constitutional government is the best form of government, because it is the most stable. Unfortunately, Aristotle says, history has given us few examples of constitutional government, partly because there has been no large middle class in most states, and partly because of the policy of the two leading Greek states, Athens and Sparta, has not been in favor of constitutional government.

THE TECHNOLOGY OF GOVERNMENT—THE DELIBERATIVE, EXECUTIVE, AND JUDICIAL POWERS: In the last chapters of Book IV, Aristotle turns to the fourth subject of his program,

methods of setting up government institutions. He recognizes three
government functions. After saying what each of these functions is,
he proceeds to show how variations in the method of setting up
and assigning these functions reflect the different types of constitutions.

THE DELIBERATIVE POWER: Aristotle first discusses the deliberative, or as we should say, legislative function. Decision-
making, he says, can take one of the following three forms in a
state: 1) all decisions can be assigned to all the population (democracy); 2) all matters are decided by a few (oligarchy); 3) some
matters are decided by all the citizens and all the other decisions
are made by the few (aristocracy and constitutional governments).
Perhaps, the most interesting aspect of Aristotle's discussion of
decision-making is his suggestion that, in a democracy, the various
parts of the state should be represented in the legislative body by an
equal number of members. Representative government was not
completely unknown to the Greeks. For example, the Athenian
League, set up in 377 B.C., had, as one part of its legislative organ,
an assembly made up of representatives from all the states of the
League. Unfortunately, however, Aristotle only makes this one
mention of a representative institution, and nowhere follows this
idea through.

THE EXECUTIVE POWER: The second element of government
is the executive, or system of magistrates. Aristotle says the system depends on four factors: 1) the number of magistrates, 2)
their respective functions; 3) their length of stay in office; and 4)
their method of appointment. There are three factors in Aristotle's
opinion which determine the method of appointment. 1) All or
some of the citizens appoint. 2) All of the citizens, or a class (on
the basis of property, birth, or merit) are eligible to hold office;
3) appointment is by vote or by lot. These factors can be combined
in any number of ways. All of the citizens, for instance, can appoint
to some offices. Again, some of the citizens can appoint a particular
class to office by lot. Each combination may be found in some
variety of constitution. Aristotle goes through all the possible combinations and assigns them to the different constitutional types.
Worthy of note in this discussion is Aristotle's emphasis on the importance of the franchise in the determination of constitutional
form.

THE JUDICIAL POWER: The third element is the judiciary, or
system of law courts. We must not think that Aristotle understands
the judicial function of the state in the same way as we understand

the function of the Supreme Court. For him the judiciary was simply the system of courts, of which, in his opinion, there are eight
different kinds.

**SIGNIFICANCE OF ARISTOTLE'S ANALYSIS OF CONSTITU-
TIONS:**   In the entire discussion of the institutions of government it must be remembered that Aristotle is only dealing with
Greek institutions familiar to him and in his treatment of constitutions and their forms he shows himself master of the Greek political
world. For this reason, Book IV and Book V make fascinating reading for the student of the political institutions of the Hellenic world
of the 4th and 3rd century, B.C. Aristotle's analysis of governmental
institutions is not relevant only to the states of his time. It has pro-
foundly influenced our concepts of government, right down to the
present time. His view that all political institutions have their roots
in the socio-economic structure of society is an accepted axiom of
political science. His designation of three governmental functions
was the starting point for the later theory of the separation of powers. His theory that there is a right inherent in the people, because
of their collective capacity to judge, to elect their rulers and to call
them to account, remains the cornerstone of democratic government
today. Finally, in our continuing distinction between those states
where arbitrary rule prevails and those where the government is the
servant of the law, we are heirs to his belief in the sovereignty of
law as the standard of right rule.

BOOK V
CAUSES OF REVOLUTION AND CHANGE IN THE STATE

INTRODUCTION: In Book V, Aristotle examines the last problem in his program of study: what are the causes of change in a
state and how can one best prevent revolution. In Book V, he
examines the general and particular causes of revolution. Many
readers will find this book resembles that famous piece of political
realism, or *Realpolitik*, of the 15th century, Machiavelli's *The
Prince*. Book V is perhaps the most useful book of the *Politics*
for modern readers, as it contains many perceptive comments on
human nature and on the nature of revolution.

THE GENERAL CAUSES OF REVOLUTION: True to his scientific method, Aristotle opens his analysis of political change with a
discussion of the general causes, or first principles (*archai*) of
revolution which govern all revolutionary situations at all times in
all places.

THE PRIMARY CAUSE OF REVOLUTION: Aristotle says that the primary cause of revolution is a feeling of inequality. The revolutionary spirit, he says, is aroused when one group of citizens feels it is not getting its fair share of constitutional rights. It is important to note that Aristotle believes the primary cause of revolution is a state of mind, not an economic ambition. One man's motive may be that he has a passion for equality, and his class is excluded from citizenship. Another man, on the other hand, may have a passion for inequality. He may feel he is superior to others and seek to take over the state. Thus, says Aristotle, inferiors become revolutionaries in order to be equals, and equals in order to be superiors.

THE SECONDARY CAUSE OF REVOLUTION: The second cause of revolution is economic and social. The revolutionary always has some object for which he is willing to fight. His profit or honor may be at stake. Or he may advocate revolt because he fears financial ruin and disgrace.

THE OCCASIONS OF REVOLUTION: Aristotle says the revolutionary's state of mind does not form all by itself in a vacuum. There must be some *occasion*, which produces the state of mind. Aristotle distinguishes eight *direct* occasions of revolutions. Two of the objects of revolution are the first two occasions of revolutions: profit-making and honor. The other six occasions are as follows: 1) when men see other persons getting a larger share than they themselves get; 2) insolence; 3) fear of wrongdoers; 4) the presence of an individual or class which is either economically or intellectually superior; 5) contempt; and 6) a disproportionate increase in some part of the state. In other words, revolutions are likely to occur when either the poorer class or the wealthy class increases more rapidly than either its opposite or the middle class. Aside from these direct occasions for revolution, Aristotle says there are four indirect: 1) election intrigues; 2) the neglect of trifling changes in the state; 3) dissimilarity of elements in the state, for example, the presence of too many dissimilar racial groups, sectional rivalries, etc., in one state, and 4) poor security screening, with the result that persons not loyal to the constitution are able to win positions of power.

SMALL OCCASIONS INVOLVE GREAT ISSUES: Aristotle warns us that the occasions of revolution may seem small and of no consequence, but they involve great issues as soon as they are directed towards the government. For example, petty intergovernmental rivalry, or family quarrels, may have a disastrous outcome. He tells us that the moral is to take precautions at the beginning of feuds and quarrels which may endanger the position of the leader of the community.

THE DIFFERENT DEGREES OF REVOLUTION:　Aristotle says that not all political changes involve open civil war. There are different degrees of political change, the most extreme of which is revolution. Some changes are purely constitutional when a democracy changes into an oligarchy, and vice versa. Such changes are due to one of two causes: 1) the growth in the reputation or power of one of the executive offices, and 2) the growth in some part (i.e., class) of the state. Revolutions tend to occur when there is no middle class, and the rich and the poor are equally balanced against each other.

THE PARTICULAR CAUSES OF REVOLUTION:　From the discussion of general causes, Aristotle turns to an inquiry into the particular causes of revolution, i.e., those causes which are particular to the various types of states. Chapter 5 lists the causes of revolution in a democracy; Chapter 6, in an oligarchy; and Chapter 7, in an aristocracy.

CAUSES OF REVOLUTION IN A DEMOCRACY:　In a democracy, revolutions are chiefly due to the policies and behavior of the popular leaders, or demagogues, towards the rich. Sometimes they attack the rich individually by bringing false accusations; and sometimes they attack them as a class, by turning the people against them.

CHANGES IN A DEMOCRACY:　1) In early times, Aristotle observes, democracies used to change into tyrannies, because society was still in a primitive state of development, and the demagogues were often military men. Later, when speech-making became separated from war-making, the demagogue who could sway the populace with his fine speeches usually had no military experience. Therefore, he was powerless to institute a tyranny. 2) Democracies may also change from the traditional form where law is supreme, to the most extreme form, where law itself is subject to the authority of the populace.

CAUSES OF REVOLUTION IN AN OLIGARCHY:　In an oligarchy, revolutions are due to two causes: 1) the unjust treatment of the masses of the population by the governing group, and 2) quarrels and rivalries within the ranks of the governing class. Revolution from outside the government occurs, for example, when a wealthy man is excluded from the right to office. A revolution from within may occur when its members have spent all their money "in riotous living," and turn revolutionary from poverty, and when an inner ring is created within the oligarchical government. In time of war or peace, the hiring of mercenaries may affect the stability of the regime. Personal quarrels or general growth in the wealth of the community which would make more people eligible for office are the most common causes of revolution in an oligarchy.

CAUSES OF REVOLUTION IN AN ARISTOCRACY: In an aristocracy revolutions arise when the circle of the governing group is narrowed through limiting the number of offices and honors to be distributed. The chief cause of revolution in both an aristocracy and a constitutional government is the lack of balance between the different classes of the state. 1) When the classes are not well balanced, a constitutional government may change into a democracy, or an aristocracy into an oligarchy—assuming that the wealthy class is that which has the most power. 2) Both types of constitutions can also change in the other direction. A constitutional government may change into an oligarchy, when the majority is convinced that political stability lies in a system based on merit. At the conclusion of this discussion of the particular causes of revolution, Aristotle comments that aristocracies are most prone to change for trifling reasons, because family quarrels and personal jealousies react directly upon the stability of the regime.

EXTERNAL CAUSES OF REVOLUTION: The foregoing discussion has concentrated on the internal causes of revolution. Aristotle says that there are other causes. Revolutions are also the result of outside pressure. In wartime, for instance, democracies have to take emergency repressive measures in order to withstand the threat to their national survival. These measures may serve as the occasion for a change to a despotic form of government.

METHODS OF PREVENTING REVOLUTIONS IN ARISTOCRACIES, OLIGARCHIES, AND DEMOCRACIES: Having determined the causes of revolution, Aristotle proceeds to examine the methods by which they can be prevented in the three states he has discussed above. Chapter VIII reads like a textbook in practical politics, and contains many sound words of advice for the prudent statesman. Aristotle's fundamental rules for preventing revolution are classic: 1) The most important rule for aristocracies is to guard against lawlessness, in general, and against petty crimes, in particular. "Revolutions have their origins in small occasions," Aristotle warns. Little changes follow one another almost unnoticed, until one day the country awakes to the realization that a big change has taken place. 2) The second basic rule is that governments must not rely on devices to trick the masses. "You cannot deceive all of the people all of the time." 3) States owe their stability primarily to the maintenance of good relations on the part of the members of the ruling class with one another, and with the enfranchised civic body. Thus, Aristotle says, in those states which have a large proportion of enfranchised citizens, governments are well-advised to introduce democratic institutions, and some measure of equality. Aristotle is firmly convinced that all governments depend on some amount of popular consent. It is not good politics to alienate either your fellow ruler or the people who elect you to office. 4) A state of crisis and tension helps keep a government in power. Maintaining a feeling of emergency may help maintain a regime. 5) The ruling class should maintain class solidarity. A split in the ranks of the rulers can bring on a revolution, as it did in Hungary, in 1956, for instance. 6) It is wise to have a regular revision of the property qualifications required to hold office. The assessment should change in proportion to the increase or decrease of money in circulation, in order to prevent either too many or too few people from becoming eligible for office, all at one time. 7) Governments should be on their guard lest one man reach a position of power because of his personal wealth or connections. Similarly, a good government should keep an eye on the rising social class of a given moment, and should at all times try to increase the strength of the middle class. 8) The most important practical rule, for Aristotle, applies to all types of constitutions. Government officials should be prevented from using their office for their own profit. It is a recurring theme of Greek political theory that political power tends to be used, and should not be used, for personal economic advantage; Aristotle's own experience confirmed the validity of this thesis. In his opinion, the general mass of men does not resent being excluded from public office, so long as they know that the office is not being used by its holder to embezzle public funds. When magistrates are dishonest, he remarks, the people feel two losses: loss of office, and loss of profit. His principal preventive remedy for political corruption is to have the magistrates give a complete accounting of their expenses to the public at the end of their term of office. A second remedy is to award public honors solely on the basis of good reputation. In this way, public office cannot be made a source of honor. 9) The last rule, which applies to democratic and oligarchic states, is that the non-governing class should be treated kindly. In a democracy, the rich should be spared. In an oligarchy, much attention should be paid to the poor. In all matters other than property, the ruled should be given equality, or even certain additional privileges. Aristotle was the first of a long line of political scientists to realize that property is the chief means to political power. It follows that the granting of extra privileges to the non-ruling citizens does little to strengthen their power position, but does a great deal to keep them contented.

POLITICAL STABILITY DEPENDS ON PROPER LEADERSHIP: It is clear from the foregoing that in the last analysis, political stability depends on the quality of a state's leadership. In Chapter 9, Aristotle discusses what the qualifications for leadership should be. These have not changed much since his day. To hold office, Aristotle says, a man should possess three characteristics: 1) loyalty to the established constitution; 2) the training and ability to do his particular job properly; and 3) "the quality of goodness and justice in the particular form which suits the nature of the constitution"; in other words, integrity.

THE BEST MAN SHOULD RULE: What happens when these qualities are not found in a single man? How are we to choose who should hold that office? Aristotle says we have to distinguish between the common characteristics and the rarer ones. In a general, for instance, we primarily look for military experience, because goodness of character is more common than military knowledge. When it comes to choosing a man to guard your property, however, you are more concerned with his moral character. In this case, goodness of character is more rare than the ability to guard property. It follows that in picking a man for an office, we must first look for that special characteristic which the job requires. Some, Aristotle says, may ask whether a candidate for office needs the third quality of goodness at all, as long as he possesses loyalty, and skill. He replies that a man cannot serve the common interest, unless he possesses goodness of character which raises him above self-interest. Aristotle's view on choosing men for office can be summed up as follows: let the best qualified rule.

POSITIVE MEANS OF PREVENTING REVOLUTION—EDUCATION: Aristotle now turns to a consideration of positive measures which would preserve constitutions from change. 1) The first important measure is the maintenance of the *rule of law*. 2) In advocating *moderation*, Aristotle repeats his advice that democracies and oligarchies should remember the value of the mean, and not go to extremes. 3) *Promotion of popular consent*. The number who are *for* the constitution should always be larger than those who are *against* it. 4) The best means of ensuring the stability of the constitution in Aristotle's opinion is the *education of the citizens in the spirit of their particular constitution*. This means that the young oligarch or democrat should be brought up to do those actions which will enable his type of constitution to survive. Wealthy young noblemen, for example, should not live a life of indolence and luxury, while the poor of their country are gathering their forces to overthrow them. Democrats, in their turn, should not hold the mistaken view that freedom means license or doing what you please. A democratic education should teach them that freedom is only possible under law.

THE CAUSE AND PREVENTION OF REVOLUTION IN A MONARCHY AND TYRANNY: So far, Aristotle has only discussed the nature of revolution in governments either by the few or the many. He now discusses the question in relation to monarchies and tyrannies, which he considers governments without a constitution, or rule of law.

THE DIFFERENCE BETWEEN THE TWO: They follow: 1) kingship is in the nature of aristocracy. Tyranny is a mixture of the extreme forms of oligarchy and democracy. This combination, in Aristotle's opinion, makes it the worst type of government. 2) Kingships have come into being for the purpose of helping the better classes against the mob with the result that kings have generally come from the upper classes. Tyrannies, on the other hand, have grown up from the struggle of the masses against the nobles. Thus, tyrants have usually sprung from the masses. 3) A final distinction is that the aim of the king is the common interest, or the good; the aim of the tyrant is his personal pleasure.

THE ORIGINS OF REVOLUTION UNDER A MONARCHY: They are similar to those under an aristocracy: unjust oppression, fear, contempt and insult. The objects of the revolution are the same as for the other types of constitutions Aristotle has considered.

IMPORTANCE OF FOREIGN AFFAIRS IN A TYRANNY AND A MONARCHY: The difference between tyranny and monarchy comes out most forcefully in the impact of foreign affairs on the stability of the two regimes. In Aristotle's view, a tyranny is most likely to be affected by the presence of a strong rival power with a rival ideology. "The conflict of opposite principles," Aristotle says, prophetically enough, "will obviously lead such a state to will the destruction of the tyranny, and where there is a will . . . there is always a way." Tyrannies are also easily overthrown from within through family quarrels, or the aroused hatred of the populace. Monarchy, on the other hand, is the form of constitution least liable to be destroyed by external causes. When it is destroyed,

Aristotle says, it is usually destroyed from within—either through personal dynastic quarrels, or through the misrule of the king.

DEFINITION OF MONARCHY: Monarchy, Aristotle says, is "a government by consent," where there is general equality, and no one is able to equal the grandeur and character of the king. He adds that monarchy has gone out of style in Greece. We might add that personal rule seems to be on the wane in our day as well. Countries have grown too big, and populations have become too large to be capable of efficient government by one man.

HOW MAY MONARCHIES BE PRESERVED?   Aristotle thinks that monarchies are best preserved by a *policy of moderation*. "The less the area of his prerogative, the longer the authority of the king will last unimpaired." Common sense leads the philosopher to the conclusion that a monarchy is most stable when the king's power is limited.

PRESERVATION OF TYRANNIES: In his comments on tyranny, Aristotle shows himself the master of what the great engineer of the unification of Germany, Otto von Bismarck, was later to call, *"Realpolitik,"* or political realism. There are two ways, the Greek says, of preserving the power of a tyrant. The first is the traditional way of *total repression*. In his opinion, any totalitarian government, if it is to remain totalitarian, must have three main objectives for its domestic policy: 1) to break the spirit of its subjects; 2) to sow distrust among them; and 3) perhaps, the most important of all, to make them incapable of any kind of action, especially, collective action. This formula for despotic rulers is still in force in many parts of the world today. Aristotle's second method is to make a *tyranny more like a monarchy*. His prescriptions for "enlightened despotism" are as realistic as those for total repression. The Renaissance thinker, Nicolò Machiavelli, offered his sovereign, Lorenzo Medici, few suggestions that had not already been made by his Greek predecessor. Examples of Aristotle's rules reveal his political astuteness. 1) Appearance counts for everything. A tyrant should *appear* to be a good king, to administer wisely, honor the good, restrain his passions, and worship in public. 2) He should *never inflict punishment* himself, but always leave punishment to his magistrates. 3) He should play the *double role* of companion to the nobles, and friend and father to his people. Aristotle says that, by following this course of action, the tyrant will prolong his rule for two reasons. First, his reign will be nobler, his subjects, free from humiliation and envy, and he himself will not become the object of their hatred. Second, by appearing to be virtuous, the tyrant will develop a character, which, although not wholly good, will not be completely bad.

BOOK VI
METHODS OF CONSTRUCTING DEMOCRACIES AND OLIGARCHIES SO THAT THEY WILL BE MORE STABLE

INTRODUCTION: In Book VI, Aristotle returns to his discussion of oligarchy and democracy to analyze each constitution in great detail. The reason he devotes so much of the *Politics* to a discussion of these particular constitutions is that they were the two most widely spread forms of government in the Greek world of his time. It will be remembered that Alexander was in the act of extending the long arm of his power as far as India while Aristotle was teaching at the Lyceum, in Athens. The possibility of a great Greek Empire was just dawning on Greek consciousness, and was soon to become very remote, indeed, when Alexander died. Aristotle's preoccupation with the idea of a superman-monarch in the foregoing passage gives us some indication of the impact his experience as tutor to Alexander must have had on his life. Nevertheless, Alexander's conquests were far away from the reality of Greek city-state life, which was clearly the principal object of Aristotle's political theory. As his discussion of voting rights, property distribution, and other related problems is thus attuned to the Greek constitutions of his day, we shall not present it here. A few of his comments on democracy, however, are worth noting, for they lead up to his inevitable conclusion that societies, like individuals, are best served by a policy of moderation. Political virtue is but the larger expression of individual virtue; it too consists in the golden mean. The underlying idea of a democracy, says Aristotle, is liberty. Liberty may be understood in two ways. First, he explains, there is *political liberty*, which refers to the democratic system of rotation in office, i.e., of the ruling and being ruled in turn. Political liberty is based on the democratic concept of justice, arithmetical equality, which makes each citizen equal to the next one in political power. In the language of today, this means "one man, one vote."

ARITHMETICAL EQUALITY: By its very nature this makes the poor the sovereign authority in the state, as there are always more poor, than there are rich. The result is that the will of the majority, or the will of the poor, is more sovereign than the will of the rich. The second type of liberty is *civil liberty*, which the democrats understand as "doing what you please." When Aristotle puts the two types of liberty together, he arrives at two conclusions: 1) the

democrat should either not be ruled at all, but live as he likes, in
complete anarchy, or else have his turn in guiding the affairs of
government; 2) the existence to a greater or lesser degree of the
two types of liberty in a state determines the constitutional arrange-
ments of every democratic society, whether an agricultural, pastoral
or a labor democracy. Aristotle proceeds to look at these types in
turn, point out the positive elements in each and show how their
faults may be corrected.

A STABLE DEMOCRACY IS A MODERATE DEMOCRACY:
It is not enough to set up a democracy on a sound basis. You also
must make sure that it endures. Consequently, the true democratic
policy is not one which gives the citizens the greatest amount of
democracy, but that which assures the survival of the state. As
always is the case with Aristotle, the best measures are the moderate measures. The rich should not be alienated by having their
wealth and property confiscated, nor should they be too much encouraged through a system of high payment for political services.
Similarly, the wise democratic government will also try to improve
the lot of the poor people through a system of public and private
social services.

SURVIVAL OF STATE: THE POLITICAL GOLDEN MEAN:
In this, and the discussion which follows on oligarchy, Aristotle expresses his conviction that the survival of a state is more important
than blind adherence to any principle. And he makes it clear that
if a state is to survive, it must be based on a policy of moderation,
not on oppression. In his discussion of tyranny, he proved that a
tyrannical government is the most unstable form of government
which exists. Ability to stay in power depends on a course of constant compromise and cultivation of the interests of the opposing
class. For this reason, Aristotle thinks that in the long run, both
the stable democracy and the stable oligarchy must approach the
most permanent of all kinds of government, namely constitutional
government, if they want to survive. Constitutional government is
thus not only *morally* the best type of government, but has been
shown to be *practically* the best type of government.

BOOKS VII AND VIII
THE END OF THE STATE: WELL-BEING

INTRODUCTION—THE IDEAL STATE: The last two books of
the *Politics* are given over to the question of the nature of the
true end of the state. Although Aristotle has already said it is

well-being, he feels obligated to define what real well-being is. To do this, he builds his own Ideal State.

THE NATURE OF WELL-BEING—THE GOODS OF THE SOUL: Since the kind of well-being of the best kind of state depends on what you think happiness is, Aristotle reviews the conception of happiness which he developed in the *Ethics*. Happiness is the ultimate good of man, for the sake of which man does everything he does. There are three kinds of goods which may be desired: external goods (wealth, family); goods of the body (health, good looks) and goods of the soul (the moral and intellectual virtues). The best of these goods are the goods of the soul for two reasons. 1) They are by nature infinite. External goods to be good, must be limited. For example, although a man should not pursue money for its own sake, he should have enough not to have to worry about starving from hunger. Similarly, with respect to bodily goods, a man cannot be too goodlooking, else he will give way to vanity. But there is no limit to the goods of the soul. You can never say a man is too virtuous, for instance. 2) The soul is more "precious" than the body, or any of the external goods, for it is the formal principle which makes us what we are. For this reason, all the other goods exist for the sake of the soul and not vice versa. This means that the goods of the soul are more valuable in the hierarchy of goods than the others.

LIFE OF VIRTUE—THE BEST LIFE OF THE STATE: If the goods of the soul, namely, the several virtues, are the most desirable for the individual, it follows that a life of virtue must be the best life for the state, since it is made up of many individuals. Aristotle insists that the other types of goods must not be lacking, however, for they are the necessary conditions of virtue. He sums up his idea of happiness as follows: "The best way of life, for individuals as well as for states, is the life of goodness duly equipped with the amount of external and bodily goods, which will make it possible to share in the activities of goodness."

IS THE BEST LIFE OF THE STATE ACTIVE OR SELF-CONTAINED? In the last book of the *Ethics* Aristotle explained why, in his opinion, the best life of goodness was the life of contemplation rather than the life of action. He now has to consider which is the best life for the state. This is a hard question for him to answer, because he has repeatedly made clear that a life of goodness consists chiefly in action directed at others. As long as you do nothing you are acting neither well nor badly. Only in action does the question of morality arise. Aristotle bases his discussion of the problem on two contemporary views of what the best life of the state should be. 1) Some say that the state should lead a life of action, i.e., a life of business, commerce, and internal and external politics. Aristotle is inclined to reject this view, because such a life, he feels, invariably leads to imperialism and the domination of other states. 2) Others say that the life of the self-contained state is best, because it enables the state to spend its time developing its own resources and culture. This view reflects Aristotle's own opinion of the matter.

WAR FOR ITS OWN SAKE IS WRONG: In his discussion of the first view, Aristotle cites Sparta as the best example of a state which leads a life of action, and asks whether that city can be said to lead a morally good life. He observes that in some people's opinion, domination by a constitutional government, such as Sparta's, over another country is unjust. It interferes with the well-being of the individual of both the conquering and the conquered state. Aristotle refuses to sanction military aggrandizement for its own sake. It is in the nature of things, he suggests, that some states are meant to be controlled by others, just as some people (the natural slaves) are meant to be controlled by others. Not all states and not all individuals are capable of self-government, in his view. Nevertheless, the only way he thinks imperialism can be justified in any qualified sense is if it helps the imperialist state *and* the conquered state attain their true end, a life of goodness. Aristotle holds that a state is justified in maintaining its power position and independence *vis-à-vis* the other nations, since national survival is one of the prerequisites for the well-being of the state. But he seems more in favor of some kind of isolationism. He says that a state which lives in isolation (if there is such a state) will have no need for, and consequently, no interest in war.

THE BEST STATE IS THE SELF-CONTAINED STATE: Aristotle re-examines the problem from the point of view of the individual citizen in order to clarify the positions of the two schools of thought he has just discussed. One school, he says, distinguishes between the life of the individual, freeborn citizen, and that of the statesman. It holds that the life of the individual is best. The others say that the man who goes into politics is leading the best life. Aristotle feels that both sides are partially right, and partially wrong. The first school is right in saying that the life of a free individual is better than the life of a despot who rules over a number of slaves. But it is wrong to consider all authority despotic. It is also wrong to prefer a life of inaction to action. The second school is wrong in thinking that the permanent management of others is the most desirable thing in life. Domination is only justifiable when it is over natural inferiors. A father naturally dominates his son, and a master, his slaves, for example. The second school is also wrong in thinking that a life of activity has to be a life which involves relationships with others. Thought, says Aristotle, is an activity. Moreover, thoughts which are followed for their own sake (i.e., are unlimited) are surely more active than action which ends in something (and is therefore limited). Furthermore, as we saw in the *Ethics,* thought is the highest kind of activity, as it is the one type of human activity which resembles the life of the gods. Aristotle concludes that a state does not have to pursue an imperialist policy to be active. It can "achieve activity by sections as the different sections of the state will be mutually interrelated." Aristotle says that a self-contained state is the only state which can know true well-being.

> **COMMENT:**   It is important to note that Aristotle reaches his conclusion with respect to the best kind of life for the state by relating this life to the needs of the individual. In making the individual of primary importance, and subordinating the state to him, Aristotle is departing from traditional Greek political theory, and opening the way for the development of the concept of individualism.

THE EXTERNAL GOODS AND BODILY GOODS OF THE STATE: In the next chapters Aristotle turns to the necessary conditions a state must have if it is to achieve a life of well-being. His standard for what the proper amount of necessary conditions should be may be summed up in one word: self-sufficiency.

1. POPULATION: The population of the Ideal State should not be too large or too small. Aristotle feels that it is particularly important that the population not be too big, as it is harder to maintain law and order when it is; and second, the state will contain too large a number of slaves and foreigners in proportion to the number of citizens. If the population is too small, however, the state cannot be self-sufficient. Aristotle concludes that the population should be small enough so that all the citizens can know each other sufficiently well to make awards and judge one another accurately. It should be large enough to enable every trade to be represented in the state so that the necessary work of the city gets done. Aristotle's rule for the ideal population is: "the greatest surveyable number required for achieving a life of self-sufficiency."

2. TERRITORY: Here too Aristotle looks for the mean between extremes; like the population of the Ideal State, it must be able to be wholly seen in a single view. It should be large enough to enable the citizens to live a life of leisure, but not too large to encourage them to excess and too many luxuries. It should be "difficult for enemies to reach the city and small enough so that the defense of the territory can be easily planned." It should also have a close connection to the sea for reasons of military security and the maintenance of proper commercial relations. Some fear that a location by the sea will make the state prey to the immigration of undesirable foreigners. Aristotle does not take this problem very seriously. As far as its economic policy is concerned, Aristotle feels that the state should have a self-sufficient market. It should import those commodities it really needs, and export only its surplus goods. Aristotle is also in favor of the state being a naval power.

3. THE NATURAL CHARACTER OF THE CITIZENS: Aristotle compares the qualities of the people of Europe, Asia and Greece, and sides in favor of his countrymen. The Europeans have high spirit, but little skill or intelligence, he says. The Asians, on the other hand, have little spirit, or vitality, but great skill and intelligence. The Greeks have both spirit and intelligence. A true chauvinist, Aristotle boasts that "The first quality makes them able to continue free; the second enables them to attain the highest poliical development, and to show a capacity for governing every other people—if only they could once achieve political unity." The legislator in the Ideal State will naturally want to combine both spirit and intelligence in the character of his people.

4. SOCIAL STRUCTURE: Aristotle has already said a good deal about the different kinds of class structure existing in different states. His discussion in this passage simply supplements his earlier observations. He distinguishes between those groups which form the "necesary conditions" of the state, and those which are an "integral part," i.e., the citizens of the state. Taking both parts together, Aristotle distinguishes six functions which are necessary to the state: 1) agriculture, 2) arts and crafts, 3) defense, 4) property and land ownership, 5) political deliberation, and 6) civil jurisdiction and public worship. The question arises whether all of these functions are to be performed by a separate class, or can some of them be combined in the same class. To answer this question, Aristotle divides his functions among citizens and noncitizens. 1) In his view, the first two functions, agriculture and arts and crafts, cannot be performed by full citizens, because citizens need free time and leisure. 2) The last three functions, defense, public worship, and civil administration, however, should in one sense be performed by the same body of citizens, and in another sense, should not. For example, the military will not consent to be ruled forever, but it should not rule because a soldier has different skills than a judge. Similarly, a judge has different qualifications from a priest. Aristotle solves the dilemma by having the whole body of citizens perform each of these functions at some time of their life. The young men enter the army. The middle-aged engage in politics and public administration, while the old men serve as priests to the community. 3) Finally, Aristotle considers the function of land-ownership. Aristotle says that the farmers should not own the land, as they are usually serfs or slaves. He believes that the best system is a system of public and private ownership. The private land is to be owned by all the citizens. Each citizen should have some acreage near the border of the state and some near the city. In this way, the distribution of land will be just, and each citizen will be willing to fight to defend his country, because he has a personal interest in its survival. The public land should be the means of providing for public services, such as a system of common meals, or public worship. The cultivation of all the land in the Ideal State will be done by slaves or serfs.

5. CITY PLANNING: We often think that city planning is a modern invention. Aristotle, however, devotes a full chapter to problems of laying out the best possible city. 1) The plan should be functional. It should not be drawn up without reference to actual conditions. One of the most vital problems in his view is the problem of health. A good planner, he says, will see to it that the city has a good exposure, preferably to the east, and an adequate water supply. 2) Defense is also a consideration. The city should have a proper internal layout; whether the city should have straight, or crooked, haphazard streets depends on the type of constitution and other related factors. The constitution also dictates the kind of fortifications a city should have. Aristocracies and monarchies usually like to have a central fortified stronghold or *acropolis* in their city, while democracies prefer a level territory. A second aspect of defense is the problem of the fortification around the city. 3) Finally, the planner has to consider the type of political activities which are to take place in the city, and provide for them. This means planning a good-sized marketplace with a law court and business area next to it. The planner must also provide for places where common meals can be taken as well as for places of worship. Aristotle recommends that temples and religious shrines be placed on "commanding sites." 4) Finally, and most important to any Greek, the whole city must be planned with an eye for beauty and taste. It must be aesthetically pleasing. The city space should be designated to accommodate all the many activities which must go on in a city. But the city must be planned as a whole, so that its various parts will go harmoniously together.

COMMENT: It cannot be repeated too often that Aristotle's views of the state are founded on the conditions which prevailed in city states of his time. Thus, in his entire discussion of the Ideal State, he means the ideal *Greek* city-state, as his sentiment indicates that Greeks have the best temperament for self-government. In this regard, there is much sense in his insisting that the city not be too large. Those who live in large cities know the degree to which lawlessness and crime run riot. In his conception of city planning, he probably has the city of Athens in his mind and wants to keep her good points and correct her faults in his perfectly planned city. The student will note that he lays great stress on both functionalism and beauty. The two are inseparable in his view.

BOOKS VII AND VIII
EDUCATION: THE CULTIVATION OF
VIRTUE IN THE STATE

INTRODUCTION: In the last section of Book VII and the whole of Book VIII, Aristotle takes up the subject which he has most emphasized throughout the *Politics,* namely, education. He has repeatedly made it clear that he believes that neither equality of economic conditions, nor any policy of economic aggrandizement produces the well-being of the state. If you want a law-abiding and happy state, you must train the citizens in the spirit of their constitution. Since the ideal state will, of course, provide the best training, Aristotle concludes the *Politics* with a description of what the "best" training is. We will not go into the details of Aristotle's educational system. The important thing is to know its principles.

THE ART OF THE LEGISLATOR IS EDUCATION: The best state is that state which possesses the best possibility of achieving happiness. Happiness, we know from the *Ethics,* is the activity and practise of virtue. The truly good man is he who possesses goodness and all the necessary material advantages which help him to make himself a good man. But these material advantages are secondary, as Aristotle never tires of repeating. In the state there are also things that are "given," such as the economic and social conditions of the country. But as a harp-player learns to play the harp from his teacher, and not from the instrument, so the citizen learns virtue not from his economic surroundings, but from the legislator. The art, or *techne,* of the legislator is education, both by law and by mental and physical training.

DEFINITION OF EDUCATION: Virtue depends on three human attributes: 1) our natural impulse to be good; 2) our ability to become good by forming good habits; and 3) our capacity, unique in the natural world, to be guided by a rule of reason, or intelligence, which tells us what goodness is. Education is concerned with the last two attributes: it is the formation of good habits by an appeal to the intelligence.

EDUCATION AND THE CITIZEN: The first problem to be solved is whether the education of the rulers and the education of the ruled should be two different systems, as Plato suggested in his *Republic.* We have already seen that in the Ideal State, all of the citizens will have a share in ruling, although they will not all rule at the same time. While the young men are soldiers, they will be part of the ruled, and the middle-aged men will form the ruling class. Aristotle's Ideal State is a government of freemen by freemen. In this type of government, therefore, the young men must begin by learning the virtue of the ruled, namely obedience. But they will be obeying a free government in which they some day will take part. Thus, while learning obedience, they will at the same time be learning to govern when their turn comes. For this reason in the Ideal State, education in obedience is not in any sense dishonorable, because the young men are preparing themselves for a glorious future, namely, governing others. They will realize the perfection of both civic and moral virtue when they come to govern others. As Aristotle made clear in Book III, in the Ideal State, the virtue of the good citizen is the same as the virtue of the good man, when the citizen actually shares in the government of the state.

PLANNING THE EDUCATIONAL SYSTEM: In planning the educational system, the legislator must organize it according to the requirements of human nature. 1) There are two different parts of the soul: the rational faculty, or intelligence, in which the end of man is to be realized; and the non-rational faculty which obeys the commands of reason. 2) There are two kinds of reason: the practical and theoretical reason. In Aristotle's opinion, human life is also divided up according to the different parts of the soul. For this reason, there is action and leisure, war and peace. The non-rational soul is concerned mainly with action and war, while the reason is directed chiefly towards leisure and questions of peace. As the non-rational soul must obey reason, so, Aristotle says, action and war must be subordinated to leisure and peace. They are good only as long as they contribute to bringing about leisure and peace.

A GOOD EDUCATION IS WELL-ROUNDED: A good educational system, according to Aristotle, must see to it that both faculties of the soul and both aspects of life are taken into account. There is nothing more harmful to the development of personality, he feels, than the concentration on one part of the soul to the neglect of the other. Similarly, there is nothing worse than presenting only one aspect of life as the best one. Education must be well-rounded. Aristotle has no patience with the men of his day who praised the Spartan educational system because it treated war and conquest of empire as the reason for and goal of a nation's existence. He asks where Sparta is today. She has lost her empire, and it is obvious that she neither was nor is a happy community. Training for war, he says, is a means not an end. It has a threefold purpose: 1) to prevent freemen from becoming enslaved themselves; 2) to put men in a position to exercise leadership in the interest of the led, and not for the purpose of establishing a system of slavery; and 3) to enable men to become good masters of those who "naturally deserve to be slaves."

> **COMMENT:** Throughout the *Politics* Aristotle has had much to say about natural slaves. As was seen in Chapter VII of Book VII, he did not hold a very high opinion of non-Greek races. In this he was no exception to his countrymen. From the very beginning of their civilization, the Greeks called non-Greeks, *barbaroi,* which means barbarians, or uncivilized people. As Aristotle suggested in Chapter VII, he believes the Greeks naturally are in a position to rule over the barbarian peoples because of their greater gifts and greater civilization. Indeed, he probably would not have called any barbarian or non-Greek peoples civilized, unless they were "Greekized." For him the distinction between Greek and barbarian is that between civilization and barbarism. For this reason, he thinks the barbarians are naturally to be ruled, while the Greeks are their natural rulers.

LEISURE: Aristotle has set forth the rather unusual theory that the rational faculty of the soul is *naturally* directed towards the pursuits of leisure and peace. Leisure, in the Greek world, did not mean "doing nothing." The word, *skole,* (leisure), is the root of our word "school." Leisure for the Greeks was an activity opposed to *askolia,* non-leisure, or occupation. Occupation to them meant working to provide the necessities of life, for example, farming, manual labor, and business. Leisure, however, referred to the specific activity of the rational soul, directed towards ends which are "pursued for their own sake." Leisure, therefore, was primarily concerned with contemplation and thinking. In between leisure and occupation came *anapausis,* or recreation. As the word suggests, recreation for the Greeks was a pause between activities. One aspect of recreation is amusement, or *paidia.* The word is derived from the Greek word for child and means literally the "type of thing a child would do." Aristotle considers leisure (the chance to think and reflect) essential for any man who wants to become good. In his opinion, however, it is not easy to achieve leisure. It demands the training of certain virtues, such as wisdom and self-control, he says. The Spartan educational system was so poor because it only trained its citizens for a life of occupation through the virtues of courage and endurance. In peacetime, however, these same virtues can become vices. Men are inclined to get bored when they are without occupations if they have not been trained differently. To relieve their boredom, they turn on one another.

WHAT IS THE BEST WAY TO TRAIN CITIZENS FOR LEISURE?
Should one educate the reason first, or train the non-rational part of the soul in the habit of obedience? Aristotle says that the non-rational faculty should be trained first as the means to the final end, namely, the education of the mind. But before either of these forms of education can take place, there should be some training of the body, so that it will become a "good servant of the soul."

EDUCATION IS BOTH PHYSICAL AND MENTAL TRAINING:
In his educational system, Aristotle shows himself a believer in the ideal: *mens sana in corpore sano,* a healthy mind in a healthy body. Having thus stated his principles, he proceeds to give his views on the training of children, on marriage and eugenics, and on the training of youth.

THE ROLE OF THE STATE IN EDUCATION: Book VIII proposes legislation concerning education, and emphasizes again the fact that different constitutional systems require different types of education. Each government has a character of its own, and it is the duty of the state to foster this character in its citizens. "We must not regard the citizen as belonging just to himself: we must

rather regard every citizen as belonging to the state." The ulti-mate responsibility for education rests with the state, for it is the responsibility of the state to look after its parts.

END OF BOOK VIII: Aristotle ends Book VIII with a dis-cussion of the value of an education in music, stressing in particu-lar the moral element in musical training. Book VIII, thus, leaves the discussion of education unfinished. We are left knowing nothing about how adults are to be trained in self-government while the analysis of the education of young people is not completed.

SIGNIFICANCE OF ARISTOTLE'S EDUCATIONAL THEORY:
In conclusion, it may be said that Aristotle's view of education laid the basis for the traditional European and American ideal of liberal arts training. Modern educators may object to his em-phasis on the moral element in education, and would probably ask for more training in specific subjects, such as the sciences and various manual skills. Yet, in the past years, well-known scientific institutions, such as MIT, have started liberal arts programs in the belief that overemphasis on pure science or engineering leaves a graduate without the proper intellectual tools which active parti-cipation in American life requires. They argue that the student may be trained in science, but he will not be able to make those decisions upon which our national safety and way of life depend. There could not be any greater tribute to Aristotle's view of education as training in the moral values of one's civilization than this.

CRITICISM OF ARISTOTLE'S POLITICAL THEORY: There is one problem which Aristotle leaves unsolved. At the end of the *Politics*, we find that the state is the whole, and man, the part of human life. The state is the moral agent which trains its members to perform their function properly. Yet, at the end of the *Ethics*, Aristotle very definitely assigns the highest place to the individual lost in contemplation of the good and the true. He makes no effort to reconcile these two views of what man *ought* to do. Should he submerge himself and identify himself with the life of the state, or should he pursue his lone individual and highly personal path towards wisdom? In other words, which is the higher moral agent, the state or the individual? This question was the consequence of the downfall of the Greek city-state system. Aristotle was on the brink between the old unified moral world of the *polis* and the new cosmopolitan Hellenic world. The value system had outgrown the city-state and was to be found by the individual, paradoxically, both in the world order and in himself.

THE *POETICS*

INTRODUCTION: Of the three works which Aristotle classifies under the productive sciences, two seem to the modern reader to belong unquestionably to the ancient world. These are the *Topics,* or "how to make a good argument," and the *Rhetoric,* or "how to give a good speech." As the Greeks were a nation of inveterate talkers, it is not surprising that, with Aristotle, argument and speechmaking should have come into their own as skills or arts which the lawyer and the officeholder must needs learn, if they are to be successful. Interesting as these two works are, the careful distinctions and logical refinement which constitute their subject matter seem like an art from the ancient past, long forgotten, and of little practical use to us. The third work of this group, the *Poetics,* however, enjoys a completely different status. Perhaps no other work of Aristotle's has had such an influence on subsequent generations of philosophers and artists as this one has had. Although Aristotle never intended the *Poetics* to be a fully thought-out philosophy of art, it nevertheless was the first attempt in history to analyze the beautiful and the pleasing from the standpoint of the individual art work itself, free from ethical principles. The subject matter of the *Poetics* is self-evident: poetry, and the poetry of tragedy, in particular.

INFLUENCE OF PLATO'S AESTHETIC THEORY: In his treatment of art in the *Republic* and elsewhere, Plato demonstrated his keen awareness of the impact of a great art work upon its audience. He realized that no matter how crude or morally bad the subject, if it were handled by a talented artist, the resulting art work would be a great work of art. For this reason, he thought a morally bad subject beautifully presented would encourage men actually to do bad deeds, by virtue of art's power of appeal to the irrational part of man's soul. To avoid this danger, Plato was in favor of controlling the production of art in his Ideal State, so that only those works appeared which were morally uplifting, and helped the citizen to live a good life. Precisely because art has such an emotional appeal, Plato thought it should be used as a tool to educate men. The principle theme of his aesthetics is that art should teach morality. This view of art as propaganda is held by the leaders of the Soviet Union today.

ARISTOTLE—ART FOR ART'S SAKE: In the *Poetics*, Aristotle considers the art work as a work of art, not as an instrument of propaganda. In his usual fashion, he sets out to discover what is the nature of art, and what good art really is. In so doing, he marks a major departure from his teacher. His inquiry into the nature of poetry starts not with a moral "ought" but with his customary observation of fact. Art can assume different forms, he says. "Making" can be of an epic, tragedy, comedy, poetry, music and dancing. After defining each of these forms in turn, he proceeds to lay down rules for what he considers the best form of art, namely tragedy. But before he discusses any kind of poetry, he first has to determine the first principles of his science.

THE PRINCIPLES OF ART: Aristotle's famous first principle of poetry, and indeed of any art, is that "art is an imitation of nature." There has been perhaps more controversy over what Aristotle really meant by art being an "imitation" of nature than there has been over any other aspect of his philosophy. Does he mean that art copies nature, for instance? If he does, then his theory can offer no explanation why we can make things which are not found in the world of nature. Perhaps he means that the artist sits down at his easel and simply reproduces faithfully what he sees. Aristotle was too fine a thinker to propose a crude "first principle" such as this.

ART THE COMPLETION OF NATURE: To understand what Aristotle's concept of art is, we must first know something about the Greek word for art, *techne*, from which comes the English words "technical," "technology," and "technique." As can be seen from the kind of words derived from it, *techne* does not refer to the fine arts at all. In fact, the Greeks had no word for fine art. *Techne* meant to the Greeks, as it still does to us in the derived words, a "skill," the "making" of a thing. The world for them was divided into the world of nature and the world where things were made. In the *Physics* Aristotle makes it plain that he thinks processes which seem unintelligible in the world of nature can be best illustrated by the world of making, or *techne*. To demonstrate his definition of natural process, for instance, he turns to *techne* for an example of motion, the building of a house. In his treatment of the four causes, he again turns to *techne* for the example of the bronze which becomes a statue. Art, the process of human making, he believes, is similar to nature or the process of natural growth. Nature herself is an artist, he says, for it is obvious that every natural process is directed toward an end. Man begets man, for instance. Moreover, one process follows another to accomplish the final purpose of nature, whatever that may be. In this respect, art has a vital function to perform for it takes over where nature leaves off. Nature makes the acorn become an oak, but only art can make an oak become an oak table. Thus, says Aristotle, in a famous passage in Book II of the *Physics*, "art brings to completion that which nature is unable to finish, and in this sense she imitates nature. If then artificial processes are purposeful, natural ones are too."

IMITATION IN ART: Aristotle opens the *Poetics* with the remark that in the world of making there are many kinds of imitation. There is music and the various kinds of poetry, for instance. These differ in their imitation of nature in three ways: 1) the means (color or the voice), 2) the object, or what is imitated, and 3) the manner of imitation.

1. THE MEANS OF ART IMITATION: Aristotle distinguishes three *means* in art imitation: rhythm, language, and harmony, or tune. Music, for instance, uses rhythm and harmony. Dancing is rhythm without tune. Prose writing imitates by language alone. Epic and elegiac poetry imitate by the use of language and rhythm, which together constitute metre. For example, "The Assyrian came down like a wolf on the fold." Only lyric, tragic, and comic poetry use all three means—rhythm, language, and tune.

2. THE OBJECT OF IMITATION: What does art imitate? Aristotle rejects Plato's view that the artist imitates the shadowy unreal world of becoming (the world that is known to the senses), because it means that the artist copies a copy of reality which is knowable to the mind alone. Consequently, he never imitates the truth. Aristotle boldly states that art imitates "men in action"; in his view art is primarily concerned with the character of men which, as we already know, Aristotle believes can only be known through action. Art imitates the world of man's soul. It is thus an imitation not of the material world, as Plato taught, but of the world of forms (for the soul is the form of man) that is known by the mind. Because art imitates the character of man, Aristotle believes the artist must represent men either better or worse than they really are. Comedy, for instance, represents men as worse than they are; tragedy as better than they are.

3. MANNER OF IMITATION: The third difference in the way art imitates nature is in the *kind of imitation*. Aristotle does not make his meaning here quite clear. Sophocles, he says, in one sense is the same kind of imitator as Homer, for both imitate ideal characters. In another sense, Sophocles is the same kind of imitator as the comic writer, Aristophanes, because both are dramatists, they write "poems representing action." In general, it seems that Aristotle's distinction sets off dramatic from narrative writing.

THE ORIGIN OF POETRY: According to Aristotle, poetry has two causes which are found in the nature of man himself. 1) The first cause is man's instinct to imitate. It is by imitation, he says, that a child starts to learn, because he experiences a definite pleasure in the things imitated. This point is important. Aristotle is saying that we delight in the work of art not only because of what it represents but also because of *the way it is made*. This explains why things which we would not like to see in the real world, such as a murder, we enjoy seeing in a work of art. Aristotle says that we enjoy art objects because of the nature of the way we learn. The artist opens our eyes, and widens our perspectives. When you look at a painting or go to a play, you take pleasure in recognizing your friends in the characters of the play, because you have learned something new about them.

THE SECOND CAUSE OF POETRY: This is man's natural instinct for tune and rhythm. We enjoy the appeal to the senses found in all art, whether it be color, music, or form. In this connection, it is important to realize that Aristotle never underestimates the sensual aspect of art. All through the *Poetics,* he draws our attention to the fact that the appeal to the senses constitutes the chief source of our pleasure in art. The first poem was written by a man who had more talent in improvising rhythm and words than his friends.

DEVELOPMENT OF POETRY: From this beginning, poetry took two directions: some poets imitated the actions of good men, and some the actions of lesser men. Homer is an example of the more serious poet, while satire represents the actions of lesser men. From these two types of poets came the tragic writer and the comic writer. Seeing in the history of poetry the progressive evolution of art forms, Aristotle makes it clear that he considers drama a more advanced form of poetry. Tragedy is thus a better means of imitating the actions of good men than the type of "seriousness" of the *Iliad* or the *Odyssey*. Aristotle even questions whether tragedy has reached its highest form or not.

EVOLUTION OF TRAGEDY: Both tragedy and comedy started, as did the first poetry, by improvisation. Spoken parts were inserted into two old forms of religious choral singing, the dithyramb and the phallic hymn. Aristotle traces the evolution of tragedy from the dithyramb to its "natural form." The first great Greek tragic poet, Aeschylus, he tells us, introduced a second actor, and deepened the importance of the chorus, so that the dialogue became the most important part of the play. The next tragic poet, Sophocles, increased the number of actors to three, and added scenery. Second, by lengthening the plot, he introduced the "grand manner" into tragedy which took the place of earlier forms of diction. Third, he made changes in meter. The trochaic meter (- ᵛ) gave way to iambic meter (ᵛ -) which in Aristotle's opinion is the more proper conversational meter for dialogue. Finally, the play itself was lengthened into five episodes or scenes.

HISTORY OF COMEDY: Although tragedy has a long history, comedy, Aristotle tells us, does not. Comedy, he thinks, had already taken the form known in his day by the time it had reached that stage of its development when it could be called comic. He thinks that the idea of the comic plot came from Sicily, but says it was the Athenian, Crates, who introduced the general formula for comedy familiar to him.

> **COMMENT:**   The *Poetics* contains much valuable material for the student of Greek literature. For a long time it was the only source we had on the origin and development of Greek drama. Recent research, however, has made a great contribution to our knowledge of the field.

THE DIFFERENCE BETWEEN EPIC POETRY AND TRAGEDY: Epic poetry and tragedy are alike in that they both are imitations of serious characters in a high type of verse. They differ in many ways, however. Epic poetry is written in only one meter and is narrative in form. An epic tells a story and does not act one. Again, epic poetry has no time limit; the action of the epic can take place over several years or even centuries. But the action of tragedy generally takes place within a single day.

> **COMMENT:**   In practice on the Greek stage, the action of tragedy was generally held within the limits of one day, or even from sunrise to sundown.

All the elements of epic poetry are found in tragedy, but not vice versa. Thus, from the standpoint of technique as well as evolution, tragedy is a higher form of poetry. After these introductory comments, Aristotle turns to an analysis of tragedy. This discussion takes up the remainder of the *Poetics*, and in many respects, resembles a manual to the budding writer on how to write a good play.

DEFINITION OF TRAGEDY: Having determined the first principles of *techne*, the nature of the species of poetry, and the difference between two very similar forms of poetry, the epic and tragedy, Aristotle is ready to say what tragedy is. "Tragedy," he says in a now-famous definition, "is an imitation of an action which is serious, complete in itself, and of a certain magnitude, in language embellished with every kind of artistic ornament which is to be found separately in the different parts of the play; in a dramatic not a narrative form; through pity and fear bringing about the purgation (*katharsis*) of these emotions." What this definition means becomes more clear as we go further into the *Poetics*, but some things can be said about it now. 1) Aristotle has already explained what he means by imitation. 2) "Language embellished" denotes the poetic means of rhythm, language and tune. 3) The "artistic ornament" found "separately" in the different parts of the play refers to the fact that in Greek drama some parts were spoken, some sung, and, frequently the chorus danced.

OTHER CHARACTERISTICS: Tragedy must have the following: 1) scenery, 2) song, and 3) diction, or the arrangement of words in meter form. 4) Since tragedy is the imitation of an action, it concerns character "that by which we say that a person has certain qualities." 5) Tragedy must have thought, i.e., it must deal with universal truths; and 6) it must have plot, or an arrangement of events.

IMPORTANCE OF THE SIX PARTS: Of the six parts of tragedy, Aristotle considers plot the "soul of tragedy" because without plot, or ordered action, there can be no tragedy and there can be no character. Plot is the first principle of tragedy in that it contains the most powerful elements of emotional interest, namely what Aristotle calls "scenes of reversal" of the situation, and "recognition." Character is second in importance to plot. It is important because it shows the moral purpose of the hero by revealing what kinds of things he chooses or avoids. Third in importance is thought, which Aristotle defines as "the ability to say what is possible and relevant in a given circumstance." Diction comes fourth. Of the "embellishments," Aristotle considers song most important. The sixth part, spectacle, has for Aristotle the least artistic merit, although he agrees that it is important as an emotional appeal to the audience.

TRAGEDY AS ACTION: Returning to his definition, Aristotle discusses what he means when he says the action of tragedy must be complete, whole, and of a certain magnitude, or length. 1) To be complete, he says, tragedy must have a beginning, a middle, and an end. The beginning must be understandable and natural, while the middle and the end must follow logically from the beginning. 2) A whole implies structure, and order. This means that a plot must show some kind of inner cohesion, or fail to be a plot. The plot must be of a certain length. The Greeks understood beauty in terms of visual proportion. In their view, the beautiful is a formal arrangement of parts with a definite limit of size relative to our power of sight. For this reason, a small animal cannot be beautiful, because the eye can see all of it in too short a space of time. A large animal cannot be beautiful for the eye cannot take it all in at once, and it loses its sense of the whole. What is the proper length for tragedy, that will permit the mind to grasp it in the proper way? Aristotle says it is that length which can be properly taken in by the memory, so "the sequence of events, according to the law of probability, or necessity, will bring about a change from bad fortune to good, or from good fortune to bad." The proper length of tragedy is a mean relative to our mental capacities.

THE CHARACTERISTICS OF TRAGIC ACTION: 1) It follows from the foregoing that there can be only one complete action or plot to a tragedy. Aristotle insists that there cannot be several plots in the same play, because this would detract from the unity and power of the drama. 2) Each part of the plot must be necessary, so that if one part is removed, the whole will seem incomplete and out of proportion. 3) Perhaps the most interesting of all Aristotle's conditions for a good plot is that the action must not relate what actually *did* happen, but what possibly *can* happen. The plot must have an inner continuity which must seem possible, but should not have happened. History, says Aristotle, relates what actually happened. But poetry relates what may happen, i.e., how a certain type of person will react in a given situation. History is only of individual events, *but poetry is of universals*. For this reason, Aristotle considers poetry superior to history. Because it is of universals, tragedy, in his view, is by its very nature more scientific than history. Thus, Aristotle does not believe that playwrights should stick to legend or historical incidents as their source of material. As long as the plot seems possible, there is no reason why the dramatist should not invent a plot of his own choosing.

COMMENT: The modern mind may be surprised that Aristotle valued tragedy and poetry in general above history. In our day, the theater tends to be a source of amusement rather than of knowledge. Yet, Aristotle's view has much sense in it. As we have seen, he believes that knowledge is only possible of universals. We can never know particular, individually existing things and events, except as we can determine what way they are similar to, or different from, other existing things. Tragedy shows us what is universal in human action and in human character. It thus enables us to interpret both personal actions and historical events correctly. Because it is concerned with particulars, and therefore, the unknowable, history can only be understood in the light of philosophy and poetry. For this reason, Aristotle ranks history as a secondary subject. In so doing, he is simply stating a fact of which every writer of history is aware. It is not so much the events that are important, but the interpretation of them that counts in the determination of historical truth.

KATHARSIS: Tragedy is an imitation not of any action, but of a particular kind of action with a particular purpose in view. In his definition of tragedy, Aristotle says that it must inspire pity and fear. He considers the aim of tragedy the purgation of these two emotions or the "cancelling-out" of the one by the other. This result is what he calls *katharsis*. The Greek word means "cleansing, or purging." Aristotle says that a *katharsis* of our emotions is brought about when there is an element of surprise in tragedy. Just what he means by *katharsis* no one really knows, and many learned books have been written on the subject. Scholars seem to fall roughly into two categories in the way they regard *katharsis*. One group holds that Aristotle understood *katharsis* as some kind of religious experience, similar to the purging of the soul of guilt, which took place in the Greek mystery religion, the Orphic mysteries. More recent scholars tend to support a second view that Aristotle considered *katharsis* primarily a medical phenomenon. They argue that the word was first used in a medical context, and referred to the cleansing of the body of ill humors. Since the idea that tragedy was supposed to arouse pity and fear was a popular theory, no doubt *katharsis* meant something particular to the Greeks that we can only imagine. In trying to discover what Aristotle might have meant by *katharsis*, therefore, we would have to know exactly how tragedy arouses pity and fear. Do we fear for the hero, and pity ourselves, for instance? Or do we sympathize with the hero, because we could be in his place, and thus fear for ourselves? Unfortunately, Aristotle never goes into what he means by pity and fear, probably because the two concepts were so familiar to men of his time. But he has given us some indication of what he means by *katharsis*. In his discussion of music in Book VIII of the *Politics,* Aristotle distinguishes three kinds of music: one for educative purposes; one for relaxation; and a third for release of emotion. This third kind, which he calls "orgiastic," or frenzied music, is not directed at the moral or cultural education of the individual, nor is it for his amusement. Its purpose is *katharsis*. Melodies which bring *katharsis,* he tells us, "excite the soul to a mystic frenzy," so that the soul is "calmed and restored as though it had gone through a medical treatment and purging." "This same sort of effect," he continues, "will also be produced on the best of us, and the result will be that all alike will experience some sort of purging, and a release of emotion accompanied by pleasure." It is clear from this passage that Aristotle considers release of emotion, or perhaps we might call it, release from emotional tensions, as necessary to the healthy individual as education and relaxation. It is the function of tragedy to bring about this necessary release, i.e., *katharsis*. Is this release the same sort of release we get today from going to a football game? Probably not. Again, although all of us will agree that we experience some sort of soul-cleansing when we go to see a tragedy of Shakespeare, even this feeling is no doubt far from Aristotle's meaning. Were Greeks overemotional, and therefore Aristotle felt they had to be given a chance to calm their emotions down? We shall never know. *Katharsis* as the aim of tragedy is still a mystery for the scholar to solve.

THE PARTS OF TRAGEDY: From a consideration of tragedy as a whole, Aristotle turns to its parts. Of the six parts mentioned above, three are related to the "object of imitation," plot, character and thought; and three to the "means of imitation," diction, song and spectacle.

PLOT: Aristotle says plots are either simple or complex. A complex plot is one in which a change of fortune takes place; a simple plot is one in which no change takes place. The change of fortune, (wealth to poverty, ignorance to knowledge), is brought about in one of two ways. The first is what Aristotle calls *reversal of fortune,* when the action of the tragedy takes the opposite course than the one it has been taking. The second way is by *recognition,* which Aristotle defines as "a change from ignorance to knowledge, producing love or hate between the characters involved." He gives many examples of these two means of changing the fortune of the tragic hero, and insists that both of these two means must come upon the viewer as a complete surprise if pity and fear are to be aroused. Unfortunately, he does not explain how the events of a play can come as a surprise, when the plot is already well known to the audience through legend and history. The third part of the plot is what Aristotle calls the *scene of suffering*, where death, murder or some painful event is enacted on the stage. The perfect tragedy to Aristotle is the one which uses the complex plot. The perfect change of fortune is the one in which "a man who is not very good and just, yet whose misfortune is brought about not by vice and wickedness, but by some error or weakness" is the hero. For example, in the great Greek play by Sophocles, *Oedipus the King*, Oedipus' reversal of fortune is brought about because he thought he could solve the problem of the plague which was raging in his city single-handed. In fact, he was the cause of the plague, but didn't realize his own situation.

RELATION OF PITY AND FEAR TO PLOT—DISCOVERY: Pity and fear can be aroused either through the spectacle attached to the play or through the element of discovery in the action of the play. Aristotle says the latter is the better way. Family situations are the source of actions which arouse most pity and fear, in his opinion, as when a son kills a mother, a brother kills a sister, or a wife her husband. Sometimes he says the murder is a result of ignorance, as when Oedipus kills his father, and sometimes it occurs with the full knowledge of the hero, as when Medea kills her children. Aristotle feels pity and fear are better aroused when the deed is done in ignorance, and the discovery or realization of what has been done comes later.

CHARACTER—THE IDEAL TRAGIC HERO: The relation of character to plot in Aristotle's analysis of tragedy is considered by most scholars to be the same as the relation of matter to form. Character is plot which has not been made actual. It is potentially plot. Plot is therefore character-in-action. You only know what sort of person a man is when you see him act. His acts reveal his character, the moral element in his soul, and, Aristotle would say, actually *are* his character. The same is true of characters in a play. There are four things which the playwright must aim at in making a tragic character. 1) The hero must be good, regardless of his station in life. 2) Character must be suitable to the hero. Manly courage is not appropriate in a woman, for example. 3) Character must be true to life, and 4) character must be consistent. The hero must act and speak as he would be expected to do. His actions must have an understandable motivation. Aristotle makes three further distinctions: the hero should be well known. The common man is not a proper subject for tragedy, says Aristotle, the aristocrat. One of his main objections to the Greek tragedian, Euripides, was that "he brought the common man onto the stage." Second, in drawing character and plot, the poet should always try to make them sound possible. Aristotle was not in favor of *deus ex machina* scenes, of which Euripides was a master, where the gods come onto the stage to unravel the threads of the plot. Finally, the character should be true to life, but yet more beautiful. The poet should ennoble the character of the hero. Aristotle has already made this point before.

FORMS OF RECOGNITION:　　In the next section, Aristotle considers different forms of recognition. As the discussion is rather technical, it is of little interest to the modern reader. Aristotle thinks the best recognition is when the discovery comes naturally and is as little contrived as possible. The key word here is vividness, and Aristotle urges the poet to keep the scene he is writing at all times before his eyes.

TECHNIQUES OF PLOT:　　In writing a play, says Aristotle very wisely, it is well to plan the plot and the scenes beforehand. Every tragedy falls into two parts, the *complication* and the *dénouement* or unraveling, of the threads. The complication leads up to the change of fortune and the dénouement goes from that high point to the end of the play. On the basis of what kind of change takes place, Aristotle distinguishes four kinds of tragedy: the simple, the complex, the ethical (where the motives are moral) and the pathetic (where the motives are passion or emotion). His last warning on plot writing is that the chorus, a typical feature of Greek tragedy, should also be considered an actor.

THOUGHT:　　Since the essence of tragedy is the imitation of action, thought plays a very minor role in Aristotle's analysis. Because moral goodness and excellence of character are revealed by action, he believes that the emphasis in tragedy must be on the plot. Thought, in Aristotle's definition, includes "every effect which has to be produced by speech," and he feels that this is a subject which is better left to the study of rhetoric. Speech is the proper objct of rhetoric, whereas action is the object of tragedy.

DICTION:　　Under diction, Aristotle discusses the language of tragedy. He spends much time analyzing the effect of the various parts of speech and the choice of words upon poetic diction. His aim is to show how the poet can combine clarity and preciseness of speech with beauty by choosing a judicious mixture of ordinary language and the rare word. His discussion is a handbook of poetic diction. A product of his culture, Aristotle has little sympathy for high-flown and obscure poetic language. The Greek concept of beauty was rooted in the ideas of limit, order, and form. Since order implied an intelligible arrangement of parts, beauty and clarity were almost interchangeable in the Greek mind. For this reason, Aristotle believes that the duty of the poet is not to indulge in lavish phrases, but to say what he has to say clearly with an eye to proportion. He sees the mark of genius in the poet's use of metaphor, because the poet's ability to get his meaning across depends upon his choice of similes. "To make a good metaphor," Aristotle says, "is to have an eye for similarities."

TRAGEDY AND EPIC POETRY: At the end of the *Poetics,* Aristotle returns to the comparison of tragedy and epic poetry which he began earlier. His purpose is to make a definite distinction between them.

SIMILARITIES: Aristotle says epic poetry is similar to tragedy in three ways. 1) Like tragedy, its action will be whole and complete, and will have a single action, thus resembling "a living organism." Aristotle sees in unity of action, one of the chief differences between both tragedy and epic poetry, and history, which is concerned with the many events which take place in a single period. Homer, he says, did not try to write about the whole Trojan War in the *Iliad,* because the whole war could not have been taken in by a single effort of the memory. 2) Epic poetry is similar to tragedy in that it can take the same forms. It too can be simple, complex, ethical, or pathetic. 3) Epic poetry has the same parts as tragedy, with the exception of song and spectacle. Furthermore, its thought and diction must also be dignified.

DIFFERENCES: Epic poetry differs from tragedy chiefly in 1) its *length.* By its very nature, tragedy is unable to imitate several courses of action which are going on at one and the same time. In the epic, however, the poet can present all the events which happened at the same time, simply by telling one right after the other. Aristotle thinks that the narrative form of writing has the advantage through its length of being able to have a grander effect upon the hearer, and to keep the listener from boredom. A monotonous incident on the tragic stage, he observes, can make the tragedy a failure. 2) The second difference comes in the use of *meter.* Whereas tragedy uses many meters, epic poetry is confined to one: the dactyllic hexameter. (— ∨∨ — ∨∨ — ∨∨ — ∨∨ — ∨∨ — —) Example: "This is the forest primeval, the murmuring pines and the hemlock." Aristotle considers the choice of this meter suitable and natural to the "grand and weighty bulk" of heroic verse. "Nature herself teaches the choice of the proper meter" in poetry, he says. 3) The final difference between tragedy and epic poetry is the most interesting; it concerns the relationship between *amazement* and the *fantastic* in poetry. Although "the element of amazement is required in tragedy," Aristotle feels that there is more room for the unexpected and irrational in epic poetry, because the characters are not seen on the stage. The pursuit of Hector around the walls of Troy, he says, would seem fantastic on the stage, but is perfectly probable and logical in the *Iliad*. In trying to define the relation of the fantastic to poetic effect, Aristotle gives us a word of caution. It is better to have "probable impossibilities than improbable possibilities," he says. Once the fantastic has been introduced, the writer should make every attempt to make us accept it as possible. Even though the artist may have been wrong to introduce the improbable into his work, he can rectify his mistake, if his use of the improbable heightens the effect of his work by contributing to the element of amazement. Aristotle condemns the use of both the improbable and badness of character, when there is no inner necessity for introducing them into the art work.

TRAGEDY IS BETTER THAN EPIC POETRY: The comparison of the two forms of "seriousness and dignity" in poetry leads Aristotle quite naturally to ask which is the better form: epic poetry or tragedy. General opinion, he points out, holds that epic poetry is better because it appeals to a better type of audience. The "many" say that tragedy is frequently overacted, and thus tends to appeal to a mass audience. Despite this strong argument, Aristotle thinks that tragedy is the better art form for five reasons. 1) It has all the poetic elements that an epic has, plus two more of its own, namely, music and spectacle. 2) It leaves a vivid impression when it is read as well as when it is acted. 3) As an art form, it is more concentrated, and its limits more defined. Aristotle believes that a more pleasurable effect is produced when an activity is concentrated than when it is spread out over a longer period of time. 4) Tragedy has greater unity of action. One epic poem, for example, will furnish subjects for many tragedies. 5) Finally, tragedy fulfills its specific function better than epic poetry, in bringing pleasure through *katharsis*.

END OF THE *POETICS*:   At the beginning of the *Poetics,* Aristotle mentions that he will later deal with the subjects of comedy, and other kinds of poetry. Unfortunately, the *Poetics* ends with the discussion of epic poetry. As it is the only work on aesthetics which

Aristotle wrote, we shall never know his view on the remaining forms of poetry.

SIGNIFICANCE OF THE *POETICS*:   As stated earlier, the *Poetics* should not be considered Aristotle's theory of art. Nevertheless, its influence on the development of the philosophy of aesthetics cannot be overestimated. Its chief contributions are of two kinds. 1) It states that art is independent from ethics in the sense that it can, and should be, judged by aesthetic standards alone. 2) Art imitates nature not by being a copy of nature, but by being the completion of a process which nature by herself would be unable to finish. These two concepts enable Aristotle to free art from dependency upon the material world, and from subservience to the "ought" of the morally good.

QUESTIONS AND ANSWERS
FOR REVIEW

1. What is the historical significance of Aristotle's ethical theory?

ANSWER: Aristotle's ethical theory marks the definite separation of individual moral values with social ethics. In making this separation definitive, Aristotle in many respects was following in the steps of his teacher, Plato. Plato took ethics out of the sphere of the purely political and made it superior to politics. His great contribution to philosophy was the recognition of *phronesis,* or moral intelligence, as the faculty in man which was able to grasp the meaning of absolute moral value. With the help of the concept of *phronesis* Plato was able to set up an objective standard of Absolute Good upon which the good of society and the individual in society depended. He took up the challenge of the Sophists, and examined the social values of the Greek city-state system of which he was a part, to show that most men did not know what real value was. They could not know what justice and truth were, because they lived in the unreal, shadow world of change and becoming. For this reason, he proposed to set up a model state according to his standard of absolute goodness, where men would be related to one another in perfect justice. In his theory of the Ideal State, Plato separated his value system from any actually existing political organization, and made the new society of his creation subject to his absolute standards. In doing this, Plato did not separate individual from public morality. On the contrary, he saw men as a part of the state, in the same way as the hand is part of the man. The philosopher first acquired knowledge of the Good, and then went back to his city to teach his knowledge to its citizens by means of education and good laws.

Plato distinguished absolute moral standards from those of a given society. He thus destroyed one of the principles upon which the Greek city state was based, namely, the identity of justice and morality with the state. Aristotle went one step further. He was the first to suggest that ethics might be primarily a matter of individual conscience, and only secondarily a matter of social behavior. He made his position clear in two ways.

First, he stated that there was no absolute objectively existing moral standard. Whether a certain kind of behavior was moral or not depended on the type of action performed, and the motivation of the agent. Virtue is a "mean relative to us," he said. It is applying general principles to individual action. Second, he subordinated the life of action in society to the life of contemplation. The best life was no longer a public life, but a private life of intense personal mental activity.

In separating individual moral standards from the moral standards of society, Aristotle took away the second foundation of Greek society, the identification of the individual with the state. He thus raised the question as to who was the higher moral agent, the state or the individual, and answered it in favor of the individual. For the first time in Western philosophy, the individual becomes independent of, and in a way superior to, the society in which he lives.

The significance of Aristotle's ethical theory is that it is essentially subjective. It is related not to an external social norm, but to some more general rule of reason, which is to be found both in man himself and in the larger context of the universe. Aristotle lived in the twilight years of the Greek city-state system, when traditional morality no longer seemed adequate to meet the more cosmopolitan demands of a Greek world which was reaching out to encircle the whole Mediterranean. With Aristotle, man turned in upon himself, and conversely out towards the larger world of natural law. Morality became a matter of individual conscience, the conforming of a man's behavior with the reason inherent in the order of the universe, and not in any particular society. This trend towards individualism was to find broader application in the later classical philosophies of Stoicism and Epicureanism, and eventually became the cornerstone of modern political and ethical theory.

2. Discuss Aristotle's view of art as imitation.

ANSWER: Aristotle's theory of art as the imitation of nature has aroused much controversy. In general, it may be considered under three topics: the way in which art imitates nature; the purpose of art; and the integrity of art.

It is clear that Aristotle did not think that art imitated nature in the sense that it copied natural objects. If art were purely representative, it would be impossible for the artist to create non-representative forms. The best explanation of how Aristotle thought art imitated nature is to be found in the *Physics*. In Book II he suggests that art imitates nature, in that it imitates natural processes. The acorn becomes an oak in a way similar to the way in which bronze becomes a statue. But nature can only do natural things. Art takes over where nature leaves off. In this sense, Aristotle says that art "perfects or completes" nature. The acorn can become an oak tree, but the oak tree can never become a table of its own effort. Nevertheless, the process by which the acorn becomes an oak, and the oak becomes a table both involve the same four elements of causation. There is the matter from which the finished product comes. There is the form which determines the kind of thing it is to be. There is the agent which brings the finished product into being; and there is the purpose or function for the sake of which the thing exists.

If art imitates nature, in the sense that it completes what nature by herself is unable to do, it is clear that art is never the same as nature. It exists independently of nature with a purpose of its own. Poetry, for example, imitates language, but it is language arranged in a special way for a special effect, which sets it off from ordinary speech. Tragedy, Aristotle tells us, imitates action, but it does not imitate ordinary action. The hero must be a man who is better both materially and spiritually than the average person, and the tragic plot must be built around him in such a way that it reveals his moral character. Tragedy, according to Aristotle, is not concerned with just any kind of action, but with that kind of action which tells us something fundamental about human nature. The purpose of all art is to give expression to the universal element in human life. Aristotle thinks that art, and especially its highest form, poetry, is concerned with the universal human condition.

To say that art is concerned with universals is not to say that art is science. In the opening chapter of the *Metaphysics* Aristotle discusses the relation of art to science, and where art stands in the hierarchy of knowledge. The doctor who cures a disease because he understands that all persons afflicted with the same disease have been helped by a particular medicine is an artist in relation to health. The scientist is the man who is concerned not with similarities but with universal principles of cause and effect. Art, according to Aristotle, is the result of our grasping those similarities in experience in view of which many separate experiences become a unified whole. In the *Poetics*, Aristotle "scientifically" analyzes the causes and effects of good tragedy, but his analysis does not explain tragedy. Tragedy is "the imitation of an action." It imitates those similarities which are universal to all human behavior. But it does not say why this universality exists.

A final characteristic of art as the imitation of nature is that it is self-contained and complete in itself. For this reason, Aristotle believes that it must be judged by standards of beauty, that is, by aesthetic criteria, which are peculiar to it alone. In the *Poetics*, Aristotle gives us his criteria for evaluating art, according to the three ways in which art can be said to imitate nature: 1) according to the means it uses, 2) according to the object, and 3) according to the method employed. Aesthetic values are essentially values relative to human demands. A true Greek, Aristotle bases his whole standard of beauty on a sense of proportion. Tragedy, for example, cannot be too short or too long. It must be just that length which will permit the memory to accept it in a single "glance." Art perfects nature, but it is a human perfection to be judged by human standards.

Aristotle views art as the imitation of nature in that nature is the material cause of art, the starting point for artistic creation, and because artistic making is fundamentally the same process as natural production. Nevertheless, the finished art work is an independent being in its own right, whose purpose is to express what is universal in human behavior and attitudes. This means that it must be judged according to aesthetic criteria which are suitable and applicable to art alone.

3. Why does Aristotle's understanding of nature and the motion of natural things necessitate a theory of a first cause?

ANSWER: Aristotle's First Cause is the logical consequence of his philosophy of nature. All natural things are in motion; they are continually coming into being and going out of being. They are thus things which can either be or not be. This means that they are always in potentiality to something else, either to being, or to non-being. According to Aristotle, if everything in the world was potential, the world would never be in the first place. The nature of our world, in his view, demands the prior existence of some being which is wholly actual. This means it must be immaterial (because matter is essentially potentiality) and eternally active (because things that stop and start can either act or not act; that is, they are in potentiality to action). Finally, the First Cause must be unmoved. If it is moved, while moving, we will have to say that there is something behind the First Cause which sets it in motion, and then some cause behind the cause which causes motion in the First Cause, and so on, back into infinity. As there can be no infinite series of regression, the First Cause must be unmoved.

Aristotle holds that there has to be an Unmoved Mover as the First Cause of the world we live in, because our world is in potentiality to time, space, and motion. In order for change to exist, there has to be something permanent underlying the change. The very permanence of change requires the existence of something which causes change to be eternal.

If Aristotle's natural philosophy requires the existence of a First Cause, the limitations of this philosophy impose limitations on the nature of his First Cause. His view of a First Mover does not include any concept of a Creator nor of an all-provident God. In the *Physics* he proves that time and motion are eternal. There always has been, and always will be time and motion, although each individual component of time, and each individual motion have a beginning, a middle and an end. If we suppose that there was a time when motion did not exist, we would have to suppose, according to Aristotle, some prior change or motion, which caused those things which were unmovable to be movable. This means that we would have to assume some motion behind the first motion which began motion, which is logically absurd. Furthermore, as time is the measure of motion, time must also have existed together with motion from all eternity. It follows, therefore, that the world cannot have been created.

One criticism of this view is that time and eternity are not the same. Eternity is not in time; it is really no time at all. In the same way, the infinite is not in space, but out of space. If time has been continuous from eternity, how do you explain the present? Aristotle says that time is potentially eternal, but actually, i.e., in the present, limited. This solution is not completely satisfactory. However, as the idea of creation was foreign to Greek tradition, it is difficult to see how he might have arrived at a theory of divine causation. Every Greek philosopher held that being can only come from something that *is*. You cannot make something out of nothing. And this is what creation means.

Aristotle's First Cause cannot be a provident God because of his understanding of natural teleology. At the end of the *Metaphysics* he raises the question as to whether the Unmoved Mover is in the world as its "battle order," or whether it is related to the world as the general is to his troops. He indicates that he holds the latter view. Yet he does not make it clear how he thinks that world is related to its First Cause. In an earlier work, *On Philosophy*, he apparently considered the idea that if there is a better, there must be a best. In other words, if nature exhibits a hierarchical system of order, there must be an apex to the pyramid. But in the *Metaphysics* it seems that his later thought did not exploit the theory of the final cause to enable his Unmoved Mover to exist as the ultimate fulfillment of the world. His natural philosophy led him to the idea that every natural object strives to realize its own final cause, which is immanent to itself, and is the perfection of its kind of form. But this theory did not bring him to any definite conclusions as to the final cause, or purpose of nature as a whole. The Unmoved Mover is thought thinking itself, a being eternally removed from the world, and related to it only as the object of desire is related to the desiring will.

Thus, Aristotle's natural philosophy leaves many unsolved problems in his metaphysics. On the one hand, it proves that a First Cause is necessary, and indicates in what way it can be said to exist. But it is not equipped to tell him what this First Cause is essentially, nor how it is related to the natural world.

4. How does Aristotle's functionalism contribute to his political theory?

ANSWER: Aristotle's functionalism may be said to contribute to his political theory in three ways. First, it lays the foundation for his view that man "by nature" is a political animal. In his opinion, man's function in the world is to act intelligently. In the *Ethics* he makes it clear that action cannot take place in isolation. In the strict sense of the word, an individual cannot act against himself. Action is social; it is related to others. Similarly, right reason is not purely subjective, but is related to the objective world around us. Consequently, it is impossible for a man to act intelligently if he lives the life of a hermit, or shuns human society altogether. A man who does this is, in Aristotle's opinion, either a monster or a god, but he is not truly human. Human society in the form of the state is the natural place for men to fulfill their function in life, just as the flock is the natural grouping in which birds fly. Second, Aristotle's functionalism determines the purpose of political society. If it is man's function to act according to right reason, then it is the function of the state to make it possible for him to do so. The political life of the state provides the arena in which moral action can take place. We are told in the *Ethics* that no man can be truly virtuous, if he lacks practical wisdom. From the *Politics* we learn that a man is most able to exercise this virtue when he is a ruler of his state. Moreover, if the rational life of man is really the essence of human existence, then the rational life of the state, i.e., legislation and statesmanship, is the purpose of the state's being. In one of the most noble expressions of the aims of political society, Aristotle tells us in the *Politics* that the state does not exist for economic purposes. It is neither an alliance for mutual security, nor an economic treaty. Its purpose is to promote human welfare. When a state loses its principal purpose, and makes economics or military aggrandizement its aim, it ceases to be a state, and becomes nothing but a contract between interests. Human happiness consists in living a life according to the dictates of reason. Social welfare must be directed towards this goal, or a state reverts to a group of households. It loses its bond which makes one body politic out of many members.

Finally, Aristotle's functionalism explains his insistence on the educative role of the state. If a man is to act intelligently, he must be trained to do so. For this reason, every state must bring up its citizens according to the value standards it exhibits in its constitution. Democracy, for example, is ruling and being ruled in turn. Consequently, young people must first be taught the virtue of subjects, which is obedience, in preparation for the day when they become rulers in their turn. Democrats must be taught that freedom is responsibility, not individual license. Oligarchs, on the other hand, must be taught to conduct themselves in such a manner that their subjects will not plot to overthrow them. All states must undertake the physical, mental and spiritual education of their citizens, in order that in a healthy body there may develop the moral and intellectual virtues necessary for a life of happiness. Aristotle emphasizes that it is the state's duty and obligation to educate its citizens. It performs its educative function through a formal system of education and through its laws, both of which are attuned to the spirit of its constitution. Man by nature is a political animal, he says. The state enables him to be a human being. Consequently, the state is the great educator of mankind.

5. How does Aristotle resolve the problem of man's subjective knowledge of an objective world?

ANSWER: Aristotle resolves the problem of man's subjective knowledge of an objective world through his concept of definition. Plato held that universal concepts existed independently from the matter in which they were found, in the pure world of forms. Aristotle rejects this view. He says that universals exist in matter as part of the definition of a thing. According to him, definition consists of the differences and similarities inherent in an object. When you say what a thing is, you say what it is like by referring to its genus and species, and how it is different with reference to its individual characteristics. Aristotle is insistent that when you say what a thing is, you are speaking about properties which actually belong to that particular thing, and are essential to its very nature. This means that the definition of a thing really constitutes the identity of that thing; it both expresses and *is* its essence. Definition, according to Aristotle, is the essential being of any concrete thing.

Definition is also the knowable aspect of a natural body. It is thus the starting-point for human thinking, the object of knowledge. When we say what a thing is, Aristotle holds that we know that particular thing, because definition is the outcome of the scientific syllogism which demonstrates the relation between the cause and the fact of a thing's existence. Moreover, our knowledge of one thing leads on to our knowledge of other things. We build on what we already know. As we progress from definition to definition, we progress from certain knowledge to certain knowledge.

The key problem in Aristotle's theory of knowledge lies in finding the principles upon which the scientific syllogism rests. In the *Prior Analytics* he states that the scientific syllogism is rooted in principles derived from experience. These principles are not things that can be learned. They are intuitively grasped by our intelligence after repeated experience with similar sets of circumstances. In many respects they are self-evident. Aristotle realizes the risk involved in accepting any principles as certain. In the *Metaphysics* he indicates that the metaphysician must found his science upon the most certain of all principles, because his science is the most fundamental to all knowledge. Yet he can find only one principle which he considers self-evident beyond a shadow of a doubt, the Law of Contradiction. And he devotes the better part of a book to proving that this most self-evident of all principles is really certain. Once, however, the scientist is sure of his principles, he can be certain of attaining the truth.

Aristotle finds the link between subjective knowledge and the objective world in the definition. The definition is at once the essence, the "what it is" of an object as distinct from its matter, and at the same time is the intelligible structure of that object which is the object of our knowledge. Aristotle was a firm believer in the value of orderly thinking based on experience. In his opinion, the two together contribute to the formation of an accurate definition which embodies our understanding of the reality of the world around us.

SELECTED BIBLIOGRAPHY

I. ARISTOTLE'S WORKS.

The Loeb Classical Library editions of the works of Aristotle (Greek text and English translation).

Oxford Translation of the complete works of Aristotle. Edited by J. A. Smith and W. D. Ross. 1908-1931.

Aristotle. *Metaphysics*. Translated by Richard Hope. Ann Arbor: University of Michigan Press, 1960.

Aristotle. *Nicomachean Ethics*. Translated by Martin Ostwald. New York: Bobbs-Merrill Company, Inc., 1962.

Aristotle. *Politics*. Translated and edited by Ernest Barker. New York: Oxford University Press, 1958.

Butcher, S. H. *Aristotle's Theory of Poetry and Fine Art*. New York: Dover Publications, Inc., 1951.

In addition, there are many other excellent editions of his major works and selections of his philosophy available in paperback.

II. GENERAL WORKS ON ARISTOTLE AND GREEK PHILOSOPHY.

Allan, D. J. *The Philosophy of Aristotle*. New York: Oxford University Press, 1952.

Barker, E. *The Political Thought of Plato and Aristotle*. London: Methuen, 1906.

Copleston, Frederick, S. J. *A History of Philosophy: Volume I—Greece and Rome*. New York: Image Books, 1962.

Guthrie, W. K. C. *The Greek Philosophers from Thales to Aristotle*. New York: Harper and Row Publishers, 1950.

Jaeger, Werner. *Aristotle: Fundamentals of the History of His Development*. Second Edition. Translated by Richard Robinson. Oxford: Oxford University Press, 1962.

Mure, G. R. G. *Aristotle*. New York: Oxford University Press, 1932.

Randall, John H. *Aristotle*. New York: Columbia University Press, 1962.

Ross, W. D. *Aristotle*. New York: World Publishing Company, Meridian Books, 1962.

Taylor, Alfred E. *Aristotle*. New York: Dover Publications, Inc., 1956.

Woodbridge, Frederick J. E. *Aristotle's Vision of Nature*. ed. with an introduction by John Herman Randall, Jr. New York: Columbia University Press, 1965.

Zeller, Eduard. *Outlines of the History of Greek Philosophy*. New York: World Publishing Company, Meridian Books, 1962.

INDEX

Motion of Animals, On the, 30
Movement: impulse of nature
  to, 54
Motive: and virtue, 152

Nation: and the state, 196
Nature: definition of, 47-48
  as form and function, 54
  as impulse to movement, 54
  as process, 40
  Sophists on, 15
Natural necessity, 60
  and mathematics, 60
  and purpose, 58
Nicomachean Ethics, 31-32
"Now," meaning of, 76-77
Number, 134-135
  the infinite in, 66-67
  Pythagoreans on, 9

Oligarchy, 222-223
  revolution in, 228-229
  stabilization of, 234-235
Origin of Animals, On the, 30
Ousia, 111-112, 123

Pain: and pleasure, 152
Parmenides, 10-12
  refutation of, 49-50, 53
Parts of Animals, The, 30
Parva Naturalia, 31
Perfection: Plato on, 18-19
Phaleas, 207
Philip II of Macedonia, 24
Philosophic method, 97
Philosophy: development of,
  94-95
  problems of, 97
  unity of, 101-102
Philosophy, On, 28
Physics, 30
  and mathematics, 55
Physics, The, 30, 47-89
Place: empty space, time, and,
  67-79

Plants, On, 31
Plato: on aesthetics, 246-247
  attack on by Aristotle, 53,
    95-97
  on ethics, 143-144
  on government, 203-205
  on ideas, 116
  on infinity, 64
  on metaphysics, 90-91
  philosophy of, 18-20
  on property, 206
Pleasure, 179-185
  and pain, 152
  and virtue, 151
Pleasure, On, 28
Plot, 254-255, 256
Poetics, The, 32, 33, 246-259
Poetry, 249
  epic, 250-251, 257-259
Poets, On the, 28
Politeia, The, 223-224
Politics, 145
Politics, The, 32, 193-245
Population: of the ideal state,
  238-239
Posterior Analytics, The, 29, 37
Potentiality, 128-131
  and actuality, 61-62, 127
  the infinite as, 67
  matter as, 125
  in process of change, 128
Prayer, On, 28
Primary being, 110-124
Prior Analytics, The, 29, 37
Privation of form: first principle
  of, 52
Private property, 205-206
Process: and function, 40
  knowing as, 42
  and nature, 40
Property: community of, 205
  management of, 200
  Plato on, 206
  private, 205-206
Protrepticus, 27

NOTES

NOTES

NOTES

NOTES

NOTES

NOTES

NOTES

NOTES

NOTES

NOTES

MONARCH® NOTES AND STUDY GUIDES

ARE AVAILABLE AT RETAIL STORES EVERYWHERE

In the event your local bookseller
cannot provide you with other
Monarch titles you want —

ORDER ON THE FORM BELOW:

Complete order form appears
on inside front & back covers
for your convenience.

Simply send retail price, local
sales tax, if any, plus 35¢ per
book to cover mailing and
handling.

TITLE #	AUTHOR & TITLE	(exactly as shown on title listing)	PRICE
	PLUS ADDITIONAL 35¢ PER BOOK FOR POSTAGE		
		GRAND TOTAL	$

MONARCH® PRESS, a Simon & Schuster Division of Gulf & Western Corporation
Mail Service Department, 1230 Avenue of the Americas, New York, N.Y. 10020

I enclose $ .... to cover retail price, local sales tax, plus mailing
and handling.

Name _____
(Please print)

Address _____

City _____ State _____ Zip _____

Please send check or money order. We cannot be responsible for cash.